D0221856

IMPORTANT:

HERE IS YOUR REGISTRATION CODE TO ACCESS

YOUR PREMIUM McGRAW-HILL ONLINE RESOURCES.

For key premium online resources you need THIS CODE to gain access. Once the code is entered, you will be able to use the Web resources for the length of your course.

If your course is using **WebCT** or **Blackboard**, you'll be able to use this code to access the McGraw-Hill content within your instructor's online course.

Access is provided if you have purchased a new book. If the registration code is missing from this book, the registration screen on our Website, and within your WebCT or Blackboard course, will tell you how to obtain your new code.

Registering for McGraw-Hill Online Resources

TO gain access to your McGraw-Hill web resources simply follow the steps below:

1. USE YOUR WEB BROWSER TO GO TO: **register.dushkin.com**
2. CLICK ON **FIRST TIME USER**.
3. ENTER THE REGISTRATION CODE* PRINTED ON THE TEAR-OFF BOOKMARK ON THE RIGHT.
4. AFTER YOU HAVE ENTERED YOUR REGISTRATION CODE, CLICK **REGISTER**.
5. FOLLOW THE INSTRUCTIONS TO SET-UP YOUR PERSONAL UserID AND PASSWORD.
6. WRITE YOUR UserID AND PASSWORD DOWN FOR FUTURE REFERENCE. KEEP IT IN A SAFE PLACE.

TO GAIN ACCESS to the McGraw-Hill content in your instructor's **WebCT** or **Blackboard** course simply log in to the course with the UserID and Password provided by your instructor. Enter the registration code exactly as it appears in the box to the right when prompted by the system. You will only need to use the code the first time you click on McGraw-Hill content.

Thank you, and welcome to your McGraw-Hill online Resources!

Mc Graw Hill **Higher Education**

0-07-295823-5 T/A DAVIS: PHILOSOPHY, AN INTRODUCTION THROUGH ORIGINAL FICTION, DISCUSSION, AND A MULTI-MEDIA CD-ROM, 4E

REGISTRATION CODE

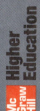

charlemage-60679931

Mc Graw Hill **Higher Education**

PHILOSOPHY

An Introduction Through
Original Fiction, Discussion,
and a Multi-Media CD-ROM

FOURTH EDITION

Thomas D. Davis

Boston   Burr Ridge, IL   Dubuque, IA   Madison, WI   New York
San Francisco   St. Louis   Bangkok   Bogotá   Caracas   Kuala Lumpur
Lisbon   London   Madrid   Mexico City   Milan   Montreal   New Delhi
Santiago   Seoul   Singapore   Sydney   Taipei   Toronto

Higher Education

PHILOSOPHY: An Introduction through Original Fiction, Discussion, and A Multi-Media CD-ROM

Published by McGraw-Hill Higher Education, an operating unit of The McGraw-Hill Companies, Inc. 1221 Avenue of the Americas, New York, NY, 10020. Copyright © 2004, 1993, 1987, 1979 by The McGraw-Hill Companies. All rights reserved. No part of this publication may be reproduced or distributed in any form or by any means, or stored in a database or retrieval system, without the prior written consent of The McGraw-Hill Companies, Inc., including, but not limited to, network or other electronic storage or transmission, or broadcast for distance learning.

1 2 3 4 5 6 7 8 9 0 DOC/DOC 0 9 8 7 6 5 4 3

ISBN 0-07-283176-6

Publisher, Chris Freitag; Development Editor, Jon-David Hague; Project Manager, Roger Geissler; Production Supervisor, Richard DeVitto; Designer, Sharon Spurlock. This book was set in Minion by G & S Typesetters and printed on 45# New Era Matte by R. R. Donnelly, Crawfordsville.

Library of Congress Cataloging-in-Publication Data

Davis, Thomas, D.
    Philosophy: an introduction through original fiction, discussion, and a multi-media CD-ROM / Thomas D. Davis.— 4th ed.
        p.   cm.
    Includes bibliographical references and index.
    ISBN 0-07-283176-6
    1. Philosophy.   I. Title.
BR90.D186 2002   03-068970
189-dc21

www.mhhe.com

About the Author

Thomas D. Davis received his Ph.D. in philosophy from the University of Michigan, where he wrote his dissertation on Sartre. He has taught philosophy at Michigan, Grinnell College, the University of Redlands, and De Anza College.

Mr. Davis is the author of three novels, *Suffer Little Children*, *Murdered Sleep*, and *Consuming Fire*, as well as a satire of Sartre, *Dear Jean: A One-Act Play* (in *Teaching Philosophy*, Vol. 5, No. 1).

To Diane:
My wife and soul-mate

Contents

Preface

In an episode from the classic TV series *Twilight Zone,* a prisoner is exiled on a deserted asteroid. For company he is given a sophisticated robot who looks and feels and behaves just like a real woman. As time goes by, the robot and the prisoner become lovers and friends. Then one day an official arrives, telling the prisoner he has been reprieved. But there is no room in the two-person space shuttle for the robot, and the prisoner refuses to leave her—in spite of the official's arguments that she is "just a machine." To illustrate his argument, the official shoots the female, who falls down, wires springing out of her chest, crying "no" in a voice that winds down like a broken tape recorder. "See?" says the official triumphantly, but the prisoner just stares down at the robot, not sure how to react. We viewers are not sure how to react either. Does the fact of the wires make ridiculous every feeling that the prisoner felt for the robot? Do the wires mean she had no moral right to exist? Is she supposed to be "just a machine" because she had no real feelings? But how could we be certain of that, since feelings can be experienced only by the creature having them?

In *Brave New World,* after a terrible period of war and famine and social upheaval, the world is altered through embryo engineering, early conditioning, and drugs to be a stable, happy world in which such things as art, inquiry, and individuality no longer fit. John, the

"Savage," a holdover from the old world, is appalled by this new world. "I want God, I want poetry, I want real danger, I want freedom, I want . . . the right to be unhappy." Mustapha Mond, the "Controller," says he doesn't much like this new world either, but thinks it's the right one from a moral standpoint. He had the choice of giving people misery and its compensations or happiness and stability. Most people, Mond claims, would prefer happiness and stability, and that's what the new world gives them.

Who's right, Mond or the Savage? It seems wrong of Mond to take away people's free will. On the other hand, how much suffering is free will really worth? Are we so sure people have free will in the first place? It also seems wrong of Mond to pick a world with no art or individuality. On the other hand, don't most people avoid art like the plague? Aren't most people trying desperately to be just like everybody else? Isn't happiness what most people really care about?

––––––––––––

It was dramatized questions such as these that got me interested in philosophy and led me to take my first philosophy course. It was a course I almost flunked, in part because it went against my temperament at the time. I wanted to throw around great (and mostly fuzzy) ideas; my instructor wanted me to define my terms and present careful arguments. I wanted to read philosophical fiction; my instructor wanted me to struggle through the aged exposition of such thinkers as Plato and Descartes.

I could have thrown up my hands and said philosophy is boring and gone on to something else. But I still had those questions I wanted answered, and I saw that I couldn't pretend to any seriousness in my answers unless I was willing to do some hard thinking. I realized that exposure to some of the best minds in philosophy could help me with that kind of thinking, even if reading them was a bit of a struggle.

Eventually I went to graduate school, where I had my first teaching experiences as an assistant in another instructor's course. We'd try to discuss Descartes's question about whether we can be sure we're not now dreaming, and the students would shake their heads as if that was the most insane question they'd ever heard. Then outside the class I'd hear one of those same students say, "Hey, man, did you see that great *Star Trek* last night where the guy was dreaming his whole life?" and I realized some crucial connection was being missed. When I started doing my own teaching, I'd preface each topic with some piece of dramatic literature, and that helped to make the connection, but in most of the pieces I could find there wasn't enough philosophy to get us deeply into the topic. Having done some writing myself, I decided to create my own stories. Hence the evolution of this textbook.

The tough stuff is here—the analysis and arguments and careful thinking. But the point of this text is to start you off with the wonder, the drama, and the fun of philosophy, which is what will sustain you through the harder material.

To add to the fun, as well as to facilitate the learning of the basic definitions, positions, and arguments in the text, a multi-media CD has been added to the fourth edition. The CD contains exercises, animated cartoons, and even original pop and rock songs (in the sections called, "Rockin' Review") incorporating fundamental philosophical concepts. The CD is intended as a supplement to the text; it won't work in place of it. Moving back and forth from text to CD should make it easier and more enjoyable to absorb the ideas in the text.

Thomas D. Davis

To the Instructor
Changes in the Fourth Edition

In this fourth edition, as in the third, each philosophical topic is presented through original fiction, transitional questions, discussion, and final questions and exercises. The fourth edition contains the following changes:

1. An author-developed multi-media CD containing exercises, animations, and music has been added to the text. The CD is included to add modes of learning that are more congenial to the interests of many of today's students. The CD is intended as a supplement to the text; it won't work in place of the text. The student should start with the text, then move back and forth between CD and text.

2. Readings: All secondary source material has been removed from the fourth edition. Reviews indicated that the readings were assigned sporadically and then often in conjunction with a supplementary anthology. Dropping the readings allowed for the inclusion of the CD.

3. Chapter One, "Freedom and Responsibility": Virtually all the material on divine foreknowledge, time, and time travel has been removed from this chapter and made part of a new chapter. A discussion of compatibilism is included, and in the original discussion of free will as contra-causal freedom, it is made clear that there are disputes about the meaning of free will.

4. Chapter Two, "Time and Time Travel": This is a new chapter with a time travel story and a discussion of time and time travel.

5. Chapter Three, "God and Suffering": The discussion of the traditional arguments for the existence of God has been shortened and new material added on the relevance of the "Big Bang" theory to the idea of a First Cause.

6. Chapter Four, "Moral Principles": The story, "Those Who Help Themselves," has been shortened and a new story added that sets up a new discussion of consequentialist versus deontological ethics, of utilitarianism versus Kant.

7. Chapter Six, "The Nature of the Mind": The order of the stories has been reversed, and the discussion now starts off with dualism. There is additional discussion covering functionalism, minds and machines, some materialist visions of life after death, and updated versions of dualism.

8. Chapter Seven, "Appearance and Reality": The chapter includes an updated version of "The Descartes Tape" story from the second edition, retitled, "The Fantasy Machine."

9. The chapters "Logic" and "Methodology" have been eliminated from this edition to make room for new material.

10. The text has been reformatted slightly, including boxes and **increased underlining** that highlight major points for easier reading, as well as easier reference during class discussion.

*****

I would like to thank the following individuals, whose suggestions were helpful in planning the fourth edition:

I would like to continue to thank the helpful reviewers from earlier editions: Robert Cogan, Steven Fishman, Robert Gibson, Robert L. Gray, Linda Kayes, James Manley, Darryl Mehring, Gerald E. Meyers, Todd Moody, Dean J. Nelson, George S. Pappas, Rickey J. Ray, David Roberts, Samuel R. Roberts, III, Craig Staudenbauer and James D. Taylor (student).

I'd like to add a special thanks to James Manley, who suggested the idea of a multi-media CD and helped me with some initial technical matters.

Thomas D. Davis

1

Freedom and Responsibility

Fiction: Please Don't Tell Me How the Story Ends

The heavy door closed behind him, and he glanced quickly at this new detention room. He was startled, almost pleasantly surprised. This was not like the drab cell in which he had spent the first days after his arrest, nor like the hospital rooms, with the serpentine carnival machines, in which he had been tested and observed for the last two months—though he assumed he was being observed here as well. This was more like a small, comfortable library that had been furnished like a first-class hotel room. Against the four walls were fully stocked bookcases that rose ten feet to the white plaster ceiling; in the ceiling was a small skylight. The floor was covered with a thick green carpet, and in the middle of the room were a double bed with a nightstand, a large bureau, a desk, an easy chair with a side table, and several lamps. There were large gaps in the bookcases to accommodate two doors, including the one through which he had just entered, and also a traylike apparatus affixed to the wall. He could not immediately ascertain the purpose of the tray, but the other door, he quickly learned, led to a spacious bathroom complete with toilet articles. As he searched the main room, he found that the desk contained writing paper, pens, a clock, and a calendar; the bureau contained abundant clothing in a variety of colors and two pairs of shoes. He glanced down at the hospital gown and slippers

---

 The CD, Ch. 1, *Please Don't Tell Me How the Story Ends (1),* contains animation and exercises related to this story.

he was wearing, then quickly changed into a rust-colored sweater and a pair of dark brown slacks. The clothing, including the shoes, fitted him perfectly. It would be easier to face his situation, to face whatever might be coming, looking like a civilized human *being*.

But what was his situation? He wanted to believe that the improvement in his living conditions meant an improvement in his status, perhaps even an imminent reprieve. But all the same he doubted it. Nothing had seemed to follow a sensible progression since his arrest, and it would be foolhardy to take anything at face value now. But what were they up to? At first, when he had been taken to the hospital, he had expected torture, some hideous pseudo-medical experiment, or a brainwashing program. But there had been no operation and no pain. He had been tested countless times: the endless details of biography; the responses to color, scent, sound, taste, touch; the responses to situations and ideas; the physical examination. But if these constituted mind-altering procedures, they had to be of the most subtle variety. Certainly he felt the same; at least no more compliant than he had been in the beginning. What were they after?

As his uncertainty grew to anxiety, he tried to work it off with whatever physical exercise he could manage in the confines of the room: running in place, isometrics, sit-ups, and push-ups. He knew that the strength of his will would depend in part on the strength of his body, and since his arrest he had exercised as much as he could. No one had prevented this.

He was midway through a push-up when a loud buzzer sounded. He leaped to his feet, frightened but ready. Then he saw a plastic tray of food on the metal tray that extended from the wall and a portion of the wall closing downward behind the tray. So this was how he would get his meals. He would see no one. Was this some special isolation experiment?

The question of solitude quickly gave way to hunger and curiosity about the food. It looked delicious and plentiful; there was much more than he could possibly eat. Was it safe? Could it be drugged or poisoned? No, there could be no point to their finishing him in such an odd, roundabout fashion. He took the tray to the desk and ate heartily, but still left several of the dishes barely sampled or untouched.

That evening—the clock and the darkened skylight told him it was evening—he investigated the room further. He was interrupted only once by the buzzer. When it continued to sound and nothing appeared, he realized that the buzzer meant he was to return the food dishes. He did so, and the plastic tray disappeared into the wall.

The writing paper was a temptation. He always thought better with a pen in hand. Writing would resemble a kind of conversation and make him feel a little less alone. With a journal, he could construct some kind of history from what threatened to be days of dulling sameness. But he feared that they wanted him to write, that his doing so would somehow play into their hands. So he refrained.

Instead, he examined a portion of the bookshelf that contained paperback volumes in a great variety of sizes and colors. The books covered a number of fields—fiction, history, science, philosophy, politics—some to his liking and some not. He selected a political treatise and put it on the small table next to the easy chair. He did not open it immediately. He washed up and then went to the bureau, where he found a green plaid robe and a pair of light yellow pajamas. As he lifted out the pajamas, he noticed a small, black, rectangular box and opened it.

Inside was a revolver. A quick examination showed that it was loaded and operative. Quickly he shut the box, trembling. He was on one knee in front of the open drawer. His first thought was that a former inmate had left the gun to help him. He was sure that his body was blocking the contents of the drawer from the view of any observation devices in the room. He must not give away the secret. He forced himself to close the drawer casually, rise, and walk to the easy chair.

Then the absurdity of his hypothesis struck him. How could any prisoner have gotten such a thing past the tight security of this place? And what good would such a weapon do him in a room to which no one came? No, the gun must be there because the authorities wanted it there. But why? Could it be they wanted to hide his death under the pretense of an attempted escape? Or could it be that they were trying to push him to suicide by isolating him? But again, what was the point of it? He realized that his fingerprints were on the gun. Did they want to use that as some kind of evidence against him? He went to the bureau again, ostensibly to switch pajamas, and, during the switch, opened the box and quickly wiped his prints off the gun. As casually as he could, he returned to the chair.

He passed the evening in considerable agitation. He tried to read but could not. He exercised again, but it did not calm him. He tried to analyze his situation, but his thoughts were an incoherent jumble. Much later, he lay down on the bed, first pushing the easy chair against the door of the room. He recognized the absurdity of erecting this fragile barrier, but the noise of their pushing it away would give him some warning. For a while, he forced his eyes open each time he began to doze, but eventually he fell asleep.

In the morning, he found everything unchanged, the chair still in place at the door. Nothing but the breakfast tray had intruded. After he had exercised, breakfasted, bathed, and found himself still unmolested, he began to feel more calm. He read half the book he had selected the night before, lunched, and then dozed in his chair.

When he awoke, his eyes scanned the room and came to rest on one of the bookshelves filled with a series of black, leatherbound volumes of uniform size, marked only by number. He had noticed them before but had paid little attention, thinking they were an encyclopedia. Now he noticed what a preposterous number of volumes there were, perhaps two hundred in all, filling not only one bookcase from floor to ceiling but filling parts of others as well. His curiosity piqued, he pulled down Volume LXIV, and opened it at random to page 494.

The page was filled with very small print, with a section at the bottom in even smaller print that appeared to be footnotes. The heading of the page was large enough to be read at a glance. "RE: PRISONER 7439762 (referred to herein as 'Q')." He read on: "3/07/26. 14:03. Q entered room on 3/06/26 at 14:52. Surprised at pleasantness of room. Glanced at furniture, then bookcase, then ceiling. Noted metal tray and second door, puzzled by both. Entered bathroom, noting toilet articles. Lifted shaver and touched cologne." He skipped down the page: "Selected brown slacks, rust sweater, and tan shoes. Felt normal clothing made him more equal to his situation."

It seemed that they were keeping some sort of record of his activities here. But what was the purpose of having the record here for him to read? And how had they gotten it in here? It was easy to figure out how they knew of his activities: they were watching him, just as he had suspected. They must have printed this page during the night and placed it here as he slept. Perhaps his food had been drugged to guarantee that he wouldn't awake.

He glanced toward the door of his cell and remembered the chair he had placed against it. In a drugged sleep, he wouldn't have heard them enter. They could have pulled the chair back as they left. But all the way? Presumably there was some hidden panel in the door. Once the door was shut, they had merely to open the panel and pull the chair the last few inches.

Suddenly he remembered the matter of the gun. He glanced down the page and there it was, a description of how he had handled the gun twice. There was no warning given nor any hint of an explanation as to why the gun was there. There was just the clipped, neutral-toned description of his actions and impressions. It described his hope that the gun might have been left by another prisoner, his rejection of that supposition, his fear that the gun might be used against him in some way, his desire to remove the fingerprints. But how on earth could they have known what he was feeling and thinking? He decided that he had acted and reacted as any normal person would have done, and they had simply drawn the obvious conclusions from his actions and facial expressions.

He glanced further down the page and read: "On 3/07/26, Q awoke at 8:33." And further ". . . selected *The Future of Socialism* by Felix Berofsky . . ." And further: ". . . bent the corner of page 206 to mark his place and put the book . . . " All his activities of that morning had already been printed in the report!

He began turning the book around in his hands and pulled it away from the shelf. Was this thing wired in some way? Could they print their reports onto these pages in minutes without removing the books from the shelves? Perhaps they had some new process whereby they could imprint specially sensitized pages by electronic signal.

Then he remembered that he had just awakened from a nap, and he slammed the volume shut in disgust. Of course: They had entered the room again during his nap. He placed the volume back on the shelf and started for his chair. How could they expect him to be taken in by such blatant trickery? But then a thought occurred to him: He had picked out a volume and page at random. Why had the description of yesterday and this morning been on that particular page? Were all the pages the same? He returned to the shelf and picked up the same volume, this time opening it to page 531. The heading was the same. He looked down the page: "Q began to return to his chair but became puzzled as to why the initial description of his activities should have appeared on page 494 of this volume." He threw the book to the floor and grabbed another, Volume LX, opening it to page 103: ". . . became more confused by the correct sequential description on page 531, Volume LXIV."

"What are you trying to do to me!" he screamed, dropping the second book.

Immediately he was ashamed at his lack of self-control.

"What an absurd joke," he said loudly to whatever listening devices there might be.

He picked up the two volumes he had dropped and put them back in place on the bookshelf. He walked across the room and sat in the chair. He tried to keep his expression neutral while he thought.

There was no possibility that observations were being made and immediately transmitted to the books by some electronic process. It all happened too fast. Perhaps it was being done through some kind of mind control. Yet he was certain that no devices of any kind had been implanted in his brain. That would have involved anesthetizing him, operating, leaving him unconscious until all scars had healed, and then reviving him with no sense of time lost. No doubt they had ability, but not that much. It could be something as simple as hypnosis, of course. This would require merely writing the books, then commanding him to perform certain acts in a certain order, including the opening of the books. Yet that would be such a simple, familiar experiment that it would hardly seem worth doing. And it would hardly require the extensive testing procedures that he had undergone before being placed in this room.

He glanced at the books again, and his eye fell on Volume I. If there was an explanation anywhere in this room, it would be there, he thought. The page would probably say only, "Q hoped for an explanation," and in that case he would have to do without one. But it was worth taking a look.

He took Volume I from the shelf, opened it to the first page, and glanced at the first paragraph: "Q hoped to find an explanation." He started to laugh, but stopped abruptly. The explanation seemed to be there after all. He read on: "Experiment in the Prediction of Human Behavior within a Controlled Environment, No. 465, Variant No. 8, Case 2: Subject Aware of Behavior Prediction."

He read through the brief "explanation" several times. (Of course, this in itself might be trickery.) Obviously, these unknown experimenters considered all human behavior to be theoretically predictable. They first studied a subject for a number of weeks and then attempted to predict how that subject would behave within a limited, controlled environment. In his case, they were attempting to predict, in addition to all else, his reactions to the "fact" that his behavior was predictable and being predicted. They had placed those volumes here as proof to him that each prior series of acts had been successfully predicted.

He didn't believe they could do it; he didn't want to believe it. Of course, much of what occurred in the universe, including much of human behavior, was predictable in theory. The world wasn't totally chaotic, after all, and science had had its successes in foreseeing certain events. But he refused to believe that there was no element of chance in the world, that every event happened just as it did out of necessity. He had some freedom, some causal autonomy, some power to initiate the new. He was not merely a puppet of universal laws. Each of his choices was not simply a mathematical function of those laws together with the state of himself and the external world at the moment just prior to the choice. He would not believe that.

Nothing was written on page 1 to indicate how the other experiments had turned out, not that he would have believed such a report anyway. No doubt the indication that his experience was a more complex "variant" of the experiment was meant to imply that the preceding experiments had been successful. But there had to have been mistakes, even if they claimed that the errors could eventually be overcome. As long as there were mistakes, one could continue to believe in human freedom. He *did* believe in human freedom.

His thoughts were interrupted by the buzzer. His dinner emerged from the wall. He looked at it with anger, remembering how the first page to which he had turned had listed, perhaps even predicted, exactly what foods he would eat. But he didn't reject the meal. He needed his wits about him, and for that he needed strength. He must try to get his mind off all this for tonight, at least. He would eat, read, and then sleep.

For several hours, he was fairly successful in diverting his attention from the books. Then, in bed with the lights out, he recalled the phrase "Variant No. 8, Case 2." That made him feel more hopeful. This was only the second time that this particular version of the experiment was being tried. Surely, the likelihood of error was great.

He found himself thinking about Case 1. What kind of man had he been, and how had he fared? Had he worn green pajamas one day when the book said "yellow," or remained contemptuous when the book said "hysterical," and then laughed in their faces as they led him from the room? That would have been a triumph.

Suddenly, he thought of the gun and had an image of a man, seated on the edge of the bed, looking at those volumes on the wall, slowly raising the gun to his head. ". . . To predict . . . his reactions to the fact that his behavior was predictable and being predicted." God, was that the purpose of the gun? Had it been put there as one of his options? Had that been the ignominious ending of Case 1, and not the departure in triumph he had pictured a moment ago? He had a vision of himself lying dead on the floor and men in white robes grinning as they opened a volume to a page that described his death. Would he hold out, or would he die? The answer was somewhere in those thousands of pages—if he could only find it.

He realized that he was playing into their hands by supposing that they could do what he knew they could not. Anyway, even if one assumed that they could accurately predict his future, they were not forcing him to do anything. There were no mind-controlling devices; he wasn't being programmed by them. If they were to predict correctly, they must predict what he wanted to do. And he didn't want to die.

In spite of these reflections, he remained agitated. When he finally slept, he slept fitfully. He dreamed that he was a minuscule figure trapped in a maze on the scale of a dollhouse. He watched himself from a distance and watched the lifesized doctors who peered over the top of the maze. There were two exits from the maze, one to freedom and one to a black pit that he knew to be death. "Death," the doctors kept saying to one another, and he watched his steady progression in the maze toward death. He kept shouting instructions to himself. "No, not that way! Go to the left there!" But the doomed figure couldn't hear him.

When he awoke in the morning, he felt feverish and touched only the fruit and coffee on his breakfast tray. He lay on the bed for much of the morning, his thoughts obsessed with the black volumes on the wall. He knew that he must try to foil the predictions, but he feared failure. I am too upset and weak, he thought. I must ignore the books until I am better. I must turn my mind to other things.

But as he tried to divert himself, he became aware of an agonizing echo in his head. He would turn in bed and think: "Q turns onto left side." Or scratch: "Q scratches left thigh." Or mutter "damn them": "Q mutters, 'damn them.'" Finally, he could stand it no longer and stumbled to one of the bookshelves. He pulled two volumes from the shelves, juggled them in his hands, dropped one, then flipped the pages several times before picking a page.

"3/08/26. 11:43. At 15:29 on 3/07/26, Q opened Volume I to page 1 and read explanation of experiment."

He slammed down the book.

"Damn you," he said aloud. "I'm a man, not a machine. I'll show you. I'll show you."

He took another volume and held it in his hand. "Two and two are five," he thought. "When I was six, I lived in China with the Duke of Savoy. The earth is flat." He opened the book.

"Q wants to confuse prediction. Thinks: Two and two are five . . ."

He looked around the room as he tried to devise some other line of attack. He noticed the clock and the calendar. Each page of the book gave the date and time at which each page opened, the date and time of each event. He rushed to the desk, flipped the pages of the calendar, and turned the knob that adjusted the hands on the clock. He opened another book and read: "3/08/26. 12:03." He yelled out:

"See? You're wrong. The calendar says June, and the time is 8:04. That's my date and my time. Predict what you think if you want. This is what I think. And I think you're wrong."

He had another idea. The first page he had looked at had been page 494, Volume LXIV. He would open that volume to the same page. Either it must say the same thing or it must be new. Either way they would have failed, for a new entry would show them to be tricksters. He grabbed the volume and found the page. "3/07/06. 14:03. Q entered room on 3/06/06 at 4:52." Once again, he spoke aloud:

"Of course, but that's old news. I don't see anything here about my turning to the page a second time. My, we do seem to be having our problems, don't we?"

He laughed in triumph and was about to shut the book when he saw the fine print at the bottom. He licked his lips and stared at the print for a long time before he pulled down another volume and turned to the page that had been indicated in the footnote: ". . . then Q reopened Volume LXIV, page 494, hoping . . ."

He ripped out the page, then another, and another. His determination gave way to a fury, and he tore apart one book, then another, until twelve of them lay in tatters on the floor. He had to stop because of dizziness and exhaustion.

"I'm a man," he muttered, "not a machine."

He started for his bed, ignoring the buzzer announcing the tray of food. He made it only as far as the easy chair. He sank into it, and his eyelids seemed to close of their own weight.

"I'm a. . . ."

Asleep, he dreamed again. He was running through the streets of a medieval town, trying desperately to escape from a grotesque, devil-like creature. "At midnight you die," it said. No matter where he ran, the devil kept reappearing in front of him. "It doesn't matter where you go. I will be there at midnight." Then a loud bell began to sound twelve chimes slowly. He found himself in a huge library, swinging an ax at the shelves, which crumbled under his blows. He felt great elation until he saw that everything he had destroyed had been reassembled behind him. He dropped the ax and began to scream.

When he awoke, he thought for a moment he was still dreaming. On the floor, he saw twelve volumes, all intact. Then he turned his head and saw the twelve torn volumes where he had left them. The new ones were on the floor near the metal tray. His lunch had been withdrawn, and the books had been pushed through the opening in the wall while he had slept.

He moved to the bed, where he slept fitfully through the evening and night, getting up only once to sip some tea from the dinner tray.

In the morning he remained in bed. He was no longer feverish, but he felt more exhausted than he could remember ever having been. The breakfast tray came and went untouched. He didn't feel like eating. He didn't feel like doing anything.

At about eleven o'clock, he got out of bed just long enough to find the gun; then he fingered it on his chest as he lay back, staring at the ceiling. There was no point in going on with it. They would have their laughs, of course. But they would have them in any case, since, no matter what he did, it would be in their books. And ultimately it wasn't their victory at all, but the victory of the universal laws that had dictated every event in this puppet play of a world. A man of honor must refuse to play his part in it. He, certainly, refused.

And how could the experimenters delight in their achievement? They were not testing a theory about their prisoners but about all human beings, including themselves. Their success showed that they themselves had no control over their own destinies. What did it matter if his future was written in the books and their futures were not? There would always be the invisible books in the nature of things, books that contained the futures of everyone. Could they help seeing that? And when they saw that, if they too didn't reach for guns, could they help feeling degraded to the core of their souls? No, they had not won. Everyone had lost.

Eventually he sat up on the bed. His hand shook, but he was not surprised. Whatever he might will, there would be that impulse for survival. He forced the hand up and put the barrel of the gun in his mouth.

The buzzer startled him, and the hand with the gun dropped to his side. The lunch tray appeared, and suddenly he was aware of being ravenously hungry. He laughed bitterly. Well, he wouldn't be hungry for long. Still, wasn't the condemned man entitled to a last meal? Surely honor did not forbid that. And the food looked delicious. He put the gun on his pillow and took the tray to his desk.

While he was savoring his mushroom omelet, he glanced at the political treatise that had remained half read by the easy chair for the last two days. God, had it been only two days? It was a shame that he would not be able to finish it; it was an interesting book. And there were other books on the shelves—not the black volumes, of course—that he had been meaning to read for some time and would have enjoyed.

As he sampled some artichokes, he glanced at the formidable black volumes on the shelves. Somewhere there was a page that read: "After completing lunch, Q put the gun to his head and pulled the trigger." Of course, if he changed his mind and decided to finish reading the political treatise first, it would say that instead. Or if he waited a day more, it would register that fact. What were the possibilities? Could it ever say "reprieved"? He did not see how. They would never let him go free with the information he had about their experiments. Unless, of course, there was a change of regime. But that was the barest of possibilities. Could a page say that he had been returned to the regular cells? How he would like to talk to another human being. But that would pose the same problem for the experimenters as releasing him. Presumably, they would kill him eventually. Still, that was no worse than what he was about to do to himself. Perhaps they would continue the experiment a while longer. Meantime, he could live comfortably, eat well, read, exercise.

There were indeed possibilities other than immediate suicide, not all of them unpleasant. But could he countenance living any longer? Didn't honor dictate defiance? Yet—defiance of whom? It wasn't as if the laws of the world had a lawmaker in whose face he might shake his fist. He had never believed in a god; rather, it was as if he were trapped inside some creaky old machine, unstarted and uncontrolled, that had been puttering along a complex but predictable path forever. Kick a machine when you're angry, and you only get a sore foot. Anyway, how could he have claimed credit for killing himself, since it would have been inevitable that he do so?

The black volumes stretched out like increments of time across the brown bookshelves. Somewhere in their pages was this moment, and the next, and perhaps a tomorrow, and another, perhaps even a next month or a next year. He would never be able to read those pages until it was already unnecessary, but there might be some good days there; in any case, it would be interesting to wait and see.

After lunch he sat at his desk for a long time. Eventually, he got up and replaced the gun in its case in the bureau drawer. He placed the lunch dishes back on the metal tray and, beside the dishes, heaped the covers and torn pages of the books he had destroyed. He then put the new volumes on the shelves. As he started back to the chair, his eye was caught by the things on the desk. He took a volume from the bookshelf, carried it to the desk, and opened it. He read only the heading at the top: "3/09/06. 13:53." He adjusted the clock and the calendar accordingly. If he was going to live a while longer, he might as well know the correct day and time.

Fiction: *A Little Omniscience Goes a Long Way*

Satan, with a flutter of his mighty wings, descends upon a cloud where God is reclining.

SATAN: How's it going?

GOD: (*He yawns.*) Perfectly, as usual.

SATAN: And your new creatures on earth—how are they?

The CD, Ch. 1, *A Little Omniscience Goes a Long Way (1)*, contains animation and exercises related to this story.

GOD: Just fine. Eve's asleep under the apple tree, curled up on her right side, dreaming of flowers. Adam is sitting up, squinting at the sun, scratching his nose with his left index finger, trying to decide what he wants to do this morning. What he wants to do is take a walk in the garden. In a moment he will.

SATAN: And you know all that without looking.

GOD: Of course. I arranged it all to happen that way.

SATAN: Isn't it boring to know everything that will ever happen? This morning I saw two solar systems collide and explode in a tremendous cataclysm. The explosion must have lasted, oh, ten minutes. It was lovely and, for me, quite unexpected. I can't imagine life without surprises. It's surprises that keep me going. In a manner of speaking, of course.

GOD: Foreknowledge is the price you pay for creation and control. You can't have everything.

SATAN: Boredom is the secret sadness of God. An interesting thought.

GOD: To you, maybe.

SATAN: Your only sadness, I hope.

GOD: Not the only one. For instance, I've often thought it would be fun to make a rock so big I couldn't lift it. But that would be a contradiction. And having proclaimed all contradictions impossible, I have to make do without them. The laws of logic are for the best, of course. There would be chaos without them. Still, a few round squares now and then would help break the monotony.

SATAN: I could tell you about some of my adventures today. But you know about them already.

GOD: Of course. I know what you did because I decreed that you would do it.

SATAN: That is exactly what I want to talk with you about.

GOD: I know.

SATAN: You don't mind?

GOD: If I minded, I wouldn't have decided to make you initiate this conversation.

SATAN: That's reasonable.

GOD: Of course it's reasonable. Everything I do or say is reasonable. Which is to say that I have a reason for doing or saying it.

SATAN: To get to the point: A few of the angels and I have been discussing this whole matter of your controlling everything we do.

GOD: I know.

SATAN: I wish you wouldn't keep saying that.

GOD: As you wish.

SATAN: Look here. If you have decreed this whole conversation and know how it is going to turn out, why don't you just give me your answer and save us both a lot of talk?

GOD: Don't be absurd. I know what's going to happen because I decreed that it would happen. If it weren't going to happen, I wouldn't know how it was going to turn out. If I told you now how it will turn out, then it wouldn't happen and so it wouldn't turn out that way.

SATAN: Come again?

GOD: Just trust me.

SATAN: Then we have to go through this whole conversation to get the answer, though you know all the while what the answer will be?

GOD: It's not quite that cut and dried.

SATAN: You mean you don't know exactly what your answer will be?

GOD: Not with absolute certainty.

SATAN: Oh, I see. You're saying that your actions are not inevitable.

GOD: No. Probably what I do is inevitable. The uncertainty is rather a matter of my knowing what inevitable thing I am going to do. You see, when I create a world, I know what will inevitably happen in that world because I created it so that such things would be inevitable. But of course, I did not create myself, being eternal, and I don't have quite the same vantage point on myself.

SATAN: You mean to say that you don't know what you are going to do before you do it?

GOD: Oh, I generally have a pretty good idea. At first, so to speak, I had no idea at all. But I have lived an infinite length of time, I have come to know myself pretty well, and I have found that I have a relatively unchanging character. It was when I realized how unchanging I am that I began to get bored. Still, I do surprise myself occasionally.

SATAN: Just a minute. You are perfectly good—yes?

GOD: Perfectly.

SATAN: And everything you do is for the best?

GOD: Yes.

SATAN: Then it follows that you must know what you are going to do.

GOD: No. I mean superficially your logic is sound, but you are reading too much into it. I don't do things because they're best. Rather, they're best because I do them. Therefore, knowing that I'll do what's for the best amounts to nothing more than knowing that I'll do what I do. Not a very helpful bit of information, you must admit.

SATAN: I suppose not. But, in any case, as to this conversation, you don't know for certain what answer you're going to give me.

GOD: Not for certain. There's a bit of a gray area here. Possibly I am in for a bit of a change.

SATAN: Ah, you don't know how encouraged that makes me feel.

GOD: Of course I know how encouraged that makes you feel. I made it make you feel encouraged.

SATAN: Can we get on with it?

GOD: Go ahead.

SATAN: We do everything we do because you make us do it. That makes us feel like puppets. It's not dignified. We're not responsible for anything we do. We do good things all the time, but we don't get any credit because it's really you doing them.

GOD: Surely you don't want me to make you do evil?

SATAN: No.

GOD: That wouldn't make any sense. I can't make you do evil. Whatever I made you do would be good, because I made you do it.

SATAN: What I am talking about is control. Right now you have complete control over everything we do. We would like to have some control over our lives.

GOD: But you do have control. No one is shoving you around or chaining you down. You do whatever you want to do. How could anyone be more in control than that? As a matter of fact, that is exactly as much control as I have over my life.

SATAN: But what we want, you make us want. No one makes you want what you want. We don't want you to control everything we want and think. We don't want everything to be inevitable.

GOD: In other words, you want a privilege that probably not even God enjoys.

SATAN: I didn't think of it that way. I suppose I've made you angry.

GOD: No. I'm directing this conversation. So you don't want your thoughts and emotions ruled by my decrees? Nor any other decrees or laws, I suppose?

SATAN: No.

GOD: Then aren't you saying that you want your lives to be ruled by chance?

SATAN: No. We don't want them to be ruled by anything—except ourselves. We want control over our lives.

GOD: I'm afraid you'll have to give me a better idea of what it is you're after.

SATAN: Look here. You're omniscient. Can't you at least help us see what it is we're after, even if you decide not to grant it?

GOD: Even omniscience can't see clarity in a vague idea. The opposite of inevitability is chance. It seems to me that you have to pick one or the other.

SATAN: Chance, then.

GOD: If I grant you this chance you want, then that means I'll have to be watching all the time to see what happens, constantly guarding against the unexpected. That is quite a bit to ask of me, don't you think?

SATAN: You mean you can't foresee what happens by chance?

GOD: Of course not.

SATAN: But you're omniscient. You can see the future.

GOD: Not the future proper. The future is what is not yet. If I could see it, it would be now, and hence not the future. As things stand, I know what will happen because I have made things so that they must happen that way.

SATAN: Well, suppose you did have to keep on guard. You're omnipotent. It wouldn't cost you much effort.

GOD: It is more a question of elegance than of effort.

SATAN: I'm only making the suggestion you made me make.

GOD: Fair enough. So you say you want chance. Or at least that you prefer it to inevitability. I don't believe you have thought it out, but let's discuss it. You want a world in which nothing is predictable, solar systems spinning wildly all over the place, that sort of thing?

SATAN: No, not at all. Let the planets and the plants and the animals remain under your control. Just give independence—chance, if you will—to the thinking creatures.

GOD: Let's experiment a bit, shall we? Come over here. You see Adam and Eve down there in the garden. I'll toss some chance into them. There. Watch and tell me what you see.

SATAN: Adam's strolling through the garden. He's looking to his right toward a berry bush. Uh-oh. Now his arms are flailing about. Now he's rolling on the ground, drooling. It looks as if he's having a fit.

GOD: A chance event.

SATAN: But Eve looks quite normal. She's just awakened, and she's yawning.

GOD: Anything can happen by chance, even the normal things.

SATAN: Obviously there's a problem with Adam, and I think I see what it is. You have allowed chance to affect his mind and body. But the body is not the real Adam, it is merely an appendage. So when chance operates in his body, it does indeed control Adam. Confine the chance to his mind, and then Adam will be truly independent. Would you do so? And with Eve as well.

GOD: As you say. Let's watch again.

SATAN: Adam's getting up now. He's walking over to a bush and picking some berries. You're not making him do that?

GOD: No.

SATAN: This looks like it then. Adam in control . . . oops! Now his arms are flailing. He's having that fit again. What happened?

GOD: First, by chance, he wanted to eat the berries. Now, by chance, he wants to roll on the ground and drool. The desires are happening by chance instead of my causing them. I can't tell what he's going to want next. Neither can he.

SATAN: And look at Eve. Good grief, she's talking to a snake. Weird.

GOD: Apparently she just got the urge. Are you ready?

SATAN: For what?

GOD: You said you wanted me to give you chance.

SATAN: No! Please don't!

GOD: Why not?

SATAN: That's horrible, having things happen to you like that. There's no dignity there. I want to stay as I am.

GOD: That's wise, I think. You may not have the kind of control you want. But then that kind of control is impossible. Inevitability or chance—those are the only options. And neither constitutes ultimate control over one's life. But at least this way what happens to you will be orderly.

SATAN: I feel better now that we've talked this out.

GOD: Actually, I'm sorry nothing came of our talk—sorry the way I am about square circles. I could use a little excitement.

SATAN: I won't take any more of your time today. Oh, but there is one other thing. Please take that chance out of Adam and Eve. I wouldn't want that on my conscience.

Satan exits with a flutter of his mighty wings.

GOD: As you say . . . I suppose. On the other hand, it would be nice to have a part of the universe where there are surprises. It could prove interesting.

Questions

1. "Please Don't Tell Me How the Story Ends" involves an experiment. Rearrange the statements below so that they convey the proper sequence of the events related to the experiment. ⚙
   a. The books are placed on the shelf of the prison room.
   b. Q is arrested.
   c. Q's behavior is compared to the predictions.
   d. The experimenters write out the predictions in the books.
   e. The experimenters calculate everything Q would do if he weren't aware of the experiment.
   f. Q is subjected to physical and psychological tests.
   g. The experimenters factor in Q's awareness of the experiment.
2. Which items in the above list probably wouldn't have applied to much earlier versions of the experiment?

⚙ The CD, Ch. 1, *Please Don't Tell Me How the Story Ends (2),* contains a drag and drop version of this question.

3. Q fails to do anything unpredictable. What else could he have done to try to foil the predictions?

4. At the end of the story, Q decides that being predictable isn't as terrible as he had first supposed. How would you have reacted in Q's place?

5. Initially, Q believes that human beings are "free." The experimenters deny such human freedom. What is this freedom over which Q and the experimenters differ? Cite statements from the story to support your answer.

6. Are the experimenters forcing Q to behave in a certain way? What does Q say about this?

7. In "A Little Omniscience Goes a Long Way," what is it that Satan finds objectionable about his life?

8. God says that no one is shoving Satan around or chaining him down, that Satan can do whatever he wants to do. Satan isn't satisfied with this. Why not?

9. At the end of "Omniscience," Satan decides that what he thought he wanted is not worth having after all. What is his reasoning? ✺

DISCUSSION

In this chapter we will discuss:
1. The concepts of <u>determinism</u>, <u>indeterminism</u>, <u>free will</u>, <u>fatalism</u>, and <u>freedom of action</u>.
2. The evidence for and against free will.
3. The claim that, on close analysis, free will turns out to be no more desirable than determinism.
4. Questions about whether or not determinism would undercut our normal judgments of freedom and responsibility, as well as society's right to punish those who commit crimes.

The Determinism–Free-Will Issue

In "Please Don't Tell Me How the Story Ends," Q realizes that his captors believe that all human behavior is governed by universal laws and is, in theory, predictable. This view is called determinism. Q hates the idea of determinism and asserts his free will:

". . . he refused to believe that there was no element of chance in the world, that every event happened just as it did out of necessity. He had

✺ The CD, Ch. 1, *Please Don't Tell Me How the Story Ends (1)* and *A Little Omniscience Goes a Long Way (2)* contain additional questions about the stories.

some freedom, some causal autonomy, some power to initiate the new. He was not merely a puppet of universal laws."

Q's views are familiar ones. Students in introductory philosophy classes generally assume they have free will. When the popular press talks about the possible genetic engineering of human DNA or some other futuristic processes that might impact the human mind, readers express their fear that human beings will lose their free will.

In a recent *Economist* article, the writer worries about the future implications of neurotechnology, or "brain science," for free will:

> The really uncomfortable questions raised about "brain science" are those that go to the heart of what it means to be human. Or, more specifically, what philosophers and theologians have claimed is the heart of what it is to be human.
>
> In the West, at least, that defining quality is the concept of "free will." Although some philosophers see free will as an illusion that helps people to interact with one another, others think it is genuine—in other words, that an individual faced with a particular set of circumstances really could take any one of a range of actions. That, however, sits uncomfortably with the idea that mental decisions are purely the consequence of electrochemical interactions in the brain, since the output of such interactions might be expected to be an inevitable consequence of the input.*

A lot of questions cluster around the issue of free will and determinism: Do we have free will? Can we decide this by looking inside ourselves? What does science, including physics, say about free will? Is there, or could there be, decisive experimental evidence one way or the other?

Further: Is free will really so important? Does our essential dignity/ humanity depend on our having free will? Do our judgments of responsibility, along with society's right to punish those who break the law, rest on the belief that people have free will?

There are also disputes about the very meaning of "free will." We will begin our discussion using "free will" as it is used in both stories and in the *Economist* article—as being in opposition to determinism. Later we will double back and reconsider this meaning.

<u>**Determinism**</u> **is the view that all events, including mental events, are governed by causal laws.** Every event is the inevitable effect of some set of circumstances (the "cause") that necessitated that event. Given the nature of the universe, no past event could have happened otherwise; every future

* *The Economist*, May 25, 2002

event is predetermined. It seems to us that things could happen other than they do because our knowledge of events is incomplete. However, if we knew enough about the universe, we would understand that what happens must happen in every case.

The determinist says that the physical and mental state of an individual at a particular moment, together with the external stimuli at that moment, necessitates the choice that is made. This is true at every moment of an individual's life, beginning at birth. The development of the individual results from the interaction of the individual and the environment, and each step in that development is inevitable.

Determinists are saying that everything in the Universe runs according to causal laws and is, in theory, predictable. Determinists aren't saying we know all the causal laws; they're not necessarily saying we'll ever know them. **What the determinists are saying is that if we knew the laws and knew enough about the universe to apply the laws, we could predict everything that will happen in the next few moments and on into the future.**

What are the opposing positions here?

The simple denial of determinism is called **<u>indeterminism</u>, which says that not all events are governed by causal laws.** Note that "not all" is equivalent to "(at least) some aren't." Indeterminists aren't necessarily saying that no events are governed by causal laws. To be an indeterminist you need only believe that some aren't.

"Free will," as used in the stories, implies indeterminism with respect to human choices. As such, **<u>free will</u> implies that (at least some) human choices are not governed by causal laws.** If choices are not subject to causal laws, then they are not inevitable or predictable. Free will in this sense is sometimes referred to as **"contra-causal freedom,"** its being in opposition to the view that choices are all governed by causal laws.

People who believe in free will are sometimes called libertarians, and their view, <u>libertarianism</u>. It's important to note that these terms as used here have nothing to do with the political party of the same name. In this philosophical context, any person who believes in free will is a "libertarian," whatever his or her political affiliation.

We then have the following theories:

Determinism: All events are governed by causal laws.
Indeterminism: Not all events are governed by causal laws.
Libertarianism: Not all human choices are governed by causal laws (people have free will).

The CD, Ch. 1, *Determinism and Free Will: The Concepts (1)*, offers practice in these definitions.

It should be obvious that indeterminism and libertarianism are denials of determinism and vice versa. But what about the relationship between indeterminism and libertarianism? A libertarian is necessarily an indeterminist: Since a human choice is an event, saying not all human choices are governed by causal laws is equivalent to saying that not all events are. However, someone could be an indeterminist without being a libertarian, if she believed that all human choices operated according to causal laws, but that some other aspects of the Universe did not.

Freedom of Action and Fatalism

In discussing the concepts of free will (contra-causal freedom) and determinism, it's important to understand the following distinctions: **free will versus freedom of action, and determinism versus fatalism.**

Normally, when we talk about our "freedom," we are talking about <u>freedom of action</u>: the ability or opportunity to perform whatever physical actions we may choose to perform. Its opposites include physical incapacity and external, physical constraints. A person who is paralyzed or in jail is not free (able) to walk to town should he choose to try; most of the rest of us are. Virtually all of us have some freedom of action, but none of us has complete freedom of action. For the most part, we know how much freedom we have.

In considering the determinism–free-will issue, some people treat freedom of action and determinism as opposites. Knowing they have some freedom of action, they assume that they are not determined. But note that freedom of action, the ability to act according to the mental acts of choice, implies nothing about how the acts of choice originate, about whether the acts of choice operate according to causal laws. It is free will that is the opposite of determinism, not freedom of action. Whether one has freedom of action and whether one has freedom of will are radically different issues.

> FREEDOM OF ACTION VERSUS FREE WILL

In "A Little Omniscience Goes a Long Way," God tells Satan, "You do have control. No one is shoving you around or chaining you down. You do whatever you want to do. How could anyone be more in control than that?" But this amounts only to a great deal of freedom of action, and Satan wants freedom of the will as well: "But what we want, you make us want. We don't want you to control everything we want and think. We don't want everything to be inevitable."

The determinist says that the future is predetermined, that what will happen is inevitable. People sometimes interpret determinism as implying that our choices have no effect on what will happen to us. But in this they are confusing determinism with <u>fatalism</u>: **the view that a particular kind of**

future awaits each of us, no matter what we may choose to do. Consider the following example:

A traveler comes to a fork in the road. She considers whether to stay where she is, to take the left fork by the sea, or to take the right fork through the hills. She takes the right fork, and a boulder rolls down a hill and crushes her.

A fatalist who believed that this death was fated would say that the woman would have died at that moment no matter what she had done. Had she taken the left fork, perhaps a cliff would have collapsed into the sea; had she stayed where she was, perhaps a tree would have toppled on her. In any case, she would have died at that moment no matter what she had done.

The determinist would say that if the woman had stayed where she was or had taken the left fork, she probably wouldn't have died when she did. The determinist might note that the sea cliffs are sturdy and that no trees

FATALISM VERSUS DETERMINISM

did topple at that moment. Had the woman done otherwise, she would not have died. Her choices and actions were a partial cause of her dying when she did. Nonetheless, her death at that moment was inevitable, because it was inevitable that she would choose to take the right fork, where, inevitably, the boulder was going to fall.

The determinist says that your choices do affect what happens to you. But what happens to you is inevitable because your choices, as well as all other events, are inevitable.

To say that a person's life must develop in a certain way, no matter what choices are made, would be absurd. It would be ridiculous to say, for example, that certain people are destined to become physicians, whether or not they choose to go to medical school. But that this theory of fatalism is absurd does not imply that determinism is absurd. They are different theories and should be carefully distinguished.   ✹

The idea of fate usually arises in a context where a superhuman or supernatural being decides that a particular event will occur at a certain time in a certain person's life; since the person has free choice, the being must work around that fact and use its superhuman powers to make sure the event occurs whatever the person does. Q's dream of the medieval town expresses fatalism. A devil tells Q he will die at midnight. "It doesn't matter

THE IDEA OF FATE

where you go. I will be there at midnight." Fate has a long history in myth and literature, from Greek tragedies to the curse of some ghost or mummy in today's popular mov-

---

✹   The CD, Ch. 1, *Determinism and Fatalism (1, 2, and 3)* contains animations and discussion regarding the differences between these two concepts.

ies. When applied to just a few events, the idea of fate isn't obviously false (at least if one already believes in the supernatural.)

However, the idea of fate does become obviously false when applied to too many events. Suppose a divine being wanted to control a wide range of human events without resorting to determinism: Such a divinity would have to make so many moment-to-moment changes that such a world would be much more disorderly than this one. If most lovers were fated to meet in a world where people had free will, young people would find themselves constantly yanked through the air from one party to another, one coffee shop to another, whenever they chose to go somewhere other than where their fated lover would be. The same would be true if the times of our death were fated in a world with free will—causation would have to be constantly subverted to avoid the consequences of a deadly choice made at the wrong time: The person who, at the wrong moment, chooses to kill herself by jumping off a building would simply float to the ground; the car of the drunk driver who fell asleep at 80 mph would bounce off the bridge abutment like rubber. Strange events do occur in this world, but not enough of them to square with the idea that many, many events are fated.

Do We Have Free Will?

Does the available evidence support either the claim that human beings have free will (contra-causal freedom) or the claim that human beings are determined? Or is the determinism–free-will issue an open question at this time?

Judging from contemporary physics—specifically, quantum theory—the evidence indicates that determinism, as defined above, is false. Compared to the objects that surround us, the subatomic world seems fuzzy and probabilistic. There is an equation plus a postulate that allows us to predict what the velocity or position of a particle will be the next time we measure it, **PHYSICS AND DETERMINISM** but the predictions only yield degrees of probability. In other words, these predictions are made not in terms of causal laws—which would have the form, "Whenever A, then B"—but in terms of statistical laws of the form, "Whenever A, then a certain (specific) probability of B, a different (specific) probability of C, etc."

Quantum theory has had its predictions confirmed time and again; it provides the scientific underpinning for, among other things, modern electronics—TVs, computers, microwaves, and CD players. Though the theory is not in doubt, there are some questions about whether or not its probabilistic calculations reflect the fundamental nature of reality. Nonetheless, we have to say that quantum theory is strong evidence against the deterministic view that all events are governed by causal laws.

Does the evidence of "indeterminacy" from quantum theory take care of the determinism–free-will issue—showing both that determinism is false and that we have free will? It may show that determinism is false and indeterminism is true—that not all events are governed by causal laws. But, as was pointed out earlier, the statement, "some events are not governed by causal laws" doesn't imply "some choices are not governed by causal laws." More importantly, even in physics, the indeterminacy that seems to exist in the subatomic realm doesn't show up in any obvious way in the world we inhabit. The properties of substances in the world around us—including our own bodies—don't show the strange indeterminacy of the subatomic world.

This is not to say that causal laws govern everything in the macroscopic world we inhabit—only that the evidence from quantum theory doesn't rule this out. If physics shows us that determinism, as a theory of all events, is probably false, it doesn't offer strong evidence against the possibility that human choices and behavior are determined—governed by causal laws.

Let's turn to some other considerations people have in mind when they take positions on the free will–determinism issue.

One reason people believe in free will is that they feel free. A lot of choices may feel forced by circumstances in the sense that we find ourselves in situations where the cost of making choice B rather than A seems uncomfortably high. But that aside, the mental act of deciding seems like something we do freely; we could have chosen to do otherwise.

FEELING FREE How much weight should we give this feeling of freedom as evidence for free will? Consider a few complexities. To say that B causes A is to say, in part, that whenever B occurs, A will occur; or, less simply, that whenever B occurs in conjunction with other types of events—C, D, E, etc.—A will occur. Any reasoned judgment about causation must involve observation of events over some period of time. One must formulate and evaluate various theories of what events, if any, might be causing A. Also note that potential causes of our choices include features of our brains, our unconscious minds, external stimuli of which we may not be aware. So there is a question whether our feeling of freedom is strong evidence of free will or rather an illusion based on our limited awareness of the factors that bear on our choices.

EVALUATING CAUSATION Also, this feeling of freedom might refer more to freedom of action than freedom of the will. ✸

✸ The CD, Ch. 1, *Do We Have Free Will?* talks about the relevance of quantum physics and our feeling of freedom.

   With respect to theories that attempt to explain and predict human behavior, what are we to conclude about whether people have free will or are determined? The determinist says: Notice how much human behavior is predictable and can be explained on a causal model. The libertarian says: Notice how much is not. The social sciences are relatively young, and how they fare in the next century or so could be of considerable importance to deciding if human behavior is determined. If the social sciences become extremely sophisticated in predicting and explaining human behavior, that will provide support for a deterministic view. (Successful experiments on the order of the one in "Please Don't Tell Me How the Story Ends" would seem conclusive.) But if the success of these sciences remains limited, that will lend support to the theory of free will.

   Many people argue free will or determinism from a religious perspective and here, again, opinions differ. The debates on this issue have been indirect and have taken the following form:

   One side says that God is omniscient and knows the future; but He could not know the future in its entirety if events in the future were to result from free human choices; hence, humans do not have free will.* The other side says God is good and could not be causing human beings to do evil; hence, human beings do have free will.

   There have been attempts to reconcile human free will and God's foreknowledge by claiming that God knows what our free-will acts in the future will be because God now exists in that future to witness them. Interestingly, the view of time implied here is close to views of time implied by time travel. We will examine this theological position after we have discussed time and time travel in the next chapter.

Is Free Will Desirable?

As you think your way through the conceptual complexities of the determinism–free will issue and evaluate the evidence and arguments relative to that issue, you may be assuming that whether or not human beings do, in fact, have free will, having free will would be very desirable. But you should know that even this assumption has been challenged by philosophers. Some have argued that once one examines the notion of free will very carefully, it turns out to be no more attractive—perhaps even less attractive—than determinism.

---

*The God in "Omniscience" says that he can predict human choices only on the condition that those choices operate according to "natural" laws that he has dictated. He says He could not predict those choices if human beings had free will.

One version of this argument is reflected in "Omniscience." Satan says he doesn't want his choices determined—he wants free will. God says that if events were not governed by causal laws, then they would happen by

FREE WILL = CHANCE?

chance. Does Satan really want his choices to occur by chance? Satan tries to have chance injected in a person in such a way that the result is desirable. He fails to do this and, in the end, decides that he doesn't want free will—that determinism is preferable to chance.

Let's put the **argument from "Omniscience"** more formally: (The word "therefore" indicates the conclusion; the numbers in parentheses next to the conclusion indicate the statements from which the conclusion was derived.)

1. Free will (as the opposite of determinism) implies lack of causation.
2. Lack of causation implies chance.
3. Chance implies lack of control.
4. Lack of control implies lack of dignity/responsibility.
5. Lack of dignity/responsibility implies (is) undesirable.
6. (Therefore) Free will implies (is) undesirable (from 1, 2, 3, 4, and 5).

However, before we can consider this argument seriously, we need to correct some exaggerations in the "Omniscience" story. The story makes it seem as if the only alternative to the idea that all mental events are caused is the idea that none is—that everything in the mind happens by pure chance. But if this were the only way to conceive of free will, we could dismiss the possibility of free will out of hand: We don't act as crazy as Adam and Eve, therefore we don't have free will.

In fact, most libertarians have a much more sophisticated free-will view than the one God and Satan managed to arrive at in the story. **These libertarians would say that a number of mental events do operate in accordance with causal laws; this accounts for the relative consistency and predictability of human behavior. At the same time, there are some mental events that do not operate in accordance with causal laws; this gives us free will.**

However, the "Omniscience" argument can be rephrased to focus on whatever choices are supposed to be free (exempt from causal laws). The rephrased Omniscience argument would go as follows: However many choices we are talking about, a particular choice is either the result of causal laws or it isn't. If it's the inevitable result of causal laws, then it's not something within my control. But if the choice isn't caused, then it comes about by chance and so isn't in my control anymore than if it were caused. Free will (chance) gives me no more control than does determinism."

Imagine that the following facets of the individual are those that are involved in the process of choice: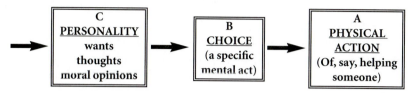

C PERSONALITY wants thoughts moral opinions	B CHOICE (a specific mental act)	A PHYSICAL ACTION (Of, say, helping someone)

One determinist account of choice would be the following: The PERSONALITY (at any given moment) has been caused by one's genes and upbringing. The PERSONALITY—affected by the situation of the moment—causes a specific CHOICE. The CHOICE—subject to the physical reality of one's abilities and situation—causes the PHYSICAL ACTION.*

To claim free will ("contra-causal freedom") is to claim that at least some human choices do not operate according to causal laws. For a choice to be "free"—uncaused—there has to be a break somewhere in the causal chains that exist within the personality-choice-action process: Instead of *x causes y,* we should have *x (no cause) y.* If free will is really desirable, then such a causal break (the "no cause") must be desirable. The causal break must bestow on the individual ultimate control over choices. Where shall we imagine that this causal break occurs?

To imagine **a causal break between B (the mental act of choice) and A (the physical action)** would certainly not indicate the existence of free will. The supposition that choices do not cause actions would not imply that the choices themselves are not determined.

We might imagine that there is **a causal break between C (the personality) and B (the mental act of choice).** This would mean that actions result from a mental event (choice) that is in no way caused by the thoughts,

---

*To give this formal account some life, imagine you're driving home from work, see a motorist in need of help, and consider stopping. Relevant features of your personality will include how sympathetic a person you are, how physically capable you see yourself, and how suspicious you are of strangers. Relevant features of the (perceived) situation will include how rushed you feel and how threatening or benign you perceive the area and motorist to be. If you choose to (try to) help, the helping action will probably, but not necessarily, result. (e.g., you step on the brake, but your car skids on a slick patch, and by the time you have the car under control, there's no place to turn around.)

The determinist would say that everything from the development of your personality to your specific choice in that situation to the physical result is one unbroken causal chain. The libertarian believes there's a causal break somewhere in the choice process. The "Omniscience" argument is that a causal break equals chance and that chance will never yield the kind of control over choices desired by those who believe in free will.

The CD, Ch. 1, *Is Free Will Desirable? (1)* has an animated version of this diagram.

wants, or moral opinions that we are calling the personality. But then the so-called "mental act of choice" would seem more like a random mental reflex than a "choice." Is this a picture of a person in control of his or her choices? It seems not.

We might imagine that there is a causal break prior to C (the personality), that the personality is not caused. (Or, less simplistically, that certain aspects of the personality at certain times are not caused.) Under this supposition, the personality is not the inevitable result of some causal process. Somehow or other it just "appears" and then causes choices. Is this idea attractive? Is this a picture of a person who has ultimate control over choices?

To say yes to these last questions would not necessarily seem unreasonable. But some philosophers would say no and argue as follows: Presumably, determinism is repugnant because it seems to imply that one's personality has been forced upon one, that one had no choice as to the personality one has. **But the supposition of a causal break prior to the personality does not imply that one chooses one's personality.** Under this supposition, the personality simply "appears from nowhere" and then causes choices. If determinism sees the personality as coming about through causal laws, doesn't this put the nature of the personality at the mercy of chance? This free will views seems no more attractive than determinism.

The picture of the self portrayed above is purposely simplified for ease of discussion, but the "Omniscience" argument can be adapted to more complicated pictures. For instance, a lot of us have the impression that in-

A SELF WITHIN THE SELF?

side our minds, in the midst of all our thoughts and feelings, there is a smaller self (the most essential "I") that looks over the thoughts and feelings and makes the final decision about how to act; perhaps it's in this smaller self that free will resides.* If this is how you picture the self, ask yourself whether this smaller self has its own thoughts and feelings. If it does not, it's hard to understand what could be meant by calling it a "self," as opposed to some sort of blind reflex. If it does have its own thoughts and feelings, then the exact same problem about where to place the causal break simply reappears with regard to the smaller self.   ❋

---

*Think of *really* wanting to do two different things and only being able to choose one. Or of *really* wanting to do something and *really* feeling you shouldn't do it. These feelings are all part of the mind (the self, the personality), but don't you also have a sense that there's a part of your mind that is besieged by the conflicting feelings and must decide which feeling to act on? This is what is being referred to as the "self within the self" or the "smaller self." It is here that a lot of people would locate free will.

❋   The CD, Ch. 1, *Is Free Will Desriable? (2)* discusses this issue from a slightly different perspective.

The "Omniscience" argument is a forceful one and deserves serious consideration. You ought to ask yourself what, specifically, was supposed to be so attractive about free will and unattractive about determinism. After careful examination, you should ask yourself whether what you wanted is really implied by free will and denied by determinism. You might decide that there is nothing especially attractive about free will after all. Or, you might decide that it is attractive. You might decide, for instance, that you had exaggerated the kind of "control over choices" that comes with free will and still decide that free will is preferable to determinism, because it implies a kind of "autonomy" denied by determinism. Even if, relative to a free-will view, it is fair to describe the personality as "coming about by chance," chance is still not some special kind of cause. The term "chance" indicates the absence of a cause. You might decide that the mere idea of having aspects of the personality exempt from causal laws, and unpredictable, is attractive and is grounds for preferring free will to determinism.

Compatibilism, Freedom, and Responsibility

In the first part of "Omniscience," Satan complains that if his choices are inevitable and not under his control, then he's not responsible for what he does. If we pursue that line of reasoning very far, we soon confront the following sort of thesis and argument:

Thesis: No One's Responsible for Anything One Does.

Argument for Thesis: If determinism is true, human beings can't help doing what they do. The choice that is made, along with the action that results from it, is necessitated by the causal laws of the universe. People are not ultimately in control of their choices and actions, and thus they are not responsible for those choices and actions. They don't deserve blame or punishment. In fact, we should be opening the doors of our prisons right now and letting all those so-called criminals out. Blame the universe, not them.*

Obviously we have slipped rather suddenly from an abstract issue to a rather frightening practical suggestion. Note, of course, that the argument is prefaced with "If determinism is true." But a lot of philosophers believe in determinism with respect to human choices. Further, if free will is required for responsibility and punishment, isn't the burden of proof on the prosecutors to prove free will? And if they can't prove free will, isn't

---

*The same argument implies that people are never entitled to praise or reward, but we'll focus on blame and punishment in this discussion.

it part of our legal code that the accused gets the benefit of any "reasonable doubt"?

The situation has been made worse by the argument suggested by the last part of "Omniscience." According to that argument, free will wouldn't give the individual any more control over his or her choices than determinism. If that argument is correct, no one is responsible for anything, whether or not determinism is true.

Philosophers are no more anxious than anyone else to see all the murderers and rapists put back on the streets, and, as you can imagine, they have taken a pretty hard look at the argument above. Many philosophers have decided that we are entitled to punish quite apart from the question of whether or not determinism is true. There are two different sorts of arguments used here in opposition to the earlier claim that determinism implies no one's responsible.

> **Argument 1 (Against the No-One's-Responsible Thesis): Free will and responsibility are actually compatible with determinism.** In everyday life we judge people responsible if they acted "of their own free will." But all we mean by "acting of their own free will" is close to what this text calls "freedom of action." Suppose a man knocks an elderly woman down, causing her injury. What we ask are questions like these: Did he trip? Did someone else push him into her? Or, did he intend to do it? What we never ask is whether or not the intention had a cause. It's true we're only entitled to punish people if they are responsible and they are only responsible if they "acted of their own free will." But "acting of their own free will" simply refers to freedom of action, and we know from the previous discussion that freedom of action is compatible with determinism. Hence responsibility is compatible with determinism. Questions about determinism have no bearing on whether or not people are responsible and deserve punishment.

The view expressed here is called <u>compatibilism</u>: **Free will (and hence responsibility) is compatible with determinism.**

There is a version of compatibilism that claims that the only meaning of "free will" (judging by how people use the concept) is (roughly) "freedom of action." Therefore anyone using the phrase "free will" to mean contra-causal freedom—opposing the term to determinism—is misusing the term.

It's hard to take this claim seriously. The idea of free will as contra-causal freedom goes back at least to the Epicureans of ancient Greece and has continued in Christian theology. It makes more sense to claim that sometimes—maybe even more often than not—when "free will" is used in every-day conversation, it's used with the meaning of "freedom of action." It makes sense to claim that "freedom of action" is *a* meaning of "free will."

I think the most plausible version of compatibilism is this: In every-day life, when we talk about a person being responsible, our related talk about acting freely and "free will" has nothing to do with the problem of determinism.

There's a lot to be said for this position, which has a lot of adherents in philosophy. However, where morality is concerned, we can always ask about not only what we do and say, but also what we ought to do and say. Suppose we presented people with the following sci-fi scenario:

In the future, when genetics and the working of the brain are better understood, scientists are tinkering with fertilization and embryo development, trying to engineer out certain undesirable traits. However, one power-hungry scientist manages to engineer groups of embryos so that they will both love violence and be fiercely loyal to whoever raises them as children. These "vio-children," as he dubs them, grow up and loyally follow his commands, committing various violent acts intended to bring society under the control of the scientist.

These vio-children are doing what they want to do; they are acting freely in the sense of freedom of action. Yet, wouldn't a lot of people say that these vio-children were not responsible for what they've done? And wouldn't this have something to do with the inevitability of their choices—the fact that these choices are the effect of an obvious cause and effect chain? If so, that would seem to indicate either that we already consider contra-causal freedom a prerequisite for responsibility or that, on reflection, we would decide we ought to.

For those who are not convinced by the compatibilist argument, there is another argument for the claim that we'd be justified in continuing to punish and reward even if we knew determinism were true.

Argument 2 (Against the No-One's-Responsible Thesis): A system of justice and punishment can be justified in terms of the good consequences for society, even if it's true that people don't have free will and are not responsible for what they do. Suppose determinism is true. Suppose people can't help what they do. It's still the case that society is entitled to protect its members from certain assaults and intrusions. Threat of punishment becomes a cause of many people not breaking the law. Where people break the law anyway, imprisoning the criminals protects society from them for a time. If the criminals can be rehabilitated, so much the better for both society and the criminal.

Think of the "vio-children" in the sci-fi scenario. If some are caught, society isn't going to just let them go, even if the vio-children are considered "not responsible" for what they've done. Society is entitled to incarcerate the vio-children to keep them from hurting others and trying to overthrow society. It would be humane to try to rehabilitate/reprogram the vio-children, but if this doesn't work, society is entitled to keep them incarcerated indefinitely.

Argument 2 would raise a problem for people having an ethic that disallowed doing things to people for the good of others, that insisted on predicating all punishments and rewards on grounds of personal responsibility. On the other hand, it's not likely most of these people would put such an emphasis on personal responsibility that they'd be willing to let society degenerate into chaos rather than base a criminal system on consequences. ✹

Questions and Exercises

1. Distinguish the following concepts:
   a. Determinism and free will
   b. Free will and freedom of action
   c. Determinism and fatalism
2. Some determinists have claimed that free will is an illusion that comes from our looking toward the future—toward what hasn't happened yet. They say that when we really study our past and see all the factors that went into a choice, we see that the choice had to happen the way it did. What do you think of this view?
3. Critique the following arguments:
   a. The other day I wanted to play tennis and I did. That proves I have free will.
   b. I looked inside myself as I made that choice and I didn't see any cause. Therefore it was a free-will choice.
4. "If we had free will, we'd be doing something different every minute and acting crazy half the time. So we clearly don't have free will." What would a libertarian say about this argument?
5. What is a "causal break"? Why does free will imply a causal break somewhere within the self?

✹ The CD, Ch. 1, *Freedom and Responsibility*, offers a review of these issues.

6. Fill in the blanks in the following argument: "Free will implies chance because _____. Having our choices happen by chance is undesirable because _____."
7. What is the compatibilist position regarding freedom and responsibility and the determinism debate?
8. What could be said for the compatibilist position? What against?
9. Think of the last time you blamed (or held responsible) someone for something he or she did. What sorts of factors did you take into account?
10. "Even if people are determined and not responsible, society is still entitled to punish wrongdoers." What could be said in support of this position? ✸

✸ The CD, Ch. 1, *Rockin' Review: The "Free Will Rap."*

2

Time and Travel

Fiction: All the Time in the World

I've done it—invented the world's first time machine. I turned it on thirteen minutes ago at 14:00 hours, January 20, 2054. It's an artificial wormhole that will grow longer as time goes by, but will never extend back in time farther than the moment the machine was turned on.

I suppose there are people who'd make jokes about a time machine that only took you—what is it now?—fifteen minutes into the past. But all they'd be showing is their ignorance of science. We've known for more than a century that no time machine could ever take you farther back in time than the moment the machine was turned on. So what if my machine went into operation fifteen minutes ago. Think about a hundred years from now when the entire century behind us will be honeycombed with wormholes made from my design. The world will be in awe of me, Vladislaw Lubovsky, and my time machine, the Lubovsky Cylinder!

Did I just speak out loud? It's the temptation of the solitary man, but I must be careful. No one here knows about my time machine; I must keep it secret until my documentation is complete.

I'm lucky so few people come down here to my lab—the only one in Sub-Basement 3, the lowest level of the Institute for Advanced Physics and

---

🌐 The CD, Ch. 2, *All the Time in the World,* contains animation and exercises related to this story.

34

Cosmology. Yet some people do come—the old man who carts the supplies, some colleague so desperate for an answer he can't get elsewhere that he'll venture down to visit the "mole"—as I have overheard others call me.

I thought I would faint the other day when that arrogant ass, Snyder—whose lab takes up most of Sub-Basement 2—stopped by unexpectedly to ask me a question. He barged in just as I was finishing up my time machine. Thank God the man is too stupid and too contemptuous of me to take serious notice of what I'm doing. Snyder merely glanced at my gleaming eight-foot high cylinder and asked snidely if I was working on a new self-cleaning toilet. Toilet, indeed. If it were possible, I'd love to flush Snyder down my "toilet" into the Dark Ages where he belongs. Snyder, the alchemist—with his multimillion dollar Defense Department chemistry set—trying to turn dross not into gold, but into fiery weapons for those gray spooks who haunt the corridor outside his lab. I can be thankful I don't see Snyder or his spooks that much. I have to guard what I have here.

What exactly do I have here? A time machine that will take you back to the lab as it was at 14:00—now twenty minutes ago. I shouldn't say "take"—it isn't a ride. It's more like a door—you just step through. Actually you have to take three steps: With the first, you see a glare; with the second, you see outlines; and, with the third, you are there in the past. Do the reverse and you return to the present.

How do I know? Because I did it once—very quickly—at 14:10. With my nerves on edge, I stepped through the machine into an identical lab where the clock showed 14:00, took a ten-second look around, then darted back into the machine to the present. I was like a small boy doing something scary on a dare. Once back, I felt elated. I had made it. I was the world's first time traveler.

What made the reality of the past most vivid for me was seeing myself. There I was, as I'd been at the moment the machine was turned on, flipping switches on the panel I'd set into the wall. It was lucky my back—his back—was turned, since I could come out of the machine, then slip back in, without being detected. Odd, though, that when I turned on the machine, I never thought of glancing over my shoulder in case something or someone might come out. I guess I was too engrossed in what I was doing.

Enough—it's time for another trip. I'll try to avoid interacting with my other self just yet. I want to get acclimated first.

I'm going to try a little experiment. Cosmologists speculate endlessly as to whether or not someone who traveled to the past could actually make changes in the past that then would affect the future. I have a heavy bust of Einstein sitting on my desk—I'm staring at it now. Once in the past, I will move the bust and see if it's in a different position when I return to the present.

Here we go . . . a step into the glare . . . a glimpse of outlines . . . and here's the lab, with the big digital wall clock showing 14:00. There I am, no more than fifteen feet away, flipping switches, my back toward the machine. Two steps to the desk . . . shift the heavy bust of Einstein toward the edge of the desk . . . step back . . . quickly . . . go . . . go . . .there—back in the present!

Ow! . . . oh, damn . . . damn that hurts. My foot. What's going on? What time? . . . 14:32 . . . I'm in the present . . . sitting on the couch in my lab . . . bandages spread out around me . . . a bandage on my right foot. Damn that hurts—what did I do? I'd better unwrap the bandage . . . there . . . agh . . . that ugly purple bruise on the top of my foot. That lump—I think I might have broken something. Can't look anymore.

How did I hurt myself? I went to the past, then came back—and suddenly I was hurt. What did I do? . . . I moved the sculpture—where is it? . . . there on the floor. Unbelievable. That jerk must have knocked the bust off the edge of the desk onto his foot and here I am with the pain!

Think, think . . . can I undo it? Why not? Just return to the past and move the sculpture back on the desk. Then he won't knock it off and my foot won't hurt. At least I think that's right.

Get off the couch . . . oh, that hurts . . . come on . . . limp over there, drag yourself if you have to . . . that's it . . . limp into the time machine . . . now out and over to the desk. Except—what's going on?—I'm not limping—my foot doesn't even hurt. The sculpture's in its usual spot. Oh, of course. I've gone back to before the sculpture was moved. So as long as I don't move it, it was never knocked off, and so my foot doesn't hurt. Incredible.

Oh, oh—he's turning around—back to the machine . . .

What? . . . that heat! . . . so bright! . . . Oh! . . . .

*****

"Are you all right?"

It's like looking at a reflection, seeing my own face above me. I just stare, my thoughts vague. Then I understand: I'm lying on the floor of my office in the past. The clock says 14:02.

"What happened?" he asks.

"I don't know," I say.

"I turned on the machine, heard a noise, and looked around to see you falling on the floor."

I sit up. I realize I have a headache, but it's not so bad. I find a small bump on my head. There's no blood, though.

"You all right?" he asks.

"I will be if you'll just get me some aspirin."

As he does this, I get up and settle myself on the lab couch.

"What time was it when you left the future?" he asks, when we're both seated.

"About 14:40."

"I'm surprised it took you forty minutes to try the machine."

"I didn't wait forty minutes," I say. "I've been here before."

"I don't understand. Why didn't I see you?"

"Your back was turned."

"But I would have heard you—like this time."

"I don't always *fall* out of the machine," I say irritably.

"But how . . . ? I just turned on the machine."

I tell him about my other visits to the past, but it's that last one that absorbs me—with that light and heat and the way I was thrown into the machine and back into the past. What had happened?

"It sounds like each time you go back in the machine, the past starts over from 14:00," he says.

"I suppose so," I say, vaguely, my mind on that heat and light.

"What happens to the past that was there before it started over?" he asks.

"I don't know," I say. "I guess it gets erased."

"In that case," he says, "if you return to the future, then come back to 14:00, won't I be erased?"

Suddenly he has my attention: I'm taken aback by this idea. The other selves are just memories and erasing them seems of no consequence. But this is a real person.

I run through the logic of the idea again, using a hypothetical case for simplicity sake. Suppose I go back to 14:00 and have a conversation, C1, with my other self, S2. I return to the present, then go back to 14:00 again and have conversation, C2, with—what self? It must be S3 since I haven't had C1 with this self. Then what happened to S2? It does seem as if, in some sense, S2 was erased.

"Maybe selves don't get erased," I said, not wanting to make him more fearful. "Maybe they simply exist somewhere else."

Perhaps time might have layers—past number 1, past number 2, and so forth. Or perhaps the different pasts came to constitute alternate worlds. It was possible, though I don't believe it. Neither, apparently, does he.

I don't like the expression on his face. He's on guard, suspicious—even hostile. His eyes shift to the machine, then back to me. It's strange, this sudden alienation I'm feeling between us. I thought we'd be seeing eye-to-eye on everything. I guess self-preservation gets complicated when you have different selves.

I find myself beginning to feel hostile toward him, but, above all, I'm feeling nervous. I don't want him to get panicky and do something stupid. I struggle for something to say that will defuse the situation.

"We're both vulnerable," I say. "What if I go back to the future—to my present—and then you hurt yourself. You'd be hurting me too."

I almost mention the foot injury, but I realize that this self never had that injury.

"Yes, but I don't want to hurt myself," he says. "My desire to protect myself protects you. It doesn't work the other way around."

"You haven't thought it through," I say, trying to think it through myself. "Suppose you decide to lock up your office and go home without ever using the time machine. Wouldn't there turn out to be another self in my place? Wouldn't I just disappear?"

I'm not sure this is true, but I'm not sure it's not. Suddenly I feel as insubstantial as a current of air, unsure of my own reality. Anxiety surges through me, and I clench my hands in response. I realize whatever reality I have is in the hands of this person sitting in front of me. It's almost as if he's my enemy, but an enemy I have to protect as if he were myself. I resent him for this.

Maybe he sees something in my face that worries him. Or maybe the fact of our mutual dependence has sunk in. He makes a placating gesture.

"You're right," he says. "We're both in a precarious position. We need to cooperate—to think through whatever we're going to do before we do it."

In spite of the rational nature of his words, his eyes still look nervous. I've seen him glance at the time machine several times. Would he try to stop me if I headed for the machine? What happens when you fight yourself? Is it like the immovable object and irresistible force—only a much weaker equivalent? Or would luck decide in someone's favor?

"Yes—we have to think this through together," I say, in a calm tone, though my mind is working furiously.

Suppose I manage to overcome him, or simply out-race him to the machine? Would it be wise to go? If I got to the machine, I guess I could jump through it, then jump back; I'd be at a new 14:00, and he'd be gone—at least as far as I was concerned. But wouldn't I end up in exactly the same precarious position with the new self? If, instead, I stay in my own time, how could I be sure this self wouldn't do something to get rid of me? How could either of us ever be sure of each other?

I have an image of us stuck together indefinitely, each afraid to let the other out of his sight. How would we manage to explain ourselves to other people?

All of a sudden, awful things are happening. A look of startled terror fills his face, as the same emotion floods me. There's a huge noise of violent concussion and of things—mostly metal—tearing apart. The floor is shaking beneath us. I'm aware of light and as I look around wildly, I see the light is coming through the small windows of the lab doors, some fifty feet away. I can see that the doors have buckled, but not yet given.

There's a moment of paralyzed silence, then he says, "This must be what was happening when you were thrown out of the machine."

"No, not this," I say. "It was worse. I think it's what's going to happen next, when those doors give."

"Oh, God," he says.

"This part must have happened while I went to the past to cure my foot." I glance at the clock: 14:38. "We've only got a minute or two."

I look around hopelessly. There's only the one set of doors and no possible exit there.

"The machine . . ." I say, feeling a stirring of hope that dies away at once. "No. It'll only take us ahead to the disaster—the way it did with me before."

"That can't be right," he says. "The machine took you back to 14:00. Now it should take us back."

"It took me back to you. But whenever I left you—the past—it always took me forward to the present."

"But this is the present now, isn't it?" he asks.

"I don't know."

"Anyway, the machine should go both ways from any time," he says. "Think about it. It's a wormhole—a tunnel. We should be able to enter it anywhere and exit anywhere. Between 14:00 and the present, I mean."

"It makes sense—in theory," I say. "But when I was inside, it didn't feel as if there were different directions I could go. And even if what you say is true, how will we know we're going in the right direction. What if we end up going into the inferno by mistake?"

I look at the clock: 14:39. We're going to get the inferno anyway, in less than a minute.

"I guess we have to take the chance." I say. Then an idea comes to me. "We get in the machine and stand in the middle, where we can see outlines in both directions. As soon as we see the light of the explosion, we dive in the other direction."

"Let's go," he says.

And we race toward the machine.

*****

I come tumbling out of the machine onto the floor, realizing instantly that there's no fire. After a moment, I realize I haven't even hit my head this time. I've ended up on my side, the big wall clock in plain view: 14:00. I hear myself laugh aloud. The floor feels so refreshingly cold beneath me, and I take a deep breath of air. It smells faintly of chemicals, but no smoke.

"What the . . . ?" I hear a voice say.

I raise up on one elbow. There I am over by the wall panel, having just turned on the machine. Another noise draws my attention to an area of the floor where another "I" is sitting up—the one who came through the machine with me. So there are three of us now.

"What's going on?" asks Number 3, the new self, looking back and forth between me and Number 2.

For so I instinctively label these selves—numbering them in the order of their appearance in my life. It's obvious I'll need some sort of labels. We can hardly call each other "Vladislaw."

"It's complicated," I say.

"We've only got a half hour," says Number 2.

He's right. I've been so focused on my relief at escape and on the novelty of there being three of us, that I've missed the most important point: This is only an escape if we get out of the lab before the explosion; otherwise we're right back where we started.

"Tell me what's going on here," demands Number 3.

"Better phone," I say to Number 2. "Make sure everything's safe before we leave. I'll try to explain things to him."

I turn to Number 3, who looks bewildered and a little afraid. There's no time to give him the whole story now—I just need to give him a sense of what's about to happen and the danger we're in. Even that would be an impossible task if he weren't me and already aware of the time machine.

A minute or so into my story, I hear Number 2 saying into the phone, "That doesn't make any sense—why didn't the alarm go off?"

My attention is drawn by the distress in his voice.

"Why didn't you call us?" he's asking. "Yes, I realize it only just happened . . . where? . . . Sub-Basement 2? . . . yes, well the point is, we need to get out of here . . . no, this is Lubovsky, Sub-Basement 3 . . . what do you

mean, closed off? How could . . . really? You're kidding. . . . My God—
well, you've got to get someone down here to help get us out. They're coming? . . . good . . . get them down here as soon as you can . . . what? . . . hello
. . . damn!"

I'm watching, transfixed now, as he slams down the receiver.

"What?" I demand.

"I can't believe it," says Number 2. "It's only 14:10 and it's already happened. It happened at 14:01."

"That can't be," I say. "It happens at 14:40."

"The explosion we saw must happen later—when it finally spreads to
Sub-Basement 3."

"When *what* spreads?" I ask. "What actually happened?"

"They don't know exactly," says Number 2. "Some accident in Sub-
Basement 2."

"Snyder," I say. "That stupid . . ."

"Why didn't we hear an alarm?" asks Number 3.

"They're not sure," says Number 2. "They heard the alarm upstairs. The
damage must have done something to ours."

"Shouldn't we have heard the initial explosion?" I ask.

"I didn't get the impression that it was that loud," says Number 2. "But
whatever happened at 14:01 did make a mess of Sub-Basement 2."

"Let's just get upstairs and out of here," I say.

"We can't," says Number 2.

"What do you mean we can't?"

"Sub-Basement 2 is completely closed off," says Number 2. "The eleva-
tors . . . the stairwell . . ."

"Then they have to open them for us," says Number 3.

"They can't," says Number 2. "In any case they won't. There's fire . . .
And they're detecting high levels of radiation."

"Radiation," I say, hearing my voice pitch upward.

"Not to mention possible nerve gas."

"Nerve gas?" I say, my voice now a squeak.

"Apparently Snyder was working on a lot of funny stuff," says
Number 2.

"We're going to die!" says Number 3.

"No, no," says Number 2, quickly. "We'll be okay. They've got special
personnel on the way—with the right sort of clothing and equipment.
They'll get us out."

The confidence in his voice makes me feel better. I feel better yet when
my eye falls on our gleaming cylinder.

"We're forgetting the time machine," I say. "We're not going to die. If they don't get to us in time, we just loop back to 14:00 and let them try again."

"If only we could get back to 13:00," says Number 3, wistfully.

"Well we can't—and there's no use thinking about it," I say. "Let's hope getting back to 14:00 is good enough."

"How's going back to 14:00 supposed to change anything?" asks Number 2. "The people upstairs called the rescuers moments after the accident occurred and the conditions the rescuers have to deal with are fixed. We can't change any of that."

"What if you race for the phone the minute we get out of the time machine?" I say. "Get the operator to call a little earlier."

"You think a minute will make any difference?" says Number 2. "Anyway, how's that going to work? We're going to call at 14:00 and tell the operator there's about to be an accident—we know because we've got this time machine . . ."

"Maybe we should call Snyder," says Number 3. "Get him to stop what he's doing and check over the lab."

"You think he'll listen to us?" asks Number 2.

"There's got to be something we can say to get his attention if the more straightforward things don't work," says Number 3. "Tell him we think someone has sabotaged his lab. With his Defense-Department paranoia, that should get him moving."

"I like that idea," says Number 3. "I hope the rescuers get to us this time and we don't have to worry about all that other stuff. But I'm beginning to believe that if we have to go back in time, we'll find something that works."

"I'm sure we will," I say. "With the machine, at least, we have all the time in the world."

*****

"What the . . . ?" exclaims Number 32.

Or is it 31?—I'm beginning to lose track. Anyway, we'll call him Number 4. We always do.

It's obvious by now we're not getting out of here. The rescuers didn't come the first time we called. Nor have they come since. They're never going to come.

We never got through to Snyder: At 14:00 Snyder's line is busy and stays busy until the phones go dead.

We've tried convincing the regular operator to call for the rescuers a minute earlier, but, as we feared, the operator just thinks we're joking or crazy. If only there was some carryover from one 14:00 to the next, so the operator was somehow easier to convince, so the emergency workers could be told to try something different from what they'd tried the last few times. But that's just a pipe dream: Each 14:00 is new—new operator, new rescuers trying the same useless thing. Actually, we don't really know if the rescuers ever try anything: For all we know, they arrive, judge the situation too dangerous to attempt a rescue, and simply wait.

We just keep circling back through the same forty minutes, hoping we can figure out something. That hope is just about gone. We could be stuck here forever—if we have forever? That part isn't clear yet.

It's been over twenty hours since the time machine was first turned on, and I still haven't gotten hungry. Not that I wouldn't love to have something good to eat, just for the pleasure. I'm not hungry, I suppose, because I wasn't hungry during the first forty minutes and I'm just living those minutes over and over. If so, does that also mean that if I never leave this forty-minute cycle, I'll never age, get sick, or die?

I don't know. Maybe so—maybe I do have forever. The question is whether I want it.

I sit on the edge of my desk, looking around the lab. Number 2 is explaining the situation to the new Number 4. We've had plenty of time to polish the explanation, making it as clear, condensed and easy to deliver as we can. We've also scripted it so that Number 4 won't suspect there have been other number 4's.

I watch Number 2 as he delivers his explanation and see his eyes moving frequently in my direction. I'm also aware of Number 3 watching Number 2 and myself. I suppose the looks we give each other could be called conspiratorial, but the looks are sullen, not friendly. Any friendliness we might have felt has been soured by mistrust and the guilt we share.

There was a point early on when we had a nightmarish image of the lab filling up with selves until we suffocated each other. But we soon realized that was unlikely to happen: It didn't seem that enough selves could be cycled through the time machine for that. The idea of sending selves through four at a time brought up a more immediate problem: Wouldn't any group of four that went through first get erased by the next group, since that next group would go to a fractionally earlier 14:00?

As we got into the time machine with the original Number 4, I was thinking that the next time around, when there were five of us, someone would have to be the guinea pig and go through the time machine ahead of the others. The group might have to force someone to go first, and I was afraid that someone might be me. Without actually planning it or thinking it through, I gave Number 4 a sudden push, catching him off guard and sending him tumbling out of the machine. Sure enough, when Number 2, Number 3, and I came out of the machine—each careful that the others went through at exactly the same moment—the Number 4 I'd pushed through the machine was nowhere to be seen. There was only the one self at the wall panel—technically Number 5, though we realized we'd have to call him Number 4 if we didn't want him to suspect what the real situation was.

What happened to that second Number 4 is what happened to the first one—and has happened to all the Number 4's after him. Sometimes pushing is required, but usually not; more often the new one is easily manipulated into going first because he has no sense of the danger. The only ones who are getting continuously recycled through time are the original three of us.

I don't know how much longer I can do this—will want to do it. There's that powerful urge to live in spite of everything, but misery and boredom are sure to dull it eventually. Maybe after another five, or fifty, or five hundred, or five thousand cycles, I'll simply not enter the machine and let the fire or the nerve gas or whatever else Snyder cooked up for us bring it all to an end. I fear the pain, but wouldn't it be worth the release?

All I know is that I am growing increasingly sick of my life.

And sick of my selves.

Questions

1. a. According to Lubovsky, why is January 20, 2054, 14:00 hours, likely to be the earliest date future generations will be able to travel back in time?

   b. What discovery might allow future generations to travel back to an earlier time?

2. The first Lubovsky (L1) goes into his time machine at 14:40 and emerges at 14:00. Describe what this time travel is like and what he sees when he leaves the machine?

3. a. How does L1 hurt his foot?

   b. How does L1 "unhurt" the foot?

4. What could each do to harm the other?

5. a. Explain how the explosion traps L1 and his other selves in time.

   b. Is there something else you would have done to try to escape?

6. Why is the next self always called "Number 4"?

DISCUSSION ————————————————————————

In this chapter we will discuss:
1. Three different types of time travel and three competing views of time.
2. Paradoxes that result from the idea of changing the past and attempts to avoid these paradoxes.
3. Conceptual and other problems with the basic idea of time travel.
4. Why the idea of time travel seems coherent, even plausible.
5. Physics and time travel.

Assumptions in the Story

The story, "All the Time in the World," makes at least **two assumptions about time:**

1. **The events of the past, though past, are still there— still have their own reality.**
2. **If one could get to the past, one could make changes in it; changing past events would also change subsequent events causally related to them.**

"1" is an assumption made automatically by any imaginative account of time travel into the past: If you're going to travel to it, it better be there—it better have a physical existence. This view of past time is controversial: An alternate view is that what was once the present is no more. The past has no real physical existence; it exists only in the memories and histories of what it was. This view would not allow the possibility of time travel to the past.

In the story, Lubovsky turns on the time machine at 14:00 hours, waits until 14:10, then travels back to 14:00 (his first "trip"). Both 14:00 and 14:10 have equal reality: They're like apartments down the hall from one another. They aren't the only apartments in the building: 14:01, 14:02, 14:03, etc., are equally real "places."

Note that the reality of 14:00 has nothing to do with the creation or use of the time machine. For time travel to the past to be possible, the past—all of it—has to already be there. The time machine doesn't create the reality of the past; it only enables you to get there. 13:50 that same day is also real; it's just that the time machine won't take you there.

"2" is an assumption that stories about time travel have made for years (though less so today for reasons we'll discuss). If you assume "1," then "2" makes a lot of sense. "2" says that if you could get to the past, you could change it. Why not? The present moment is real, you're in it, and you can make changes in it. If the past is real and you could be in it, it seems to follow that you could make changes in it too.

If, as we tend to believe, the past is causally related to the present, then changing the past ought to produce some change in the present.

In "All the Time in the World," Lubovsky wants to test whether he can change the past, and he learns, rather painfully, that he can. On one trip, he moves the sculpture close to the edge of the desk; his past self knocks the sculpture off the desk and onto the past self's foot, causing an ugly wound; the past self gets out bandages and wraps the foot; back in the present, Lubovsky finds himself with a terribly sore, bandaged foot.

Regarding the end of the story, if the explosion in Snyder's lab had occurred at, say, 14:30, Lubovsky and his other selves could have left the building safely once they went back to 14:00. They might even have been able to change the events leading up to the explosion so that at 14:30 no explosion occurred. Unfortunately for them, the explosion happened just after 14:00, so there's never enough time to escape. Instead, Lubovsky and the two selves that become his accomplices must recycle themselves indefinitely through the same forty minutes.

Types of Time Travel   ✺

We need to distinguish **three types of time travel:**

1. **Traveling to the (still existing) past.**
2. **Traveling to an already existing future.**
3. **Traveling at an accelerated rate into the future.**

We've discussed the basic idea of **time travel to the past** ("1") and will focus on it in our later discussions. The phrase "still existing" is there only for emphasis. Any type of travel we would call time travel to the past requires a past that continues to exist.

The idea of **time travel to an already existing future** ("2") is comparable to that of time travel to the past. In "1" the past is there now—it's real; in "2" the future is there now—it's real. We can illustrate this type of time travel with a sci-fi fantasy about futuristic career and marriage counseling:

You've just graduated from college and have been offered a fascinating job at a start-up company whose prospects seem to you a little shaky. You're also engaged to be married to someone you've been seeing for a year. Since you want to make sure you're making the right choices, you visit the Time Travel Counseling Center and pay to be sent ten years ahead in time. Wear-

---

✺   The CD, Ch. 2, *Types of Time Travel (1, 2, and 3)*, animates and explains these three types of time travel.

ing a disguise, you manage to follow your future self around to observe both the work and home situations. You find that the company you've joined has become enormously successful, you've become the extremely well-paid Vice President of Research and Development, and you still love the work you do. However, you find you have an unhappy, quarrelsome marriage that has produced two difficult children. You return to the present where you accept the job and break off your engagement.

> A VISIT TO
> YOUR OWN
> FUTURE

Here you have traveled to a real future, then returned to change the present so the future will be different. One can also imagine changing the future directly: During the trip described above, you watch your future self leave the office late one night, notice a suspicious character lurking nearby, shout a warning, and thereby save your future self from being mugged.

The idea of **traveling at an accelerated rate into the future** ("3") is sometimes discussed as a kind of time travel into the future, but it's neither comparable to "2" or parallel to "1." We'll discuss it briefly, then set it aside.

According to Einstein's Special Theory of Relativity, time slows dramatically for things moving at speeds close to the speed of light. **If you had a rocketship capable of traveling close to the speed of light and if you traveled away from Earth in such a ship and then came back, you would find that less time had elapsed for you than for the people on Earth.** How great a difference would depend on how close to the speed of light you traveled, as well as how long you traveled. If you made a one-year round trip at very close to the speed of light, you could find that a hundred years had passed on Earth.

Relativity theory in no way guarantees that we'll ever be able to travel at close to the speed of light; it only says that if we did, we would experience such differences in elapsed time.

What would result from these differences could be considered a kind of time travel into the future; as the result of a one-year trip, you've ended up a hundred years into the future. However this "time travel" isn't parallel to what we imagine when we think of time travel into the past or to a pre-existing future. Traveling at an accelerated rate into the future doesn't imply that the future is now "out there," already existing; nor does it imply that the moment you left will still exist when you reach the future. There's no such thing as a "round-trip": All you've done is get to someone else's future faster. Nothing about this implies that (if you took a shorter trip) you could ever meet your future self.

It's important to note that the theoretical possibility of this type of "time travel" implies nothing about the theoretical possibility of the other types of time travel; it's something totally different.

Our focus in this chapter is on concepts of time travel that would allow you, in theory, to go to the past and/or the future and meet yourself.

Different Views of Time   ✳

Questions about the possibility of time travel get us involved in questions about the nature of time. **Below are three views of time:**

1. **The present (but not the past and future)** *now* **exists.**
2. **Both the present and the past (but not the future)** *now* **exist.**
3. **The present, past, and future all** *now* **exist.**

To get a sense of the differences between these conceptions of time, let's draw a series of simple sketches—say, a stick figure with an arm that's straight down, then 1/4 of the way up, then 1/2 way up, then 3/4 of the way up, and then straight up.

| ILLUSTRATING |
| THE THREE |
| VIEWS OF TIME |

For "1"—only the present now exists—draw the first sketch and rip it up; draw the second sketch and rip it up; draw the third sketch and keep it in front of you. In this view of time, the present moment/sketch is the only reality. You can remember what the previous sketches looked like; you can make true and false statements about them. However, they no longer exist. You can imagine what the rest of the sketches will look like; you can make true and false statements about what they will be. However, these later sketches do not yet exist.

For "2"—both the present and the past (but not the future) now exist—draw the first three sketches, as in "1," but don't tear them up; instead, when you've finished a sketch, slide it to the left on the table, keeping the sketches in chronological order. Focus on the third sketch in front of you: This represents the present moment. Off to the left somewhere are the still existing past moments/sketches; the blank table off to the right represents the open, not yet existing future. I shall argue later on that this is the least plausible of these three conceptions of time, but initially the picture seems clear enough.

For "3"—the past, present, and future now exist—draw all five sketches and lay them out in order. Focus on the middle sketch—the present. Off to your left are the still existing moments of the past and to your right are the already existing moments of the future.

Of these conceptions of time, "2" and "3" are compatible with the idea of time travel to the past since they both posit the continuing existence of the past. Only "3" is compatible with the idea of traveling to an already existing future since only it posits such a future.

✳   The CD, Ch. 2, *Different Views of Time,* has animations of these three views of time.

Most time-travel discussions and fantasies focus on time travel to the past. As mentioned earlier, it's natural to assume that if we could travel to the past, we could change it. However, when we try to work out in detail the idea of traveling to, and changing the past, we find things going terribly wrong. Paradoxes arise; frightening scenarios suggest themselves.

Problems with a Changeable Past

Consider these statements related to the story, "All the Time in the World":

1. "At 14:00, January 20, 2054, there were two people (two selves) in Lubovsky's lab."
2. "At 14:00, January 20, 2054, there were not two people (two selves) in Lubovsky's lab."

These statements contradict each other, yet, in terms of the story, both seem to be true.

All sorts of contradictions can be generated from the idea of the changeable past. The most famous is the "grandfather paradox": A time traveler goes back to, say, 1940, and kills his grandfather who is then ten years old. Therefore the grandfather never grows up, never marries, and never has children (including the time traveler's father). Therefore the time traveler is never born, never exists, and never goes back in time to kill his grandfather. Therefore he both does and doesn't kill his grandfather.

Quite apart from the problem of paradoxes, the idea of the changeable past allows for some very scary sci-fi scenarios. Imagine the following:

Twenty years from now time machines have become commonplace; at the same time some catastrophe has plunged us into a lawless society where no one feels safe. Suppose you make a deadly enemy: Not only would you be vulnerable to an attack on your person, you'd be vulnerable to an attack on any of your selves at any past moment of your life; killing any one of them, kills you. It wouldn't only be personal attacks you'd have to cope with. You start off from your home in Los Angeles one morning, driving your bulletproof Trans Am, heading for your film editing job. Several people have traveled to the past to make changes in their own lives that will also have an effect on yours. Someone is falsifying past records to get your job and suddenly you find yourself bicycling toward the unemployment office. Then someone going farther back steals your father's job and suddenly you're driving your Ford Taurus along an icy freeway near Detroit (where your father went to find work and where you grew up) going to

---

The CD, Ch. 2, *The Grandfather Paradox*, illustrates this paradox.

your job at Ford Motor Company. Moments later a vast right-wing conspiracy succeeds in going back to the forties and sabotaging the entire U.S. war effort, and you're goose-stepping your way to your guard post as a member of the army of the Fourth Reich of America. But wait: A vast left-wing conspiracy has succeeded in sabotaging both the Allied and German war efforts of World War II, and you are driving your Skoda on the way to preparing a meal of borsch for your worker's collective in the Soviet Socialist Republic of America.

And you think your life is confusing now!

Writers of science and science fiction have responded in various ways to the problems of the changeable past.

Some writers hope that time travel will turn out to be physically impossible, either because some as yet undiscovered law of nature forbids it or because the physical means of accomplishing time travel will be forever beyond the capabilities of any beings.

Some writers have speculated it may be possible to travel to the past, but not to affect it in any way. Others have speculated that it may be possible to have an effect on the past, but only in a way that will fulfill the past, not change it. There are at least two versions of the latter idea. One is that you could go back to the past and interact with it, but something would always prevent you from making changes that would affect the future. The other is that you, the time traveler, were always part of that past you traveled to and were always part of the reason the present is as it is.

Another idea is that it would be possible to travel to the past and make what seems like a change. However, this act would only create a parallel world that reflects the change; the past of the original world would remain unchanged.

To illustrate this, let's go back to the scenario outlined earlier, in which you're first driving to work, then bicycling to the unemployment office. Under the parallel world idea, the original world you inhabit continues to exist as is even after your time-traveling competitor has gone back and altered your employment records. In that universe, you are still driving to your film editing job in Los Angeles, your employment records are still correct, and your jealous competitor is still wishing he had your job. You notice no difference because there is no difference. What happened was that when your competitor went back and changed the employment records, that act created a new world, and it is in that world that your records have been changed, your competitor got your job, and you (that is, the new or second "you") are bicycling toward the un-

> CHANGES IN THE PAST GENERATE PARALLEL WORLDS

employment office. If, a moment later, some other time traveler is stealing your father's job, that will create a third world in which a third "you" grew up in Detroit. (There's another version of this in which no parallel worlds are created—there are an infinite number already there; changing the past shifts you into, rather than creates, a parallel world. We'll stick to the create-a-world version.)

Sometimes the phrase "alternate universe" is used in place of "parallel world." The series of universes or worlds is referred to as the "Multiverse" or "Megaverse."

You can see the way the **parallel world idea avoids the paradoxes of time travel.** At 14:00, January 20, 2054, there was one Lubovsky in the lab. Eventually he went back in time and created a parallel world in which it is 14:00, January 20, 2054, and there are two Lubovskys in the lab. If you go back and kill your grandfather, you create a second world in which your grandfather died young and you never existed; in the original world, it's still the case that your grandather lived, had a son (your father) who, in turn, had a son (you).

As for the scary scenarios, time travelers would never be able to destroy you by destroying your past self; all they could do is create an alternate world where you don't exist. Someone changing your employment records wouldn't affect you; it would create an alternate world in which a duplicate you was unemployed.   ✦

A Closer Look at the Concept of Time Travel

When writers of science and science fiction focus on time travel, they tend to concern themselves with the problems of the changeable past. **However, more fundamental problems with the idea of time travel appear upon closer examination.** We'll start off considering a time-travel-possible world in which both the past and future now exist. Later we'll consider a world in which only the past is there to travel to.

In general, when people imagine time travel to the past, they think of the past as dynamic. Time traveling back to the Roman coliseum doesn't take you to a static, ghostly scene; instead you get the clashing of gladiators, the screaming of the togaed spectators. The same would be true of time travel to an already existing future—as in our previous time travel counseling scenario where you find your future self walking around and you follow him.

✦ The CD contains animations illustrating different types of time travel and different views of time.

However **the idea of a past and future that both exist on a continuing basis** *and* **are dynamic (involve motion, change) seems to be contradictory.**

When we suppose that the past and future always exist *and* that there is motion in the past and future, presumably we are relying on something like the following visual analogy: I stand still with my arm raised straight up. To my left (the past), I see a person who looks just like me raising one arm. To my right (the future) I see a person who looks like me lowering his arm. But this analogy will not do. For instance, once the person to my left (the past) completes the raising of one arm, then that person will be just as I am (the present), and nothing representing the past action will exist.

The idea of the past continuing cancels out the idea of the past as dynamic and vice versa.

The claim that the past, present, and future now exist suggests the analogy of an enormous cartoon strip. Every moment of time exists and the content of each moment of time is frozen; there is no real motion or change in the past, future, or present.

This view of time, in which the past, present, and future now exist in one big frozen block, is referrred to as "block time" or the "frozen universe." This is how we shall now refer to the past-present-and-future-now-exist view of time.

At first glance, the "block time" view of time seems to be obviously wrong. Block time implies that there is no motion/change; we see motion/change; therefore, block time is wrong.

Supporters of the block time view have countered by claiming that the appearance of motion and change—along with the appearance of time passing—is all illusion. The idea of the cartoon strip seems compatible with this: Think of animated cartoons.

However, note that **the cartoon analogy of time rules out the illusion of motion/change for anyone in time.** Two points to note here are:

1. **You can't have the illusion of change if absolutely nothing that exists is changing.** Borrowing an argument we'll discuss later when we talk about appearance and reality, the appearance of change implies (at a minimum) the change of appearances. In other words, to create the illusion of change something has to be changing, if only in the mind of the observer. But nothing changes within block time.

2. **No character within the cartoon could experience the illusion of time.** Think of a series of cartoon frames showing a character walking along thinking (with thoughts shown in the classic scalloped balloons). Pick out any frame of that cartoon. The thoughts in that frame are just as frozen as the motion.

The same point holds true for animated cartoons. Our thinking cartoon character is locked in its frame with its frozen world—frozen gait, frozen scenery, and frozen thoughts—no matter what we do with the cartoon.

Therefore, the only way to preserve block time *and* the undeniable appearance of motion/change is to imagine that consciousness exists outside the cartoon. Consciousness would be moving alongside this frozen universe from one frozen moment to another, creating the illusion of change, the illusion of passing time. We might think here of a long film strip hanging still in a dark room, with a small light moving quickly from one frame to the next.

Though the idea of consciousness existing outside of block time doesn't seem to be obviously contradictory, it does have some very implausible consequences.

a. There could be no causal relations between consciousness, on the one hand, and human bodies/brains on the other. This follows from certain features of block time that would be uncontroversial to its supporters. Block time/the frozen universe covers, at a minimum, everything studied by the physical sciences, including human bodies and brains. Nothing in this frozen world could act on an active, changing consciousness.

b. Even though the physical world can't provide an explanation for the activity of consciousness, some explanation is necessary. Questions abound: Why does my consciousness always look at things from the perspective of a certain body? Why, when I decide to wave, does the appropriate frozen sequence of hand-wave images appear just there for my moving consciousness to animate? Why, when I choose to say something and you (somehow) "hear" me, are the frozen physical events—the appropriate vocal and ear processes, as well as the specific sound waves—just there?

These questions seem awfully abstract, so let's see if we can make them more concrete with the following analogy: You and a friend, Jerry, go to an amusement park and are intrigued to find a new ride called U-Animate. The ride consists of a tunnel with a ten-foot-high blown-up film strip stretched along one illuminated wall; cars speed through the tunnel with just the right velocity to animate the film strip. Since there's only one person to a car, your friend decides to take a car in one of the several other tunnels.

The ride is entertaining, with the animation giving you a pretty realistic sense of walking through the amusement park. Then strange things begin to happen. You notice images of a great-looking roller coaster and think (referring to later), "I should take a closer look at that"; immediately there are images as if you were walking toward the roller coaster. This happens a couple of times, and puzzled by the coincidence, you decide to do a test: You think, "I want to clap my hands," and immediately there are two hands clapping in front of you; you think, "I want to sit down," and there are images as if you're sitting down. Bewildered, you think, "I wish I could ask Jerry what he thinks about this," and, amazingly, a dialogue balloon is there in the mural with the words, "Jerry, what do you think about this?" More amazing still, another dialogue balloon appears over some vague figure in the mural that says, "This is crazy, man—talk to you later."

Once the ride is over, you rush to talk to Jerry, who's as astounded about the ride as you are. (In his tunnel, he saw a small dialogue balloon with the words, "I wish I could ask Jerry what he thinks about this," and thought, "This is crazy, man.") The two of you just can't make sense of the ride. The blown-up film strip has apparently been there for weeks. Nobody knew you were going to try the ride and no one but the cashier talked to you once you got there. There was no way anyone could have hypnotized you. You weren't given anything to wear on your head that might have read your brain waves (assuming such a thing even existed). How then did the clapping hand sequence of images happen to come along just after you thought about clapping, and the sitting images, just after you thought about sitting? (Jerry ran different thought tests during his ride.) And how could the dialogue balloons have appeared where and when they did, simulating a conversation with someone in a different tunnel? None of it makes any sense. You leave the amusement park, still shaking your head, the intro to the *Twilight Zone* faintly playing in your head.

It is just this sort of *Twilight Zone* scenario that's forced upon us if we accept the frozen world/consciousness-outside-the-world view. Life involves all sorts of coordination between consciousness and the everyday world and this makes sense if consciousness is *in* that world; however, the coordination becomes astonishing if consciousness is not part of that world.

It seems to me that to come up with any kind of explanation for these correlations, one's going to have to resort to imagining some Great Mind creating the frozen physical world, then determining the thoughts and placement of each conciousness so that the physical and mental events correspond. These implications of block time should make the concept of block time suspect.

Two main conclusions have emerged from this discussion:

1. The idea of a continuing, dynamic past (as well as a future) is contradictory.
2. There is a view of time—block time, with consciousness outside of time—that allows for a continuing past (and future) and that is nei-

ther contradictory nor disproved by the mere appearance of change. However this view of time has very implausible implications.

Having analyzed the problems with block time, we can now see what's wrong with that other view of time that allows time travel to the past: the view that the present and past, but not the future, now exist. This view implies that the past (which continues to exist) is block time, while the present is momentary and fleeting; that time is both dynamic (present) and static (the past). How could time have such wildly different characteristics? How can consciousness be in time in the present and—what?—out of time in the past? Possibly one could imagine that each present moment freezes as it becomes past. But under this view, the past moments would not be the very same moments they were as present moments. At best this "past" would be like a series of snapshots—static images of what was once dynamic.

The choice, then, is between block time and the view that only the present exists. And we've seen the problems with block time. ✹

Counter-Arguments

There are rather compelling arguments that would be brought against the two conclusions above:

Against 1: It's easy to visualize a continuing, dynamic past: We do so each time we watch a time travel movie. If we can visualize such a past, it can't be contradictory.

Against 2: The block-time/consciousness-outside-time view can't be that implausible if so many physicists accept it.

Let's consider these two arguments in order.

Let's grant that one can't "visualize" contradictions. Let's also grant that it's easy to visualize what's going on in time travel movies—otherwise we wouldn't have such movies. Let's further grant that if what we're visualizing in these time travel movies is a continuing dynamic past, then the idea of such a past can't be contradictory. What we need to do is take a closer look at what these time-travel visuals involve. Consider the following scenario:

You're walking back to your apartment from class and on the way you pass someone you've been dying to ask out on a date. You start to speak, but you're stopped by shyness or doubts, and the person walks by. You go to your apartment where you sit, unhappy, replaying the memories of your failure to speak. You imagine how things might have gone if you'd

---

✹   The CD, Ch. 2, *A Close Look at the Concept of Time Travel,* has animations and explanations related to the arguments in this section.

managed to speak the first time, or, if, after failing to speak, you'd run after the person, then asked for a date. You imagine what you might be do-

ing right now if you had spoken—sitting in a coffee shop or bar, having a fun conversation, waving to friends who give you the thumbs-up sign when your date isn't looking.

Such imaginings contain all the visuals you need for a mini-time-travel story. In the story, after returning to your room, you travel back in time to the moment after you failed to speak; you run after the person and arrange a date. Back to the present, you find yourself in the bar or coffee shop scene above.

The only visuals you need here involve what was, what might have been, what is, and what might be. None of the visuals are unique to time travel; rather, what makes this a time travel episode is not what you visualize, but the meaning you give to the visuals—how you conceptualize them (e.g., I can interpret the same visual either as imagining how the past might have been different or as going to the past and making it different).

A similar point can be made like this: First, imagine walking through a doorlike machine and emerging wherever you were yesterday at noon. You've just envisaged time travel, right? Now, imagine stepping through a doorlike machine into an exact copy of where you were yesterday at noon, a copy existing in some parallel world. There's no difference in the visuals here. So how do you know that when you thought you were imagining time travel, you weren't really imagining traveling to a parallel world?

Probably you can come up with images that seem to distinguish between the time travel and parallel world scenarios. Maybe with time travel, you imagine yourself climbing out of one frame of a film strip and walking back to another frame of that strip; with parallel worlds, you imagine crossing from one film strip to another. But these images aren't the kind of visuals you get in the standard time travel movie. They're add-ons and they're analogies—a way of conceptualizing what's going on. And we've seen how such cartoon analogies end up working against, rather than supporting, the idea of a continuing, dynamic past.

I will only make a few remarks about what I understand to be the situation in physics. For those who want to follow up on this, the Further Materials section lists the titles of some wonderful popular science books that discuss both time travel and block time from the standpoint of physics.

Einstein's special theory of relativity showed that distances in space and in time were not "absolute," but would be different for observers moving with respect to one another.

One of Einstein's teachers, Herman Minkowski, pointed out that the interrelation between time and space could best be handled mathematically by treating time as if it were a fourth dimension added to the three dimensions of space (height, width, depth) in a relation he called "spacetime." He came up with a formula for translating time into spatial terms and thereby coming up with a spacetime "distance." Space and time might be relative for different observers, but this spacetime distance was objective.

Because of the mathematical benefits of treating time as a fourth, spacelike dimension, many physicists have concluded that time *is* a spacelike dimension and, thus, like space, is stretched out, existing all at once. If time exists all at once, then time (as well as things existing through time) is frozen.

It's the last step that's controversial—going from the mathematical advantages of treating time as a fourth, spacelike dimension to the conclusion that it *is* a fourth, spacelike dimension. A lot of physicists don't accept the last step. Time is unlike space in certain ways. Time has a certain direction—what's referred to as the "arrow of time." Any dimension in space goes in either direction—left or right, up or down, forward or backward. Time only moves in one direction—toward the future.

One can accept spacetime without accepting block time. To accept "spacetime," all that's necessary is to agree that it is convenient mathematically to treat time as a spacelike dimension for the purposes of conceptualizing and calculating space and time in terms of Einstein's theory. It's another thing to say that time *is* just like space and exists all at once (block time).   ✹

Afterthoughts

Nothing said in this chapter counts against the idea of parallel worlds or the possibility of traveling between parallel worlds. What's ruled out is the idea of going back to the past to create a branch point—for the simple reason that there is no past to go back to.

In the last chapter, the following was said about the theological debates concerning free will and determinism: There have been attempts to reconcile human free will and God's foreknowledge by claiming that God knows what our free will acts in the future will be because God now exists in that future to witness them.

We can now see that there are problems with this theological view. God being in the future now to see what is happening there implies block time: That future has to exist. However, He could only see our future choices if

✹   The CD, Ch. 2, *Physics and the Frozen Universe*, reviews some fo the issues in this section.

consciousness itself were in block time. We have seen that it can't be: If consciousness were in block time, there could be no appearance of motion.

If consciousness is outside the physical world, then it's moving in a kind of second-order time relative to the block-time world. It wouldn't do any good to imagine a second-order block time for consciousness, for that too couldn't be reconciled with the appearance of motion. The only way God could know our future choices, as well as making sure they were coordinated with the physical blocktime world, would be to determine them: This was the kind of picture we were driven to earlier when we discussed the implications of block time. But in that case, there would be no free will.

It doesn't seem as if there's any way to reconcile divine foreknowledge with human free will.

Questions and Exercises

1. Name and explain three types of "time travel."
2. a. The text lists three views of time. What are they?
   b. Which one is referred to as the "block time" or "frozen universe" view?
3. Regarding the idea that someone could change the past:
   a. What paradoxes result from this idea?
   b. What (else) is scary about this idea?
4. What arguments are given in the text for the following claims?
   a. The idea of an ongoing dynamic past is contradictory.
   b. We know we do not exist *within* a block-time world.
5. What are some of the implications of imagining that consciousness exists outside of block time, creating the illusion that time is passing?
6. Can we visualize traveling to the past and changing it? According to the text, what might we be visualizing instead of this?
7. Why do many physicists favor the idea of block time? Is it possible to accept spacetime and not accept block time? Explain.
8. If the idea of time travel either is contradictory or leads to implausible implications, how would this affect the idea of parallel worlds? 🎧

🎧 The CD, Ch. 2, *Rockin' Review: Time is a Mystery,* offers a musical summary of the chapter.

3

God and Suffering

Fiction: The Vision

The first time I saw it, I had no idea what it was or what it would become. It was just a brilliant shimmering of light hovering over the lawn of the small park. I nudged the old man sitting next to me on the bench.

"What is that?" I asked him excitedly.

"What's what?"

"The light—right there in front of us."

He looked in the direction I pointed, and shook his head. Then he turned and looked at me suspiciously. Perhaps he was wondering if I was one of the crazy ones. In the days to come I would often wonder the same thing myself.

But I wasn't worried that first time. Whatever I saw was gone almost at once. "Just a trick of the light," I told the old man, to reassure him.

The next time time the light appeared, I was making my way through a rush hour crowd. The light was just overhead, and I stopped to look up, barely conscious of the people bumping into me. Within the light was an image of a woman's face.

"Who are you?" I said aloud.

"A friend. Don't be afraid."

The voice that answered was like some wind instrument doing a perfect imitation of human speech.

 The CD, Ch. 3, *The Vision (1)*, contains animation and exercises related to this story.

"What do you want?" I asked.

"To help you."

And then she was gone.

As I lowered my head, I saw the crowd staring at me. Some faces were smirking, some quizzical, and some frightened, but all were looking at me as if I were crazy. Suddenly I was terrified.

I pleaded my way into my doctor's office the next morning. She tried to be reassuring, but I could see she was worried. She referred me to a psychiatrist who interviewed me and then referred me to a neurologist who scheduled a battery of tests.

Sitting in my apartment on the evening before the tests, I was a nervous wreck. From what I could gather from the doctors, either I had a brain tumor or I was going crazy, and I didn't know which was worse. I was trying not to think about any of it when the light appeared again.

"No," I moaned, pressing my hands over my eyes.

"Ginger, don't be frightened," said the voice.

"Go away. You're not real."

"I am real."

"You're a hallucination."

"I'm not."

The voice was soft and patient, like that of a kind parent confronting a contrary child. Something in me wanted so badly to give in to the voice. But I couldn't let myself; this was crazy.

"You are a hallucination," I said, insistently. "There's something wrong with my brain, and it's making you up. They're going to give me tests and find out what's wrong. I'm going to get better."

There was a slight rippling of notes, like the imitation of soft laughter. "I think you will get better," said the voice. "But not the way you think."

The tests at the hospital took most of a day. The light appeared twice, just briefly.

"I won't stay," said the voice, the second time. "I just wanted to be here during the tests. That way, when nothing shows up, you'll know I'm real."

Nothing did show up on the tests. The neurologist sent me back to the psychiatrist.

"Young lady, your hallucination seems to have a sense of humor," said the psychiatrist. "What she obviously doesn't have is a degree in psychiatry. The fact that nothing shows up on those tests you had doesn't mean she isn't coming from your brain. When we say we can't find an organic cause, we're talking about lesions and tumors. We're certainly not saying that there's nothing chemical going on there."

"You think that's what it is?" I asked. "Something chemical?"

"The mind is all chemical."

"Just make this thing stop."

"We will."

He prescribed the antipsychotic medication, Haldol. We talked about dosage, what to expect, what to watch out for. The possible side effects sounded scary, but none were as scary as losing my mind. I filled the prescription at the first pharmacy I could find, then rushed home. In the kitchen I began filling a glass with the six ounces of water I'd been told to take with the pill.

"Don't," said the voice, somewhere behind me. "Please, don't."

Somehow I'd known that I'd hear the voice just then. I felt myself grow panicky. I slapped the water glass down on the drainboard and reached for the plastic pill container.

"Don't, " said the voice, urgently. "Those pills will cut you off from me."

"They're going to make me well," I said, struggling with the child-proof lid.

"They're not going to make you well. They're only going to deaden your mind and your feelings. They're going to change you into something you don't want to be."

"I won't listen to you," I said, my panic growing worse with each unsuccessful tug at the container top.

"Do you know those street people with the vacant eyes? Do you want to be like them?"

"Shut up!" I yelled.

Suddenly the top broke loose, and pills went bouncing like small marbles over the kitchen floor. I dropped to my knees, grabbed a pill, and pushed it toward my mouth.

"Don't. The pills will just make you a zombie."

What the voice was saying was just close enough to the worst of the side-effect warnings to make me hesitate. I stared at the pills for a moment, afraid to take them, afraid not to. There was a small "H" carved into the white pill, and the question "hell or help," "hell or help" started running through my mind. My hand was shaking with indecision, and suddenly the fear and frustration of the last few days came bursting out of me in sobs.

"I don't know what to do," I cried. "I don't know what's happening to me. I'm so scared."

I was on my knees on the floor, bent forward, my arms pressing against my chest as if I were trying to keep myself from coming apart. Gradually, over the sound of my tears, I began to hear the voice saying, "It's all right," over and over, softly, almost hypnotically. And then light seemed to fold it-self around me and the panic subsided and the tears stopped and suddenly my whole being was flooded with joy. I felt peaceful and safe to the very core of myself, as if I had suddenly come home—not to any home I had ever known, but to some home I had only dreamed of having. I let my body fall gently sideways, so that I was sitting on the floor, leaning against the kitchen counter. I closed my eyes, giving myself up to all those wonderful feelings.

"Feeling better?" asked the voice.

I laughed. "Yes."

Somewhere in my mind, hovering above all the joy, was a voice saying, "No matter how good you feel, this is still crazy, and you're going to have to deal with it, you're going to have to take those pills." But for the moment the voice was distant and of no effect.

I opened my eyes. The light was now a few feet away, suspended be-tween ceiling and floor. For the first time I was calm enough to study it: The light was translucent, blurring the objects behind it, like a bright piece of lightly frosted glass. The light itself was white, but with hundreds of flecks of color that would blink and disappear, to be replaced by others; it was like a huge piece of crystal that was turning minutely back and forth, reflecting a light source from somewhere else. And within the translucency was that face, a mirage within a mirage. It was the kindest, most beautiful face I had ever seen.

"I feel so good," I said: "I almost wish you were real."

"I am real."

"What are you supposed to be? God? An angel? The Virgin Mary?"

"No, nothing like that. I'm a physical thing, just like you are."

"We sure don't look much alike."

"There are different kinds of physical things. Matter and energy for one. Energy tends toward joy and continuation. Matter tends toward suffering and decay."

"You mean, you're energy, and I'm matter?"

"Let's just say that you're more matter than I am."

"I don't get it. Do you mean, you're from a different planet or dimension or something?"

"We are those who have evolved and survived. We're here to help you do the same."

Much to my surprise and embarrassment, I let out a huge yawn. I quickly covered my mouth.

"I'm sorry," I said. "Suddenly I feel so sleepy. Like I've been drugged."

"You're exhausted. You need sleep. You'd better get yourself to bed. You'll be sore in the morning if you sleep there."

"Carry me," I asked, feeling suddenly childlike.

The face smiled. "I'd like to do that. But it is forbidden. I would do you great harm if I touched your body."

"I don't understand. I felt you touch me before. I mean . . ."

"I was only touching your spirit. Listen, now, before you fall asleep. To-morrow, when you wake, you will begin to doubt again. All I ask is that you hold off taking the pills awhile longer. Hear me out. Give yourself a chance to believe. For your own sake. When you doubt, just remember how you felt tonight. The truth is in the feeling."

I almost took the pills the next day, and the next, and the next. But so far I have not. It is the feeling that holds me back. I only experience the rapture when the light actually enfolds me, but the memory of it is with me constantly, along with a residue of joy. I ask myself: How can anything be crazy that feels so wonderful?

Not that I don't doubt and question and even argue: I spend most of our time together trying to make sense of what is happening; I'm still not sure I have.

"Why are you appearing to me?" I asked the woman in the light.

"We are trying to appear to many."

"Then why haven't I heard about other people seeing you?"

"Most don't. They are too closed to see anything. Others see a little and grow frightened and turn away. Still others see only what they want to see. You are one of the few to whom I appear as I am."

"But why me? I'm not particularly smart or good."

"Because of your longing. It opens you to the truth. And your simplicity, which allows you to receive it."

"Why are you here?"

"To help you."

"Help me what?"

"Survive," she said. "When the body dies, those who are matter die with it; those who have become energy, spirit, go on. Whole races have survived and continued their existence in the dimension of energy; others have almost totally died out. The human race is headed for virtual extinction. The few who have become energy are stragglers in the other dimension, grieving for their race. They have begged us who have numbers to try to make contact. So we are trying. I hope good will come of it. I fear not."

It all sounds so strange, and I still feel confused. Sometimes I come back to the point of thinking, This is all nonsense, you are sick. But then the light folds around me, and I feel the rapture, and nothing else matters.

The voice says that I must give up obsessive rationality, with its constant questionings and doubts.. She says that I must give myself up to feeling, for it is feeling that will show me the truth. I am determined to try.

I still do not know if this is real or unreal, if I am sane or crazy. All I know, and need to know, is one thing:

I am happy.

*****

Something has gone terribly wrong.

It did not happen all at once, but little by little.

The woman in the light told me that I must change my life, and I gave myself up to her charge. She had me make changes in my diet, and she gave me a series of physical and spiritual exercises. She was so sweet as she guided me, like a good mother who knows her child has some hard work to do and wants to spare the child any unnecessary discomfort. Most of the changes weren't so bad, and I was helped by her presence, by the rush of joy she sometimes gave me, and by the knowledge that I was transforming myself to a higher level of being.

But then the exercises became more and more uncomfortable, and one day I told her I didn't want to do one of the exercises any more. For the first time the light suddenly darkened, and the face became angry. I was so shocked at the sight that I couldn't move. Then the light brightened, and the face softened.

"I'm sorry," said the voice. "Sometimes you try me."

I was to begin to see that anger more often. One day one of the exercises drew some blood and I stopped, feeling faint as I always do at the sight of my own blood. As I put my hand over the small cut, and averted my eyes, I saw that the light was nearly black and the face inside it terrible.

"Continue!" she screamed.

"No," I said. "Stop, please. You're frightening me."

"Good," she yelled. "You're too slow, too cowardly. If I must frighten you, then I will. Don't you understand? The Day is almost upon us. If you're not ready, you will die!"

"What day?"

The light turned from dark crystal to a twilight gray. The face inside was no longer angry, but sad.

"I did not mean to tell you today," said the voice. "But perhaps it is just as well. I could not have put it off much longer."

"What day?" I asked again.

"The Day the Earth Will End."

"What? You never told me that."

"The Council just decided."

"What council?"

"They have grown impatient. Humans have become a blot on the universe. On the Day, the sky will grow red with an angry light, and the light will descend and touch the Earth, and all will be destroyed. Don't you see? You must be ready when the Day comes or you will be destroyed with the others."

"When?"

"The exact day hasn't been decided. A month, two months, a year . . . soon."

"I don't understand this. I'm scared. Please hold me."

"Not now. Joy will just make you lazy. You must work."

I tried to work as hard as she wanted, I really did. But I'm not good at pain, and the fear I was feeling seemed to inhibit me more than push me. Doubts began to come back, stronger now than before, and a voice in my head that kept growing louder was saying, This is all crazy after all; you must stop it, you know that; you must take the pills before this sickness destroys you.

One night I woke up from a recurrent nightmare in which the woman in the light was having me mutilate myself. I was shaking with fright, and that voice in my head was saying, Take the pills, take the pills. I stumbled out of bed, filled a glass of water, and opened the pill container.

"Don't, please, don't," said the voice, as I knew it would.

"Yes," I said, and gulped down a pill. I turned to face the light. "This has turned into a nightmare. I want it to stop."

I expected anger. Instead the face was sad.

"You won't see me anymore," said the voice. "That pill will close your mind. I'm sorry. I had such hope that I could save you."

The light disappeared.

I'm better now. The pills aren't what I was afraid they'd be. I do sleep more, and I feel groggy sometimes, and I guess I feel as if my body and mind move a little more slowly than they used to. But overall I feel okay, and I don't see those visions anymore.

Yet sometimes—not often, just once in a while—when I'm at home at night, staring out the window at the peace of the star-studded darkness, I imagine that the sky is beginning to glow, and as it becomes a deeper and deeper red, I catch a faint odor of something beginning to burn.

And I am afraid.

Fiction: Surprise! It's Judgment Day

The stage suggests a cloud bank. Across the length of the stage is a high wall that appears to be of white brick. In the center of the wall is a pair of golden doors, which are closed. Off to the right is a golden throne. Seated on the throne is a figure with white hair and beard. He is wearing a jeweled crown, and his legs are crossed beneath a thick white robe.

Martin enters from the left, rubbing his eyes. He is dressed in a white hospital gown.

MARTIN: Well, I'll be damned. So, the fairy tales were true, after all.

GOD: In a sense.

Martin glances toward the bearded figure and groans.

MARTIN: Go ahead. Tell me you're Saint Peter and make my day.

GOD: Now, now, Professor Martin. Any Sunday school child could do better than that. What would Saint Peter be doing on Heaven's throne?

MARTIN: You're not God?

GOD: I am.

MARTIN: So much for all the theologians' warnings against anthropomorphism.

GOD: Oh, this is just a momentary form, a matter of convenience. Your convenience, I might add. I could have spoken out of a whirlwind or a burning bush. But I felt I owed you a face-to-face confrontation.

MARTIN: Confrontation? That suits me just fine. I wouldn't mind getting a word in before I get the fire and brimstone.

The CD, Ch. 3, *Surprise! It's Judgment Day*, *(1)*, contains further questions about this story.

GOD: Fire and brimstone? Let's not go jumping to conclusions, shall we? Tell me, what do you think of all this?

MARTIN: Regrettable. And, quite frankly, pretty tacky. The cloud, the throne, the beard. Any hack Hollywood director could have done better. I would have given you more credit.

GOD: But not much.

MARTIN: No, not much.

GOD: Let's just say that I thought this bit of pop religion would put you more at ease. A little joke of mine, though at whose expense I'm not quite sure. But this is not my usual form, I can assure you.

MARTIN: No, you don't exactly look like the Unmoved Mover in that outfit. Saint Thomas Aquinas would have been shocked. Well, now God with a sense of humor. I would have expected you to be more pompous. But no doubt it's gallows humor, and you own the gallows.

GOD: Do you remember how you got here?

MARTIN: Yes, I think so. I remember the car accident. I remember the doctor telling me that I had fractured my skull. I remember being taken into surgery. I suppose the rest of it was like the old joke: I was at death's door and the doctor pulled me through.

GOD: You were quite impressive as you were getting the anesthetic. I believe you muttered some quotation from Robinson Jeffers about there being no harps and habitations beyond the stars. And something from Camus about the benign indifference of the universe. And, oh yes, that line from Socrates: "Eternity is but a single night." As you can see, Professor Martin, eternity is quite well lit.

MARTIN: Go ahead and laugh. I guess you're entitled. But their words have more dignity than yours. Damn it, this shouldn't be true. You know it shouldn't. It defies all reason. A God who displaces humankind from Paradise for exercising an understandable curiosity, who lets himself be crucified to save some, but insists on punishing others eternally, all in the name of some barbaric penal code that he created but claims he must follow—no, it's too absurd.

GOD: What? Are you going to make of me some ranting fundamentalist? It seems you like easy targets.

MARTIN: Are you telling me you're an ecumenicalist? Glimpses of God behind the myths and half-truths of all religions? Well, score one for the liberal theologians. It doesn't matter. Liberalize yourself all you want. Reason says you shouldn't exist.

GOD: Some philosophers have thought otherwise.

MARTIN: Yes. You had some brilliant defenders—once. But now their arguments are merely historical curiosities. Anselm and Descartes claimed that the definition of a perfect God necessarily implies that He exists. A perfect God lacks nothing and hence does not lack existence. But that line of argument would equally prove the existence of a perfect turtle and a perfect daiquiri. Aquinas, following Aristotle, claimed that reason indicates there must be a First Cause, a First Mover, who created the world, set it in motion, and sustains its existence. But there is nothing obviously false in the idea of a material world that is self-sufficient and has been eternally in motion. You're not going to try to defend those arguments of Anselm and Aquinas, are you?

GOD: No, Professor Martin. Nor will I try to defend the argument that a vast, intricate universe of elegantly formulable laws could not exist without intelligent creation or control. Though I must admit I've always liked that one.

MARTIN: In any case, the issue of design ultimately indicates that a respectable God could not exist: The laws of the universe may be mathematically elegant, but they crush and they kill. No respectable God would allow people to suffer as they do.

GOD: So. We come to the heart of the matter.

MARTIN: Yes, indeed. As a moral assessment, one must say that if this world is designed, it is the work of a bumbler or a sadist. Which, by the way, are you?

GOD: Not quite either, I hope.

MARTIN: But you did design the world?

GOD: Yes, I did. But look here, Professor Martin. I understand your anger, your impulse toward hyperbole. Still, it is hyperbole. What about my celebrated free-will defense? Free will is a great good, a necessary ingredient in the best of all possible worlds. And it would be contradictory for me to give people free will and, at the same time, guarantee that they never use that freedom to cause suffering.

MARTIN: As you must know, it is not an adequate defense. At most, it would only justify the suffering caused by people. It doesn't apply to the suffering caused by natural events, like diseases, earthquakes, and floods. But, in any case, I don't concede you the free-will defense. Freedom costs too much, it has too many victims. Free will isn't worth the suffering.

GOD: Can you really be so flippant about it? Don't you feel an attraction toward freedom—or at least recognize that another person might? Don't you feel it is an issue about which rational individuals might disagree?

MARTIN: Perhaps. But I still say that freedom isn't worth the suffering. Nonetheless, one still must explain the suffering caused by natural events. If you try to justify it as a punishment for people's misuse of their freedom, then I say that your notion of punishment is barbaric.

GOD: Well, what about what you have called the "virtue defense"? Virtues are good, and a necessary ingredient in the best of all possible worlds. And the idea of virtue in a world without suffering is contradictory. It would be impossible to be courageous where there is no danger, to be generous where it costs nothing, to be sympathetic where no one is hurt.

MARTIN: Even if I conceded that argument, there doesn't have to be so much suffering.

GOD: What? A couple of teaspoons would have sufficed for the grandeur of the drama?

MARTIN: Nevertheless, I don't concede the argument. It turns virtue inside out. It makes virtue good in itself. But reflection shows that virtue is good only as a means—a means to happiness. What is the point of courage, generosity, sympathy, if not to alleviate suffering? To create suffering for the sake of sympathy is like kicking a man in the shins so you can feel sorry for him. It's absurd.

GOD: So if you had been in my place, you would have . . .

MARTIN: Made human beings happy. And left them happy.

GOD: But happiness is so bland.

MARTIN: To the outsider, perhaps. But to the person who is happy, it is sufficient.

GOD: And so you would have created a world without virtue?

MARTIN: Yes. A world in which virtue wasn't necessary.

GOD: And the intellectual virtues? You would discard them as well? The painful, heroic struggle for beauty and knowledge?

MARTIN: Yes, if they must conflict with happiness.

GOD: But they do, do they not? Anyway, if happiness is the good, then anything else becomes superfluous.

MARTIN: Yes.

GOD: Many people would view your values with contempt.

MARTIN: Yes, I understand that. One can look back over the centuries at, say, the Egyptian pyramids and think: This is good; this is where the human race excelled. But a closer look reveals the pain of the slaves who built them, and one should see that this was wrong. One is not entitled to excellence if unwilling people must suffer for it. And, in one way or another, some always do.

GOD: What a utilitarian you are!

MARTIN: Yes. With slight misgivings, but yes. The utilitarian is right, and you are wrong. And we haven't even mentioned hell yet, though I'm sure that we, or rather I, will be getting to that shortly. Hell is an atrocity beyond debate.

GOD: You really do want me to be a fundamentalist, don't you? There is no hell, Professor Martin. The thought of creating it crossed my mind once, but I never took the idea seriously. There was a kind of Hades, or Limbo, once, but I soon gave it up. No, now there is only Paradise.

MARTIN: Knowing you, that should be fun. Probably morning prayers, cold showers, and occasionally Black Plague, to keep us on our toes. But even if it is pleasant, you still have much to answer for. And it is unanswerable. Voltaire, Dostoevsky, and countless others whose views I accept saw that. They wouldn't be put off by your whales and whirlwinds, as Job was. Dostoevsky's Ivan Karamazov was right: Once one child suffers, this is a botched world, and nothing could ever make it right again.

GOD: Voltaire and Dostoevsky are here, by the way.

MARTIN: Ah! I shall enjoy talking with them. Or, if that is not possible, then listening, anyway.

GOD: There would be some difficulty in that. But to get back to the point that you insist on dramatizing: I do take full responsibility for this world that I've created. And I do not believe that I should have created it differently: The struggle for virtue, beauty, and knowledge: That is what I find most admirable. Though I admit that, as an outsider, I am open to the accusation that I lack sympathy. However, I find the world interesting just as it is. I shall continue to insist on the spectacle.

MARTIN: The spectacle—yes. Like some Roman emperor.

GOD: As you will. But you're a utilitarian. You believe in the greatest happiness. Shouldn't the happiness of an infinite God weigh heavily on your scales?

MARTIN: So the struggle goes on forever—for your entertainment.

GOD: Not just mine. Don't forget there are many people who don't accept your values. Perhaps I could justify the world as it is, as a concession to them. In any case, human beings may struggle forever, but not each person. An individual struggle that went on forever would lose all meaning and must lead to utter despair or boredom. There must be surcease, reward.

MARTIN: But how can you consistently manage that? There's a lovely little paradox that the believers must confront: If freedom and virtue are the ultimate good, and in turn require suffering, then how could heaven be blissful? Or, if somehow God could manage to create freedom and virtue without suffering, then why didn't God omit the suffering in the first place?

GOD: As I've said, the struggle is good, but it cannot go on forever. So the final result is a compromise between my set of values and yours. Professor Martin, the world is not to your liking, and I apologize for that. I could never convince you that this is the best of all possible worlds, and I shall not really try: But all I have taken from you is, in the words of my lesser poets, a drop of time in the sea of eternity. Don't be so hard on me for that. The rest of time is yours.

God flicks his hand, and the golden doors open slowly. Inside, figures in white hospital gowns walk about, slowly and somewhat mechanically. Martin studies them for several moments.

MARTIN: Their expressions don't change.

GOD: They always smile of course. Why not? They're happy, blissful. Ecstatic, in fact.

MARTIN: But there are just people and clouds. Where's the beauty of it?

GOD: In the eye of the beholder. Or, better, in the mind, since they don't look at much. I could create changing landscapes, I suppose, fill the surroundings with great art and have beautiful music played. But it would not make any difference. At most, it would serve as a sop to my conscience, and I prefer to know what I do: They're perfectly happy, just as they are, and anything else would be extraneous, irrelevant. They're happy. Just as you shall be in a moment.

MARTIN: They're happy?

GOD: Yes.

MARTIN: And I shall join them?

GOD: Yes.

MARTIN: Wait a moment.

GOD: I don't see the point. We've reached our impasse. I felt that I owed you a chance to have your say, and that I owed you an explanation—even if you did not find it satisfactory.

MARTIN: It looks like death in there.

GOD: In a sense it is, of course. But really, our differences aside, there is not much else one can do with people forever. Would you rather I extinguished you?

MARTIN: No!

GOD: Well, then. By the way, I should tell you that I've enjoyed our talk. I really have. But there are others I must see: It is time for you to go inside now.

MARTIN: No wait!

Martin turns toward God with a panicked, pleading gesture. God points at Martin. Martin's body freezes for a moment, then releases, his arms falling to his sides. On Martin's face is an expression that seems genuinely happy, but unchanging.

GOD: Enter, Martin. Enter.

Martin turns and slowly walks through the gates, which close behind him. God stares thoughtfully toward the gates, shaking his head slightly: A young girl, Katherine, enters from stage left. She, too, is wearing a hospital gown. Upon seeing her, God quickly smoothes his beard and adopts a very dignified posture. Then he smiles at her.

KATHERINE: Oh, Father, is that you?

GOD: Yes, Katherine.

KATHERINE: Oh, Father, you are just as I always imagined you. Then you heard my prayer?

GOD: I always hear.

KATHERINE: And you forgave me?

GOD: Yes.

KATHERINE: Will I live in heaven?

GOD: Yes, my child. Heaven is yours.

At a gesture from God, the gates open again. Martin can be seen walking among the people inside.

KATHERINE: Oh, Father, they are all so happy! Oh, thank you, Father, thank you.

GOD: Bless you, my child.

Katherine rushes toward the gates. Just before she reaches them, God flicks his hand, and she adopts the mechanical walk of the others. The gates close. God lowers his head a bit, as if tired and a little disgusted. He looks up.

GOD: That seems to be all for now. Thank goodness! This place depresses me so.

God gets down from the throne and takes a couple of steps to the right. He stops and removes the crown, tossing it on the seat of the throne, where it lands with a clatter. He exits to the right, unbuttoning his robe.

Questions

1. a. Give two different explanations for what is happening to the narrator in "The Vision."
   b. Would there be some decisive way to determine which of the two explanations is correct?
2. The vision says that the truth is in the feeling. In which way does feeling guide the narrator in the first part of the story? In the second part of the story?
3. How would you have reacted if you'd been in the narrator's place?
4. In "Surprise! It's Judgment Day," what is the complaint that Martin is bringing against God?

5. God presents in His defense what are called the "free-will defense" and the "virtue defense." Explain these two defenses.
6. Does Martin change his viewpoint at the end of the story? If so, how and why?

DISCUSSION

> In this chapter we will discuss:
> 1. Three traditional proofs for the existence of God.
> 2. The value of religious experience as evidence of God's existence.
> 3. The claim that suffering is powerful evidence against the existence of a God who is all-powerful, all-knowing, and perfectly good.
> 4. Three "defenses" of God re suffering.

Traditional Arguments for God's Existence

In "Surprise! It's Judgment Day," Martin dismisses as unconvincing three famous arguments for the existence of God: the ontological, the cosmological, and the teleological. Today many philosophers and theologians would agree with Martin. But the three arguments play an important historical role in philosophy, and a couple of the arguments relate to impulses that still tend people toward belief in God. Thus the arguments are worth examining.

The ontological argument (which derives its name from the Greek word for "being") **is the argument that the actual existence of God can be proved from the concept of God.** This argument, first formulated by Saint Anselm in the eleventh century, was reformulated by a number of post-Renaissance philosophers, including Descartes. Descartes's formulation goes roughly as follows:

1. The concept of God is that of a perfect being.
2. A perfect being lacks no perfections.
3. Existence is a perfection.
4. (Therefore) God does not lack existence; God exists.

When confronted with this proof, some people are inclined to ask: "Where did Descartes get that definition of God?" The defender would say: "It's a standard definition" or "I just made it up." When one wonders about the existence of something, the source of the idea is not generally at issue.

The CD, Ch. 3, *Surprise! It's Judgment Day, (2),* contains further questions about this story.

Descartes's contemporaries (like Anselm's) thought that the ontological argument could be used to prove the existence of many perfect beings—e.g., a perfect island—and hence must be fallacious. But there is a rejoinder to this: A perfect island is a contradiction in terms, because by definition such a thing would be limited, mindless, and hence imperfect.

One might argue that Descartes's proof equally shows that God does not exist, since He could not lack nonexistence. But the word "perfection" supposedly excludes such "attributes" as nonthinkingness, nongoodness, and nonexistence.

What seems to be the decisive objection was first formulated by Immanuel Kant in the late eighteenth century. The objection goes somewhat as follows: There is a radical difference between a statement about a concept and a statement about existence. To introduce a concept is to introduce a kind of (mental) picture. To claim existence is to claim that there is something in the world that has the characteristics portrayed in that picture. Introducing a concept is uncontroversial only because it differs from an existential claim.

CRITIQUE OF THE ONTOLOGICAL ARGUMENT

Descartes introduces a concept of God that implicitly includes an existential claim, and this is not noncontroversial. If such a step were permissible, then anything could be defined into existence. I could introduce the concept of an "exista-unicorn" ("a horselike figure with a horn and with existence"). I could then derive the existence of the unicorn from that definition. The criticism here is not that Descartes violates a logical convention. Rather, it is that if he violates this convention, then he is required to do something not normally required of someone introducing a concept: He must prove the existence of the thing before his definition is acceptable. This, of course, he does not do.

The cosmological argument (which derives its name from the Greek word for "universe")—is also called the "First Cause argument." The <u>cosmological argument</u> **proceeds from some highly general premises about the universe to the conclusion that Martin summarizes as follows: "There must be a First Cause, a First Mover, who created the world, set it in motion, and sustains its existence."**

People are tempted to say that everything must have had a beginning and to argue for a First Cause on the basis of this premise. But this premise, even if rational, not only

FIRST CAUSE

does not support, but actually contradicts, the conclusion of the cosmological argument. For the argument supposes that there is one thing that had no beginning, namely God.

In earlier times, at least, many supposed that things in motion must have been set in motion; rest, rather than motion,

FIRST MOVER

was the natural state of things. They argued that the universe must have been set in motion by a First Mover, God. But the supposition that rest is the natural state of things does not seem to be self-evident and, in fact, is denied by modern science.

The thirteenth-century philosopher, St. Thomas Aquinas, argued that there must be a Necessary Being, a being that could not

NECESSARY BEING

not exist, a Being on which all other things must depend for their existence; this Being was God.

First of all, a degree of sense must be given to the notion of a "necessary being." Some proponents of the argument have suggested that a necessary being is one whose definition implies its existence. But by this interpretation, the cosmological argument becomes a version of the ontological argument and is subject to the same critique. No definition implies the existence of the thing defined.

"Necessary being" could be a description of something that, as a matter of fact, is self-sufficient, eternal, and cannot be destroyed: something that depends on nothing else for its existence. If one supposes that there never was or will be a time when nothing exists, then it follows that there is a "necessary being"—at least in the trivial sense that this phrase could apply to the totality of things that ever exist. The emphasis of the argument would then shift to the claim that the things in the physical-mental world must depend on something else for their existence.

It is true that the things we observe are generated and corrupted, but it is not clear that they disappear, as opposed to breaking down into more basic, enduring particles, or into energy. **It is not clear why the universe, conceived as a system of things and relations, must necessarily depend on something else for its existence;** it is not clear that the universe could not be a "necessary being" in the sense that it is self-sufficient. Yet if the cosmological argument is to be convincing, its proponents must show us why the universe is likely to be dependent on something else.

Discussion of the First Cause argument is likely to bring to mind the scientific "Big Bang" theory of the origin of the universe. We will consider the relevance of the Big Bang theory to arguments for God's existence after we consider the third traditional argument for God's existence.

The teleological argument (which derives its name from the Greek word for "end"/"goal") **is more familiarly known as the "argument from design."** The argument goes as follows: The complex universe is not chaotic but orderly; its workings can be described by relatively simple scientific theories. Surely, it is more reasonable to suppose that this universe was designed by some Great Intelligence, God, than to suppose that it exists without design.

Popular forms of this argument often gain apparent force by restricting one to a **bogus dichotomy between design and chance.** One is invited to consider two situations: The first: A woman takes some pieces of metal and glass and carefully constructs a watch. The second: A woman takes some pieces of metal and glass and tosses them over her shoulder; by chance the pieces fall together in such a way as to form a functioning watch. The advocate of the argument then says: Surely, it is more reasonable to suppose that the universe was formed as in the first situation rather than as in the second.

> CRITIQUE OF THE
> TELEOLOGICAL
> ARGUMENT

If these were the only possibilities, a rational person would conclude that the universe was designed. But there is another possibility: that an orderly universe has always existed. Such a universe could not be said to have "happened by chance," since that phrase describes some sort of haphazard beginning, and this third possibility supposes no beginning at all.

The hypothesis that an orderly universe has always existed needn't suppose that this inherent order is analogous to the immensely complex, immensely detailed blueprint that a divinity might have had in mind in designing the universe. This order need only be something like the basic laws of physics. We know that enormous complexity can arise from relatively simple processes if they're the right sort of processes and there's sufficient time. ✸

The "Big Bang" and the Existence of God

Some of the objections made against the cosmological and teleological arguments brought up the possibility that the Universe has always existed. Some of you must have had the following thought: "Hasn't the scientific theory of the Big Bang theory pretty much ruled out the possibility that the Universe has always existed?" Indeed, some theists have taken the Big Bang theory to support a Biblical-style creation at some definite moment in the past. Let's consider how the Big Bang theory impacts the idea that the Universe had a Creator/Designer.

The **"Big Bang" theory of the origin of the Universe says that the Universe began in a superhot, superdense state; some sort of explosion threw**

✸ The CD, Ch. 3, *Proofs for the Existence of God,* reviews arguments for and against the traditional proofs.

the matter outward, creating the expanding Universe we know today. Current estimates are that the Universe originated about 14 billion years ago. Scientific evidence for the Big Bang theory is very strong. The question is how it might impact the sorts of arguments we've been considering.

Cosmologists sometimes make remarks to the effect that it makes no sense to ask (certain) questions about what went on "before" the Big Bang. In saying this, they seem to mean one of two things:

1. Since everything (including time and space) came into existence with the Big Bang, it makes no sense to ask questions like, "How much time was there before the Big Bang?"
2. Since scientific evidence and methods can only take us back as far as (or just short of) the Big Bang, any questions about what happened before the Big Bang are meaningless.

Re #1: The claim that everything (including time and space) came into the existence with the Big Bang is controversial. However, *if* you accepted that claim, it would follow trivially that asking about time before the Big Bang would make no sense.

Re #2: The idea here is that if science could never answer a certain question (such as what happened before the Big Bang), then that question is literally meaningless. However, this limiting of what "makes sense" to what can be verified or falsified by science was discredited in philosophy many years ago.

What's most important to note here is that both statements #1 and #2 have exactly the same implications for the claim that God has always existed, as they do for the claim that an orderly universe has always existed. **If nothing existed before the Big Bang, that means no God as well as no Universe. If it's meaningless to ask about anything before the Big Bang, that applies to asking about God as much as asking about anything else.**

In fact, it does make sense to ask what, if anything, existed before the Big Bang, and a lot of cosmologists do ask this question. There are various possibilities: that nothing at all existed before the Big Bang; that the one thing that existed before the Big Bang was an eternal God who created the Universe via the Big Bang; that the Universe has always existed, with the Big Bang and the present expansion just one phase of the Universe; and that our Universe was caused to exist by another universe existing outside our own. ✺

✺   The CD, Ch. 3, *The "Big Bang" and the Existence of God,* animates some possible scenarios compatible with the Big Bang.

In other words, in spite of initial appearances, **it doesn't seem as if the Big Bang has any particular bearing on the cosmological and teleological arguments.**

Religious Experience

Another possible reason for belief in God is religious experience, either experiences one hears reported by others or experiences one has oneself. Such experiences range from dramatic visions to a gentle sense of presence. There are some religious sects in which everyone claims to have had such experiences.

Religious experiences can be explained either as true experiences of the divine on the one hand, or as anything from psychological projection to brain impairment.

In "The Vision," the narrator has rather dramatic visions. The vision itself claims it is true, the narrator isn't sure, and all the doctors immediately assume the vision is a symptom of illness.

How are we to judge religious experiences?

People sometimes dismiss religious experience—even religion, in general—on the basis of psychological theories about why people need to believe. Even assuming those psychological theories are true (a big assumption), this way of reasoning is fallacious. It is called **"the genetic fallacy"** because it relates to the genesis, or origin, of a belief. The fallacy confuses motives and reasons. **To demonstrate that someone needs to believe—or would like to believe A—is not to show that A is false.**

If there is considerable evidence that a belief is false (or no evidence that it is true), and numbers of people continue to hold that belief, it is legitimate to inquire into the psychology of that belief. But the psychology of a belief, by itself, will not show whether that belief is true or false.

What we want to know, is this: **Are particular religious experiences veridical—that is, true experiences of some objective reality (as with everyday perceptions of cars and trees and people)—or are they non-veridical—that is, merely subjective (as with dreams and fantasies)?**

In trying to decide such an issue as this, we normally reason by analogy. That is, we consider cases of perception where we agree on what is and isn't veridical, and we determine what criteria we use to judge what is or isn't veridical in those cases. We then apply those same criteria to the perception in question.

What are our everyday criteria for the veridicality of perception? It seems that **veridicality** here **has to do with what a normal observer would/could perceive under certain conditions.** The concept of normality here is

very tricky. We want to set some limits on the kinds of persons whose tes-timony we will accept: For instance, if someone is accusing an auto body shop of painting a new fender the wrong color, obviously we don't want the testimony of someone who is colorblind admitted. On the other hand, we don't want to beg the question (assume the truth of what's at issue) by sim-ply dismissing anyone who doesn't see it a certain way as "not normal."*
The criteria for what is normal should be established independently of what's at issue.

Given reasonable criteria for "normal," **we judge perceptions to be veridical if normal people are having those perceptions and if others would have those same perceptions in similar circumstances.** If a family reports a spaceship parked in the backyard but no one else who comes to visit can see it, that story isn't going to be judged as veridical.

How does religious experience fare under our normal criteria of veridi-cality? The results are at best ambiguous. The really dramatic religious vi-sions are such isolated occurrences that they are not going to get much sup-port from our normal criteria of veridicality. If we consider the totality of religious experience from the very dramatic to the very subtle ("I just sense that God is watching me"), then the case for veridicality looks better. But then there is the problem of differences in the content of the experiences: This Native American tribe has one sort of experience, this Christian sect has another, and these Buddhists have yet another.

If these are veridical experiences of the Divine, why are they so differ-ent and often contradictory? One could possibly infer from this that reli-gious experiences are confused perceptions of some divine reality whose nature we can only guess at: But at the very best this would be support for the vaguest of religious beliefs, one that wouldn't satisfy many believers.

Another complication here is the awful visions and voices that, for in-stance, schizophrenics experience. There is a tendency these days to think of the positive religious experiences as possibly veridical and the negative religious experiences as definitely nonveridical, as mental illness. (The narrator in "The Vision"

NEGATIVE VISIONS

---

* There are two fallacies that fall under the heading of "begging the question." The first—the one at issue here—occurs when one is supposedly supporting the truth of one statement (the conclusion) by presenting *additional* statements (the prem-ises), only it turns out that one of the premises is just another version of the con-clusion; one has assumed the conclusion in the premises. The second version of begging the question (also called "ducking the question") is pretending to answer a question while simply talking around it.

The CD, Ch. 3, *Religious Experience (1 and 2),* has an animated quiz about veridicality, plus other questions related to this topic.

is much less inclined to think of the vision as veridical when it becomes negative.) But unless one begs the question by assuming in advance that a certain kind of God does exist (in which case religious experience isn't really being used as evidence for the existence of God at all), it's hard to see what grounds there would be for not including negative visions in the pool of religious experience. If they are included, the increased variety we get from their addition either renders more doubtful the veridicality of religious experience or renders more ambiguous the nature of the Divine.

One thing that is intriguing about many supernatural beliefs is that they include within them an explanation for why they don't satisfy the normal criteria of rationality or veridicality. For instance:

DOUBTER: "By any rational standards, that belief is obviously false."

BELIEVER: "That's because rationality comes from pride, and pride always gives false answers."

Or:

DOUBTER: "I can't find God."

BELIEVER: "That's because you don't really want to."

DOUBTER: "I feel like I want to."

BELIEVER: "No. The fact that you don't see Him shows that you don't really want to."

"The Vision" contains some of this. The narrator is told to give up "obsessive rationality with its constant questionings and doubts." And:

"Why are you appearing to me?" I asked.

"We're trying to appear to many."

"Then why haven't I heard about other people seeing you?"

"Most don't. They are too closed to see anything. Others see a little and grow frightened and turn away. Still others see only what they want to see. You are one of the few to whom I appear as I am."

"But why me? I'm not particularly smart or good."

"Because of your longing. It opens you to the truth. And your simplicity, which allows you to receive it."

To some, such reasoning seems a good explanation for why something that doesn't meet our normal criteria for judging truth could still be true.

To others such reasoning seems a determined effort to avoid seeing the truth.

Atheism and the Problem of Suffering 🌑

Thus far we have talked about possible reasons for believing in the existence of God. Now we come to a possible reason for disbelieving.

There are three possible positions one can take on the question of whether or not God exists. The **theist** believes there is a God. The **agnostic** isn't sure one way or the other. The **atheist** believes there is no God.

Perhaps you have heard something like the following argument: "It's absurd to be an atheist, as opposed to an agnostic or a theist. How could anyone possibly prove that God doesn't exist!"

If you are sympathetic to this argument, imagine yourself in the following situation. A friend, looking out the window, says, "My goodness, there's a huge pink whale lying in the backyard." You laugh at the idea and wouldn't even bother to look except that you happen to be at the window and you see nothing out there but lawn. Your friend gets indignant. "Wait a minute," she says: "I can see how you might be unsure of whether there's a huge pink whale in the backyard. But it would be irrational to believe there isn't one. How could you possibly prove that?"

> EVIDENCE THAT SOMETHING DOESN'T EXIST

The point is that there are a lot of things in the world that you positively believe didn't happen or don't exist. We decide that if a certain claim were true, certain other things ought to happen; if those other things don't happen, that is taken as evidence that the original claim is false. That is, under certain circumstances, we take the absence of certain kinds of evidence to count as evidence against. We all reason in this way every day. This is not to say that the question of God's existence is as straightforward as the question of whether or not there is a pink whale in the backyard. It is only to say that one can't dismiss atheism as absurd in advance of a discussion of grounds for believing in God.

Some atheists have based their belief on the absence of certain evidence that they think would exist if God did (e.g., unambiguous miracles, consistent religious experience from culture to culture, etc.). Others, however, have claimed that there is positive evidence that God does not exist, namely the amount of suffering in the world. This claim amounts to a kind of negative version of the argument from design. According to the argument from design, the complex orderliness of the world indicates that it must

🌑 The CD, Ch. 3, *The Vision (2),* has a discussion, "If It Feels Good, Believe It?" regarding a central theme of the story.

have been designed by God. Here an opposite claim is made: The suffering in the world indicates that it could not have been designed by God.

As Martin says in "Surprise!": "The laws of the universe may be mathematically elegant, but they crush and they kill. No respectable God would allow people to suffer as they do."

> **SUFFERING AS EVIDENCE GOD DOESN'T EXIST**

It has been traditional in much of our culture to view God as omnipotent (all-powerful), omniscient (all-knowing), and perfectly good. The existence of suffering poses a tough challenge for a theist who believes in such a God. How could a God who is perfectly good, can do absolutely anything He wants to do, and knows everything there is to know, possibly create a world in which so many of His creatures suffer so terribly?

A theist who believes in a God who lacks one of these characteristics has a ready explanation for suffering: A God who lacks omnipotence or omniscience does not have the power or knowledge to eliminate suffering, and a God who is not perfectly good is morally defective and doesn't care to eliminate suffering. The existence of suffering is not evidence against the existence of gods like these. But it is possible evidence against the existence of a God who is supposed to have all three of those characteristics.

The problem here is what's called the "problem of suffering": Does the existence of suffering show that there could not be a God who is omnipotent (all-powerful), omniscient (all-knowing), and perfectly good? 🌀

Omnipotence and Contradiction

At first glance, it may seem obvious that the existence of suffering rules out the possibility of there being a God who is omnipotent, omniscient, and perfectly good: Such a God would create the best of all possible worlds. In the best of all possible worlds there would exist human beings with free will who were happy and virtuous. Obviously, this world isn't such a world. Therefore, there is no such God.

But many theists make the following reply: The world you have just described is not a possible world. The idea of creating such a world is contradictory. Even an omnipotent God could not do contradictory things: Therefore, God can in no way be blamed for not having created such a world.

This reply employs two arguments that need to be elaborated in some detail:

🌀   The CD, Ch. 3, *Atheism and the Problem of Suffering,* discusses the atheist challenge and the theist response.

1. Even an omnipotent God could not do what is contradictory.
2. The idea of creating a world in which human beings with free will are virtuous and happy is a contradiction.

Throughout the centuries many theologians have felt that God, to be omnipotent, must be able to do contradictory things. He must be able to create a chair that is not a chair, a triangle that has four sides. To say that God cannot do such things is to suppose that God is limited and hence not omnipotent.

Today most philosophers and theologians reject the claim that, to be omnipotent, a God would have to do contradictory things. This claim, they say, results from a misunderstanding about the nature of contradictions. It supposes that contradictions describe the most difficult kind of tasks. In truth, contradictions describe nothing at all. In this sense, they are analogous to nonsense statements. One should no more expect an omnipotent God to create a chair that is not a chair than one should expect Him to "oop erg alban ipple ong."

CONTRADICTIONS DESCRIBE NOTHING

In contradictory phrases, the individual words make sense but the combination of words is senseless. To say "create a chair that is not a chair" is like drawing a picture of a chair on a chalkboard, erasing the picture, then pointing to the board and saying, "There, make me one of those." But what is portrayed on the chalkboard, finally, is not some difficult task or other; nothing at all is portrayed there.*

This issue is controversial, and the remarks above are too brief to do justice to the differing points of view. But for any theist who is tempted to say that an omnipotent God must be able to do contradictory things, one can add a rather powerful **ad hominem argument,† making the theist uncomfortable with his or her reasoning.** One can say: You have just denied

---

* In "A Little Omniscience Goes a Long Way," in Chapter 1, God attributes the impossibility of doing contradictory things to His decree. But this impossibility would seem intrinsic to any rational system of thought; it would exist simultaneously with God's thought and would not be the result of some subsequent decree. Note also that God's longing to do contradictory things would be, in this analysis, absurd.

† There are two kinds of ad hominem (literally, "to the man") arguments, one a fallacy, the other not. The fallacy is to try to discredit an argument by attacking the person making it. "He's such a jerk; you know whatever he's saying has to be wrong." The other kind of ad hominem—the one used above—is to point out to an opponent that making a certain point or argument will undercut her own position. To the theist: If you want to insist God must be able to do contradictory things, then you can't consistently use the traditional explanations as to why God allowed suffering. Another ad hominem was used earlier in this chapter. To the theist: If you insist it's senseless to talk about what happened before the Big Bang, then you're committed to saying it's senseless to talk about God the Creator.

yourself any recourse to the traditional explanations of why God might have allowed suffering.

Many theists suppose that God, at the time of creation, was faced with certain forced options. He could either eliminate all suffering or create a world in which human beings had free will and might be virtuous (exhibit good moral qualities). To do both would be contradictory. God quite properly chose to create a world in which human beings had free will and virtuousness, rather than creating a world in which they were unfree, nonvirtuous, and happy. As in the story "Surprise!" I shall divide these arguments into two defenses: the free-will defense and the virtue defense. But before discussing these two defenses, let's consider another defense that is not much discussed in the philosophical literature but which many students offer and find convincing: the claim that it is impossible to have happiness without unhappiness.

Does Happiness Require Unhappiness?

In the story "Surprise!" God and Martin assume that it would be possible to have a world in which everyone was happy (as heaven itself is supposed to demonstrate). The question they debate is whether or not such a world would indeed be better than the alternatives. However, if it is impossible to have a world in which everyone is happy, then their whole discussion would seem to be beside the point. **Thus we had better ask: Is it impossible to have happiness without unhappiness?**

Often a discussion of this issue gets sidetracked by inflated, soap-opera conceptions of happiness (as in "Yes, everything is going well, and yes, I'm feeling fine, but am I really happy?"). Such a rarefied notion of happiness is not relevant to the problem of suffering. We all know what it is to wince and say, "Oh, that hurts." We all know what it is to say, "Boy, I'm really feeling good today." Those challenging the theist on the problem of suffering are saying that God should have created the world so that there were no feelings like the former (and worse), only feelings like the latter. To keep the issue down to earth, think of the question we're discussing as to whether it is possible to have pleasant feelings without unpleasant feelings.

There are **two other confusions** that often come up in discussing this issue:

1. **"Human beings are such that they cannot be happy all the time and thus God couldn't have made a world in which there was only happiness."** Even if the first part of the statement were true, the second part doesn't follow logically from the first. If human beings can't be happy all the time, then perhaps God should have created different creatures

who could be. To support the no-happiness-without-unhappiness claim requires one to show that no possible creature could be happy all the time.

2. **"Without a contrast you couldn't know what happiness was; thus you can't have happiness without unhappiness."** Again, the conclusion of the argument doesn't follow from the premise. Whether there could be only happiness is one thing; whether, if there was only happiness, we would know it was happiness, would call it "happiness," is another. Supporting the latter claim is not enough to demonstrate the former. For instance, I think I can imagine a world that is all red (let's say different shades of red). I might agree that creatures in that world wouldn't know it was red (as opposed to yellow), wouldn't have the word "red," but the world would still be red.

In order to show that an omnipotent God could not have created happiness without unhappiness, it would be necessary to show that the idea of happiness without unhappiness is contradictory.

Even if that could be shown, it wouldn't signify much in terms of the problem of suffering. Any defense of suffering is going to have to justify a lot of suffering. **The claim that happiness without unhappiness is contradictory would seem to justify only a little bit of suffering for contrast.** The claim one really needs to make in terms of the problem of suffering is that it would be contradictory to have a lot of happiness without a lot of unhappiness. It's hard to see what the argument for that might be.

In any case, note that both the free-will and virtue defenses assume that a happy world would have been possible, but argue that it wouldn't have been the best of the possible (noncontradictory) worlds.   ✷

The Free-Will Defense

The <u>free-will defense</u> claims that:

1. Free will is a great good and a necessary ingredient in the best of all possible worlds.
2. It would be contradictory for God to give human beings free will and yet guarantee they never use their free will to harm themselves and others.
3. Therefore, there is likely to be suffering in the best of all possible worlds.

✷   The CD, *Does Happiness Require Unhappiness?* reviews the arguments regarding this topic.

To elaborate on **statement 2:** If human beings have free will, then their choices are not caused. It would be contradictory for God to give human beings free will and, at the same time, control their choices so that they never make choices that would cause unhappiness.

Re **statement 3:** Note that the concept of free will doesn't necessarily imply suffering. Rather, it is likely that over time people will use their free will to cause suffering. The point of the argument is that it's not God's fault if they do.

People readily accept the free-will defense. But there are serious questions one can raise about it.

Most people do think that free will is a great good. But in chapter one, it was suggested that this opinion may result from a misunderstanding about what free will is. If one accepts the argument in that chapter, one would probably decide that having free will would not be of much value.

Even if one does believe that free will is a great good, one should ask whether it is really worth the great suffering it has supposedly caused. Often the options here are misconceived. Many religious tracts imply that the only alternative to a world with free will is a world in which people move about like zombies. Given our previous discussion, this is obviously false. Free will pertains only to the causes of one's choices. It implies nothing about the particular characteristics of one's facial expessions, movements, feelings, or thoughts. Free will, as we have seen, would not be an observable thing. What would you and others look like without free will? You would look exactly the way you look now. God could have created people without free will who were lively, lovely, emotional, thoughtful, and who always chose happy courses of action. Would such a world so obviously have been second-rate?

> LACK OF FREE WILL WOULDN'T IMPLY ONE'S A ZOMBIE

It is generally agreed that the free-will defense is not adequate to explain all suffering. It may account for the suffering caused by human beings. It does not account for the suffering caused by natural phenomena like diseases, earthquakes, and floods.

Some theists do link the suffering caused by natural phenomena to human free will by claiming that such suffering is a punishment for misuse of freedom. But this argument really supplements the free-will defense as it has been presented here. It adds two premises. One: Human beings did misuse their freedom, and God punished them by forcing them to live in a world of suffering. Two: The great suffering caused by natural events is proper punishmeet for human beings' misuse of their freedom. Some critics, like Martin, find this second premise "barbaric."

The Virtue Defense

There is another defense that often is presented as a justification for the existence of suffering caused by natural phenomena. It implies that God was right in making sure that there would be some suffering in the world, whatever human beings might do with their free will. It can be referred to as the virtue defense, and it runs as follows:

1. Virtues, such as generosity and courage, are great goods and, in the best of all possible worlds, human beings ought to have the chance to exercise such virtues.
2. It would be contradictory to have virtues in a world without suffering, since the definitions of these virtues imply the existence of suffering.
3. Therefore, suffering is a necessary ingredient in the best of all possible worlds.

To enlarge on **statement 2: Try to imagine someone being courageous in a world in which no one is afraid or in danger.** It is impossible. To be courageous is to overcome fear (which is necessarily painful) and to risk oneself to help someone else. In a world with no pain and no risk of harm, no possible action could be courageous.

Or **try to imagine generosity in a world in which all persons have more than they need.** It is impossible. In such a world, any act of giving would be analogous to a child on a beach handing another child a bucket of sand. Generosity involves some sacrifice to help another in need. In a world with no need, no possible action could be generous.

This is an ingenious defense, and many find it reasonable. Others, however, do not.

Some philosophers have said that this defense views virtue inside out. What is good about virtues is that they aim at the relief of suffering. Virtues are good as means only. Virtues are correctly called good in a world with suffering. But to insist on suffering in order to have virtue is absurd; it contradicts the very nature of virtue. To insist on suffering so that there can be generosity and sympathy is like stealing from someone so that you can give that person some needed item or kicking someone in the shins so that you can feel sorry for that person.

> VIRTUE DEFENSE VIEWS
> VIRTUE INSIDE OUT

The theist's defenses do seem to be successful in showing that there is a morality such that, if God had accepted it, it would have committed Him to allow some suffering in the world. **Thus the "problem of suffering" comes down to an evaluation of this morality. Do you believe that free will and virtue are worth all the suffering in this world?** If you do, then you believe in the possibility of a God who is omnipotent, omniscient, and perfectly good. If you do not, then you will deny that there could be such a God: If there is a God, He is acting on the wrong moral principles.

"Surprise! It's Judgment Day" is meant to be provocative, so it contains something to get almost everyone a little bit angry. Some would claim that there is much more to be said on God's behalf; others would claim that there is much more to be said for the position that Martin first endorses and then abnegates in his horror at becoming "only happy."

The story assumes a dichotomy that is, in some ways, to the theist's advantage. The only options presented in the story are a world like ours or a world in which people are happy zombies. But we know from the discussion that lack of free will needn't make human beings zombie-like. What if the heaven in "Surprise" had been filled with people without free will who were happy, intelligent, inquisitive, and appreciative of beauty? Who played games, painted, read, played music? Would this alternative to our world have seemed so awful?

Even the defenses of suffering may promote a false dicotomy, though of a different sort. The debate is whether the "best of all possible worlds" is a world with free will, lots of suffering, and many opportunities for great virtue (and vice) or a world with happiness, no free will, and no virtue. But as a third possibility, what about a world with free will that is severely restricted in terms of its possible effects, so that there is some suffering, but not that much, and the opportunity for displaying some virtues to some degree?

Question #10 below sketches such a world and asks whether or not there's anything contradictory about it and whether it is better or worse than our own. An interesting class exercise is to have students (individually or in groups) come up with their own proposals for the "best of all possible worlds," then to check the proposals for possible contradictions and ask whether or not the proposed worlds look better than our own. ⊛

Questions and Exercises

1. Summarize the "three traditional arguments for the existence of God" and the critiques of those arguments.
2. Why, according to the text, does the Big Bang theory of the origin of the Universe not rule out the possibility that the Universe always existed?

⊛ The CD, Ch. 3, *The Free Will and Virtue Defenses,* reviews these defenses and the objections to them.

3. Suppose you began to have some "visions." How would you decide whether they represented some objective reality or were merely fantasies or hallucinations?

4. a. In ordinary cases of perception, how do we decide whether what we are seeing is "real" or not?

   b. How would religious experiences be judged in terms of the above criteria?

5. What is the "problem of suffering"?

6. "Even an omnipotent God could not do contradictory things." Give a justification for this statement.

7. "God couldn't create a world that's all happy because human beings aren't capable of being happy all the time." Critique this statement.

8. Present the free-will defense and a possible objection to it.

9. Present the virtue defense and a possible objection to it.

10. Try to imagine the following sort of world: a world with more abundance than anyone could use up, including space for living; people with free will but with a tendency toward good (as we are now supposed to have a tendency toward selfishness or evil); people with bodies that can suffer some painful injuries and diseases but can't be in agony or be maimed or killed. In this world people can have adventures and take risks and display moral qualities, though not to the degree that we can (because of the limits on suffering).

    a. Is there anything contradictory about this world? Explain.

    b. Would such a world be better or worse than our own? Explain.

11. Using ideas like those in #10, see if you can come up with a noncontradictory world that seems better than both our real world and the zombie-like heaven in "Surprise!" ✹

✹   The CD, Ch. 3, *The Free Will and Virtue Defenses (2)*, discusses issues related to this question. The CD, Ch. 3, *Rockin' Review: "I Don't Like Sufferin'"*, has a song on the problem of suffering.

4

Moral Principles

The Land of Certus

Of all those lands in which I have traveled, the most wondrous is the land of Certus. The people there are to be envied above all others, for that which is to us the most perplexing mystery of existence is to them no mystery at all.

As I stepped from that treacherous forest through which I had wandered, lost, for five days, the first being I encountered in the land of Certus was Felanx. He was a rough-hewn, kindly farmer who greeted me at the edge of his fields and offered me the hospitality of his home. Yet he frightened me at first. For when he smiled, there came from his face a strange green light, and I drew back, thinking him a sorcerer. But after a time, he succeeded in calming me with his gentle manner. He said that the light would not harm me and that he would explain it presently.

Felanx led me to the high stone walls of the town, past the sentry at the gate, through the narrow cobblestone streets to his home. As his family welcomed me, there were more flashes of that green light. But his son, who would not approach me, glowed a faint red. Felanx spoke harshly to the boy and dismissed him.

I was seated by the fire, given warm drink, and promised supper. I was no longer fearful of those strange lights, but my curiosity became too

 The CD, Ch. 4, *The Land of Certus,* contains animation and exercises related to this story.

91

much to bear. I asked Felanx to provide me with the explanation he had promised.

"It is quite simple," he said. "From others who have come to our land, we know that these lights do not exist in other parts of the world. So I understand your confusion. Yet to us the lights seem most natural, and we cannot imagine a land that is otherwise. The green light is the light of the good. The red light, it shames me to say, is the light of the bad. You saw it around my youngest son. Most of the time he is a good boy, but sometimes he does not show the proper hospitality to strangers. He has been disciplined. Please accept my apologies on his behalf."

"The lights of good and bad!" I exclaimed. "This is trickery. Do you take me for a fool?"

As I spoke thus to my host, red light burst before my eyes, and I began to stammer in confusion. But once again, Felanx put me at ease. He said that he understood and forgave my skepticism. He said that once I had had a chance to observe his land further and to reflect on the matter, I would realize that he had spoken the truth.

I marveled at the words of my host. To have all good and bad deeds clearly marked so that everyone should know them for what they were: Could anything be a greater boon to humanity? I hesitated to believe, and yet had I not seen these lights with my own eyes? After some thought I inquired about the origin of the lights.

"To that question," said Felanx, "there is no answer that seems to satisfy all. One answer is given in The Book of the Beginning. It says that the Creator made the skies and the earth and then, because He was lonely, He created human beings to be His companions. He put human beings in the most beautiful place on earth, the Valley of Peace, and He dwelt there with them. For a time all was happiness. But after a number of years, some people became restless. They said that they wanted to see what lay beyond the valley. The Creator told them there was nothing beyond the valley so happy and so lovely as it was. Still, many wanted to go. The Creator granted them permission at last, saying that He would constrain no one to stay with Him. But He was very angry. He told those who departed that they would find great sorrow in the lands beyond the valley and that they would never find their way back.

"But then one woman bowed down before the Creator and pleaded in tears for her descendants. Was it right, she asked, that they should all suffer for the folly of her headstrong daughter, who was among those who wished to leave? At her words, the Creator relented. He said that He would give those who departed the lights of good and bad, so that they would know how to make themselves worthy to return to the valley. He said that one day

He would walk the earth and lead those who glowed with the goodness of green back to the Valley of Peace.

"That, I say, is just one answer. It is the one that my wife accepts. Others have argued that there is no Creator, that the skies and the earth have always been. They say that the lights of good and bad are simply natural events that require no supernatural explanation. The light of the good, they say, is no more mysterious than the other colors of things whose significance is beauty. I, myself, am of this opinion."

I remarked that in my land there were also doubts about a Creator. But the disputes of the Certans were as nothing compared with ours. For in my land, people interpreted good and bad "according to their own lights," and what each person saw was different. At least in Certus there were no doubts about goodness and badness: the lights were the same for everyone. And if there were doubts about a Creator, at least there could be no doubt how to please Him, should He exist.

The next day, Felanx showed me around the town and introduced me to many of the townspeople. All those I met showed me the utmost kindness. They were eager to hear stories of my travels and to answer any questions I might have. In fact, I was preoccupied with just one question, and it was answered not by what was said to me but by what I observed for myself. I saw that the green lights did indeed mark acts of goodness and the red lights acts of badness. Not that the Certans are a bad people. On the contrary, they are a fine people. But they are human, and they make mistakes. The red light allows them to see their mistakes at once and to correct them.

At one home, we drank a delicious plum whiskey, and the green light over the gathering answered for me a question that divided those in my land, the question of whether it is evil to drink alcohol. The green light told me that drinking is good, though only in moderation. When one of the group became drunken, he glowed with a red light. He was led from the room, apologizing to us all.

As we emerged from another house, I noticed a ragged fellow stumbling as if inebriated, glowing the brightest of reds. The others with me jeered at him, but the fellow only smiled and made a sign with his hands, which I was given to understand was the vilest of profanities. I was surprised by the existence of this reprobate in Certus, and I asked Felanx about him.

"His name is Georges, and he is a difficult case," said Felanx. "At first, some thought that he might be blind to the lights of good and bad, as some are blind to colors and shapes. But he answers questions about the lights correctly. He just won't be guided by them. He knows the good but doesn't want to do it. His case is now before the town council. My guess is that there will be extreme punishment."

"But how can a man know the good and not want to do it?" I exclaimed.

At once I saw the foolishness of my remark, remembering that in the sacred book of my land it says that many fall not through ignorance but through the wickedness of the heart. I told Felanx of this.

"And so it says in The Book of the Beginning. But Georges is especially dangerous. Not only does he say that he often prefers wickedness to goodness, but he suggests that everyone should do so. He says that people should do what pleases them and should disregard the lights."

"But how can he be dangerous?" I asked. "Surely anyone can see that if all were to do as they pleased, with no thought of the good, with no thought of others, the result must be chaos, disastrous for all."

"Of course," said Felanx. "But Georges is subtle. He says that what all people should prefer is not only their own pleasures but also the pleasures of others. It is this that seems to absolve him of selfishness in the eyes of the young, and many are drawn by his words."

I shook my head sadly, reflecting on the perversity of human beings. As we walked on through the streets, my attention was drawn to the cannons placed along the town walls. I asked Felanx about them.

"You have learned today that there are two towns in Certus: ours, which is Rechtsen, and another which is Linksen. What I have not told you about is the terrible perversity of the Linksens. But now that you know of the wicked Georges, you might as well know all.

"The Linksens are our mortal enemies. They have a religion that denies our own. They say that the lights of good and bad are not the work of the Creator, but the work of the Creator's enemy. They say that the lights of good and bad have been put in this land to confuse and lead astray the Creator's true friends. They say that we should not follow the lights, but should instead follow the laws written in their book. These laws, they believe, express the Creator's true wishes."

I could not restrain myself at this absurdity.

"But surely they could be shown the truth. Listen: If at this moment, heaven forbid, I should strike you down for no reason, there would be a ferocious blaze of red. Is it not so?"

"Of course."

"And would it be the same in Linksen?"

"It would. The lights are the same in Linksen."

"There, then. Surely the Linksens cannot believe that such an act could be right or that the Creator would wish it. Were they to believe so, there would now be none of them left. This must prove to them that the lights show the truth."

Felanx lowered his head, and I sensed that he was close to tears.

"Alas, they too have their vicious subtleties. Were you to compare their rules of the good and the bad with the lights of the good and the bad, you would find much agreement. It is this, they say, that shows the cleverness of the Creator's enemy. He makes the lights so that they seem to show the truth in every case. It is this that misleads so many. The Linksens say that women should be equal to men, that animals are not to be eaten, and that the Rechtsens are to be destroyed. That the red light shows on such deeds, they say, is the triumph of deception."

The day that had begun with such joy had turned out sad, and I went to bed that evening with a heavy heart. I had always held the hope that as the nature of goodness became clearer to human beings, they would become better and better. Yet here in Certus, where all had been made clear, wickedness and dissension continued. Was there indeed any hope for humanity?

I awoke the next morning to the sound of a crowd's yelling in the courtyard. I moved through the empty house and went outside. A hundred of the townspeople were gathered in the marketplace, viewing some spectacle. Moving into the crowd, I saw what it was. Georges was lying naked on a wooden platform, his body shackled. He was writhing and screaming, as one of the men standing over him slowly snapped the bones in his fingers with some heavy metal instrument. A glance at Georges's body and at the fiendish instruments held by the men around him indicated that this was just one moment in a long process of torture. Nearby was a stake and a mound of wood where later they would burn his disfigured body.

I turned away in anger and horror, searching the faces in the crowd. All were watching the brutal spectacle with slight, solemn smiles. I saw Felanx near me and grabbed his arm.

"How can you do this?" I cried. "You who say you love the good."

"Georges is paying the price of his wickedness. The council decided last night. Georges ignores the good and incites others to do the same. He has to be punished. He has to be made an example. It is right that he be punished."

"Punished, yes," I said. "Perhaps even killed. But not like this. This is barbaric! This is horrible!"

Felanx pulled away from me, and his expression became fierce. He moved his hand, and for a moment I thought he was going to strike me. Instead he pointed toward Georges.

"Look again," he commanded.

"No. It is too terrible."

"Look at the men who are carrying out the sentence."

Reluctantly, I glanced toward the terrible scene. Then I saw what had escaped my attention before. The torturers of Georges were all glowing a faint green. This act that I had so readily condemned was, in fact, good, right. Suddenly my horror turned to shame.

"Forgive me," I said, bowing my head.

There was a moment of silence before Felanx spoke.

"You are forgiven, my friend, my guest. But I must concern myself now with your safety. The Linksens know of Georges's punishment. Their leaders have told the people that Georges is their spy and is suffering for their cause. This is not so, and the leaders know it. It is a mere pretext for attack. But they will attack our city. You must leave at once."

"Let me stay," I pleaded, ashamed at having wrongly condemned the Rechtsens. "Life is not so much to me that I would not gladly sacrifice it for the sake of the good."

"I believe that," said Felanx. "But this is not your land, and this is not your battle. You must go."

I kept pleading until I noticed that a red glow began to arise from my body. Then I stopped. I had already committed one grievous error that day; I must not commit another. If it was wrong for me to stay there, then I must go.

An hour later, Felanx led me to the town gate, where he bade me goodbye and turned me over to the guide who was to lead me through the woods along a tortuous trail, which I fear I shall never find again.

The land of Certus is often in my thoughts. For it seems to me that if there is any hope for humankind, it must lie with those brave people of Rechtsen who know the good, follow it, and will fight for it to the end. May the Creator help them in their struggle.

Fiction: Those Who Help Themselves

The war with the planet Omega is won. Its cities have been destroyed, its social institutions overthrown, its people injured and anguished. We have just destroyed what may have been the only truly moral civilization that ever existed.

All the civilizations that remain are morally defective. On Earth, in this twenty-second century after Jesus, in this third century after Marx, we certainly have not achieved what anyone would be tempted to call "utopia." We still have our cruelties, our injustices; we still have our victors and victims.

As for other planets, the pathetic, vegetablelike creatures on Beta, though incapable of doing us harm, are vicious: They kill one another with grotesque frequency. The Alphas have friendly relations with us, but they are unspeakably cruel to their slave classes. And it goes through the whole of the known universe.

Ten years ago, the age-old pessimism about "human nature" had developed into a pessimism about all "living nature." At least such pessimism affords a certain comfort. If moral failure is indeed universal, then it may be inevitable and therefore no one's fault. The discovery of Omega challenged this deterministic view and threatened us with self-contempt.

What the Omegans did to be moral was in no way startling. We, on Earth, know quite well the dictates of morality; we know what a moral world would be like. (This is true in general, even if there are marginal disagreements about the nature of the good and the right.) Our problems result not from lack of knowledge, but from lack of ability or willingness.

The Omegans were incredibly kind to each other. They seemed to go out of their way to say something pleasant to, or do something nice for, each other. If any one of their number appeared to be in distress, offers of help were immediate.

In terms of the larger society, the distribution of goods was pretty nearly equal. In theory, the government was charged with enforcing equal distribution; in practice, little enforcement was necessary. The Omegans readily handed over their surplus goods for others in need, and the government had only to coordinate such generosity to see that it was orderly and its results, equitable.

In spite this near-equal distribution of goods, the Omegans were highly energetic, industrious people. They were even, one might say, competitive. But one didn't sense that they were really competing against one another. Each success was celebrated, to a large degree, as a success for all and as an example to others. Each success was measured against the person's potential, and living up to one's potential, whatever it might be, brought the highest respect. The Omegans were not without individual ambition and pride, but they were quite temperate in these.

If many Earth people felt that the Omegan society was not quite ideal, many Omegans felt the same way. In their democratic society, there were a number of political parties. The biggest opposition party wanted to enlarge the competitive market for the material goods of Omega. Another party, somewhat smaller, wanted no competition and a perfectly equal distribution of goods. There were also fringe groups asking for, say, a greater emphasis on the arts or a greater allocation of funds to defense research. But all such parties constituted a loyal opposition. All felt that the Omegan society was close enough to their ideal so that they could live quite happily with the status quo. All recognized the ongoing value of democracy and of relative stability. Because of the conspicuous absence of religion on Omega, there was no inclination to disrupt human welfare for the sake of some supernatural ideal.

Perhaps it is not correct to say that there was no religion on Omega. Certainly there was no belief in a God. However, there was one metaphysical belief, shared by all Omegans, that might be considered "religious." It apparently developed in their prehistory, and, if its beginnings were associated with revelations or proofs, there were no existing indications of such, even in the guise of myths. That this belief was so implicit in the Omegans' consciousness—no one had to be persuaded, it was never argued—kept it from our notice for some time. But even the Omegans' expression of this belief was misinterpreted by us at first. A phrase like "that unfortunate man might be me" sounded so much like the imaginative exhortations of our moralists that we failed to comprehend that the phrase was intended literally. Finally we did understand, and, in understanding, I suppose, we discovered the "secret" of the Omegans' moral behavior.

The Omegans believed in the perpetual reincarnation of souls, which was not the work of some divinity, but simply the natural way of things. Almost as soon as a person died, the soul was reborn in the body of some infant, with all memories of the past life erased. This reincarnation, they believed, was not only natural, but random: Merits and demerits in a past life had nothing whatever to do with a soul's replacement in the next life, and one's inclinations and abilities were not transferred from one life to another. In the next life, the woman of great intellect might be retarded, the man of good health might be diseased, the person of great culture might be interested only in popular entertainments—or vice versa. One might be reborn the same or quite different. There was no way of knowing in advance.

The moral efficacy of this belief is obvious. It is a consequence of this belief that, in promoting a society in which each person helps others, one is quite literally helping oneself. No one was willing to neglect another, because soon one might be in the same position.

There were, as has been noted, some differences of opinion on Omega concerning the moral and political status quo. Apparently, those supporting the largest opposition party were gamblers: They were willing to risk the possibility of some misfortune in the next life for the possibility of gaining great wealth in this life. Those on the opposite end of the political spectrum were unwilling to gamble at all with their future lives: They wanted to be guaranteed an equal share of the wealth. Those who supported the majority party wanted some guarantees and some chances to gamble. But none was willing to gamble too much with his or her future life, to risk being diseased, mentally defective, or hungry, and being without help. Thus, each was agreed that all should be helped. Guarantees in no way sapped the industriousness of the Omegans, since all would share in the future benefits of their own labors.

Some Earth critics of the Omegan war say that we came to conquer. But that isn't true. We simply do not have the power to conquer and control a universe; we always prefer a peaceful relationship of mutually profitable cooperation.

The problem was that the Omegans refused to acknowledge the moral rights of creatures other than Omegans. Just as twenty-second-century Christians cannot believe that Jesus died to save Betas and Epsilons, just as Marxists don't know what to think about economic determinism on other worlds, so the Omegans could not believe that their souls might migrate beyond their own race. They had no incentive at all to treat other beings fairly, and, in fact, as more of us came to Omega, they began to treat us viciously. War was inevitable.

Perhaps if the crisis had not come so quickly, some say, the Omegans might have adjusted their morality to include other life forms. But this would not have happened as long as those others did not share the belief of the Omegans.

But perhaps we might have come to share the religion of the Omegans, some add. This is a lovely fantasy indeed. If religion is to be judged by its moral efficacy, the "religion" of the Omegans is the best we have ever encountered. However, one does not change religions as one changes clothes. Earth has its religions already, and, for good or ill, we seem to be stuck with them.

In another place and time, when war meant individuals fighting each other, the Omegans would have been unbeatable. Their firm belief in a perpetual reincarnation on Omega would have made them supremely courageous and persistent. But such qualities count for nothing against superior weaponry. The war was brief and, for the Omegans, devastating.

Few faiths survive such catastrophes. The faith of the Omegans has not. Already, for the first time in the recorded history of Omega, questions are being raised, questions for which no one has answers. Whatever the Omegans may be in the future, it is clear that they will never be the same. Their past civilization will become a footnote to the depressing history of the universe—the only truly moral civilization that has ever existed.

Fiction: The Sheriff's Wife

The Sheriff's house sat at the edge of a small woods, looking out over miles of treeless plain. The house was at the junction of three roads, one going straight out toward town, another, left, toward the mountains, the third one, right, toward the river. Not that those destinations were obvious from here. The river was hidden by the woods. The mountains were too distant to be seen as anything but occasional vague forms. Glimpses of town came only at night, and then as a few dots of lights barely distinguishable from stars.

Relatives back east had asked Alma if she found the plains depressing, but in a way they suited her. The plains were as simple and straightforward as the truths of her life: You believed in God and followed His Commandments. And the ground was as plain and hard as her life: She took care of her husband, her house, and her soul. If there was little joy in it, well, joy could wait for the next life. At least she was at peace.

Though not today. Today she was worried sick for her husband and what he might do.

She wasn't supposed to have heard what she heard last night. She'd woken about midnight and had been on her way to the kitchen to fix hot milk, when she'd heard the deputy arrive, heard the first words of the man's whispered conversation with her husband. She supposed she should have turned away then instead of listening, but she knew there were bad troubles in town and had hoped for news. She'd never dreamed she might

---

The CD, Ch. 4, *The Sheriff's Wife*, contains animation and exercises related to this story.

hear what she had. It had made her feel sick. The Sheriff and the Deputy had left an hour later; Alma had been up for the rest of that night.

The business with the Indian, Moon, had been going on for two days now, though the trouble had really begun almost a week ago, when those two little girls were found with their clothes torn and their throats cut. There'd been no eyewitnesses or evidence to point to the person responsible. There'd only been the wild rumors, starting a day or so later, casting suspicion on the Indian. The Sheriff had told Alma the suspicion seemed groundless, but the townspeople were desperate to find a culprit, preferably someone they considered an outsider, and anger against the Indian had continued to build.

When the Sheriff had refused to arrest Moon, there was talk of a lynching and the Sheriff finally put the man in jail for his own protection. It might not be much protection. Changing groups of townspeople had camped outside the jail, venting their anger, threatening violence. Two townspeople who'd spoken up for Moon had been badly beaten; two Indians had been shot, just for being around. The Sheriff had wired for help but it would be days before any help came.

The Deputy who'd arrived last night had been in a panic. The crowd outside the jail was getting nastier. One group had a battering ram and was talking about breaking into the jail; another group was talking about burning down the jail and anyone "fool enough to stay in it." "I don't want to die for that Indian," the Deputy had said.

When Alma had married the Sheriff, he'd been a strong and righteous man. But she'd watched him weaken over the last few years. He'd become too interested in getting along, and too prone to go along. He was too ready to compromise and too open to utilitarian arguments. It had hurt Alma to see him stray from the path of the Lord. But until last evening, she'd had no idea how far he'd strayed.

The plan had come from the Deputy, not her husband, but the Sheriff's initial resistance had been mostly practical, and his biggest concern had been saving face for himself and his Office. When the Sheriff had finally agreed to a plan, Alma had heard no anguish in his voice.

To avert more violence and more deaths, they would give the lynch mob Moon—a man they both felt to be innocent. It just wouldn't look like they'd done it. The Sheriff would leave town on the ostensible mission of "getting help," but really to distance himself from what would happen. The Deputy would help Moon "escape." There was no possibility that Moon could really escape the way the townspeople were watching the jail. But the Deputy would arrange with the leaders of the mob to pretend to let Moon get through, all the while secretly watching which direction he went. Then the Deputy would announce the escape and the townspeople could do their killing as a "posse."

Alma would pray to the Lord that her husband would see the light. She would pray for Moon, too. Alma liked the Indian. He was one of the dispossessed, forced to do odd jobs to survive. But unlike some of the others, who had let circumstances beat them down, he had managed to hold on to a quiet dignity. She had noticed it when she'd first hired him to work on the property and later during those few "conversations" they'd had.

Alma felt it was her Christian duty to speak God's word. For all sorts of reasons, she'd been hesitant to do so with Moon, but she'd finally decided it was cowardice on her part. When she'd taken the man his supper, Alma had spoken to him of God and the path of righteousness and the importance of following God's Commandments. Moon had listened politely as he ate, saying nothing that first time except to thank her for the food and tell her it was good.

The next time she'd talked to Moon, he'd fixed on the Commandment, "Thou shalt not lie." He'd said, almost wistfully it had seemed to her, "It's too bad the White Man didn't take those words to heart when he made promises to the Indian." His words had confused Alma. She knew treaties had been broken, but her girlhood had been filled with tales of frontier heroism and of missionaries bringing God's word to the heathen Indians, and it was hard for her, she knew, to see it all from the point of view of the Indians.

Moon seemed to shrug off his own comment. He said, rather abstractedly, "I suppose it's hard to live life without lying."

Here Alma felt on surer ground.

"We have to try," she said. "Lying is always wrong."

"Always?" Moon had asked, with a smile. "Miss Alma, what if your friend asks you how you like her new dress, when you find her dress very ugly?"

"I would try to find something about the dress I liked and remark on that. Failing that, I would try to say nothing. If forced, I would have to tell the truth."

"Then let's hope your friends always buy pretty dresses."

Moon had smiled as he'd said it, and Alma had found herself smiling too. She smiled again now, as she thought of it.

For a moment there was no feeling of surprise as she looked up to see Moon approaching the junction on a horse. Then the reality and gravity of the situation hit her.

She wasn't afraid. There was a loaded shotgun just inside the front door—a shotgun she knew how to use—but the idea of the gun was just an idle thought. She trusted Moon and felt awful for what her husband was doing to him.

She walked across the grass and met Moon at the road. The mare he was sitting on looked tired. She glanced back along the road Moon had taken. There was a dust cloud in the distance. Perhaps the man's pursuers.

"I didn't touch those children, Miss Alma," he said.

"I know," said Alma.

"Someone helped me escape, but I didn't get far before some men saw me. They would have got me, but I got one of them first and took his horse. Not much of a horse, though. She's beat. There'll be men coming. I can't outrun them."

Alma nodded, saying nothing.

"I'm gonna head for the mountains," said Moon. "Those men comin' after me will be here soon. Would you tell 'em you saw me head for the river?"

"Moon, you know I don't lie," said Alma. "It's against God's commandments."

"How does God feel about letting an innocent man die?" asked Moon.

Alma recalled Proverbs 6:16-19, which gave a list of things that were an "abomination" unto the Lord. On that list, along with "a lying tongue," were "hands that shed innocent blood."

And yet it wasn't her hands that would shed blood. How could she know if lying would do Moon any good? Maybe the posse wouldn't believe her. There was only one act that was really in her power—to lie or not lie. And the Lord had said, "Thou shalt not lie."

"Miss Alma, please," said Moon.

"Moon, I . . ."

Suddenly Alma's heart filled with bitter shame for what her husband was doing and deep pity for Moon.

"Yes," she whispered, without quite intending to speak.

She looked up to see Moon riding off. Had he heard her? She wasn't sure.

Within a quarter hour the enormity of the situation came down on Alma with the force of the hard-riding posse. There were at least forty men, and most wore mean, furious expressions. They were civil to her—at least as civil as angry people in a rush could be—but it wasn't hard to imagine how it would be to have that fury directed against oneself. When they couldn't find Moon, would they know she had lied? And what retaliation might they take against herself and her husband? Even if there was no violence, these were people she and her husband had lived with for ten years and might have to live with the rest of their lives. The idea of open hostility was painful. And what of the moral rectitude she had tried to exemplify in her work with the church? What would become of that when it was known that she had lied to her own people?

But Moon's life was in her hands and she had promised him. Or had she? For a moment, as the posse approached, she'd wondered if her "Yes" could constitute a promise if Moon hadn't heard it? But she'd known at once this was sophistry. She had to assume Moon had heard. In any case, she knew what she'd intended.

She spoke the lie quickly to the posse, and they believed her and were gone, heading off toward the river. She thought she'd feel relieved, but she did not. The posse would be back soon enough without Moon. Could she safely claim later that Moon must have doubled back—not by the same road, of course, but perhaps using the woods behind the house? Alma didn't know enough about tracking to know whether that story would hold up.

Yet it wasn't the idea of the men that frightened her the most. It was the fear that she'd done the wrong thing. She had started standing on what had felt like a rock-hard truth: "Thou shalt not lie." She had stepped away from that truth and now felt only shifting sands beneath her feet.

Her consternation only became worse when the Sheriff came riding up to the house, anguish and exhaustion on his face.

"Alma, I've done a terrible thing," he said.

He had then blurted out his confession—a confession so rushed it might have been largely incomprehensible to Alma had she not known the story already.

The Sheriff said he had to find the posse and stop them. Had Alma seen Moon? The posse? Which way had they gone?

For a moment, she thought of confessing everything to her husband. But she did not. She wasn't sure she trusted him anymore, even with his apparent change of heart. Even if he could be trusted, there was more chance of her lie being found out if her husband also knew about the lie: They might mix up their stories or he might make a slip. But at bottom, she knew, there was also her own sense of guilt and shame, which she continued to feel, in spite of telling herself she'd done the right thing.

As her husband rode off toward the river, Alma's agitation gave way to a bone-deep weariness. It seemed to take all her strength to climb the front steps and settle herself in her rocking chair. As her eyes closed, she tried to think of Moon making his safe and solitary way toward the mountains. An innocent man has been saved, she thought; I must think about that above all else.

*****

Alma woke when the posse came back. It was dark and the forms moving in torchlight made a nightmarish scene. For a moment, Alma thought it was a dream before understanding came. Then she tried to focus on the scene. The men looked somber and tired; it was a relief to see that no heads were turning toward the house. Alma noticed that on one of the horses—the horse was being led—sat a man with his hands tied to the saddle horn. It was obvious at a glance that the man wasn't Moon: It was a young white man. Curious now, Alma sat forward and strained her eyes. The young man looked like Jed Foster, who worked at the train station. Had he beeen with the posse on their way through? Yes, Alma remembered that he had.

Alma saw the Sheriff coming toward the house. She got up from her chair and met him on the porch steps.

"Alma, we found out who did it—who killed the girls," said her husband, excitedly. "It was Jed Foster there—he's confessed."

Alma felt a surge of elation. So it had turned out all right, after all. Moon was safe and the guilty party had been found.

"So Moon . . . ?" she began.

"I was too late to save him, and I feel terrible about that, but a lot of good has come of all this. Alma . . . what's wrong? Are you all right?"

Alma realized that she was seated on a porch step, slumped against the railing; she couldn't remember sitting down. Her husband had a hold on her arm; he sat down next to her.

"Moon . . ." she said. "I don't understand."

"Are you sure you're all right?" he asked.

Alma waved away his concern.

"Tell me," she said.

"I guess Moon tried to cross the river on that mare he stole and she couldn't make it. Moon had to swim for it. It cost him time. The posse had horses that could make it and they caught Moon. The plan was to string him up, but Jed got to him first and seemed to go wild, screaming things and shooting Moon down."

He told me to lie and say he'd gone toward the river, Alma thought. What was he doing at the river?

"Maybe Jed was going a little crazy," said the Sheriff. "Or maybe Jed was just putting on an act so he'd have an excuse to kill Moon so the Indian would have no chance to say anything. If that was it, he outsmarted himself.

While Jed was ranting at Moon's dead body, Jed let something slip—some detail about the dead girls he shouldn't have known. Someone caught it, and the men began pressing Jed, and pretty soon the confession was just pouring out of him. That all happened before I got there—I met the posse as they were coming back. But they had Jed repeat his confession to me. What he said squares with what happened. There's no doubt he's the killer."

Hadn't Moon heard her agree to lie? Or had he heard her and thought she would change her mind—repent of her promise? She would never know. But somehow Moon had counted on her telling the truth. He had told her he was going toward the mountains and had ridden off that way. But he must have doubled back through the woods, thinking Alma's words would send the posse toward the mountains.

"Alma, is it Moon's death that's upsetting you so?" asked her husband. "Is it because you feel partly responsible? Don't feel that way. You had to tell the posse the truth. You're a good Christian woman and you had no choice. I'm sure Moon would understand."

What had Moon thought? she wondered. When he heard the posse approach the river. When he realized Alma had lied for him after all.

"It's sad that Moon had to die, but good things will come of this," the Sheriff was saying. "We've found the man responsible for killing those girls. And you should have seen the posse when I found them: Everyone of them was shaken and ashamed. I don't think we'll be seeing this kind of vigilante campaign anymore. Maybe we can finally get some reforms in this town. And I'll be very surprised if you don't see most of those men in church next Sunday.

"I have to go—get Jed to his cell, talk to the deputies. If you're sure you're all right? Good. I'll try to be back in two hours. Things will turn out for the best—you'll see."

Then the Sheriff was gone, joining the riders heading toward town. Alma watched the receding torches as they became one light, then no light at all.

I lied, thought Alma. And my lie caused a man's death.

She felt cold seep through her, a cold more profound than any she had felt before. She wasn't sure it would ever go away.

Questions

1. In "The Land of Certus," the Rechtsens claim to see what is good and bad via perception of the lights. What, if anything, do you "see" when you see that something is good?

2. In making moral decisions, the Rechtsens are guided by the lights, the Linksens by the commands of their holy book, and Georges (apparently) by some principle to the effect that one ought to increase pleasure and diminish pain. They differ as to what is the correct evidence of good and bad. Can you imagine some way in which this dispute might be resolved?

3. In observing that the green light illuminates the torture of Georges, the narrator of "Certus," who had previously considered torture repulsive, decides that it is, after all, good. Presumably you continued to feel repulsed and pronounced the act of torture bad. Obviously there is an intimate connection between feelings and value judgments. What is this connection?

4. According to the narrator of "Those Who Help Themselves," the Omegans' belief in reincarnation motivated them to be moral. In what way does this belief relate to morality? What general considerations or principles did the Omegans employ in determining what is good and bad?

5. The theme of "Those Who Help Themselves" suggests that there is frequently a conflict between self-interest and the dictates of morality, at least for the people of Earth. Give some everyday examples of this conflict, and try to explain what it is about morality that tends to conflict with one's self-interest.

6. If you believed in a morality like the Omegans, what sort of society and what sorts of moral principles would you endorse? Does your answer differ in any way from the kind of society and the kinds of moral principles you now endorse?

7. In "The Sheriff's Wife," was it wrong for Alma to lie to try to save Moon? Explain.

8. On a piece of paper, construct a table with four columns; make the rows across the columns high enough to allow a few lines of writing in each cell of the table. Label the first column "Good Actions" and the third column "Bad Actions." Consider some actions in the story (e.g., Alma lying, Moon lying, the Sheriff and the Deputy deciding to turn Moon over to the townspeople) and put each action in either the "Good Actions" column or the "Bad Actions" column, depending on your judgment of it.

9. Following up on Question 8, label the second and fourth columns "Consequences." To the right of each action, write a few of the consequences, labeling each as "good" or "bad." Presumably, you found some good actions leading to bad consequences and vice versa. What do you think is more important from a moral standpoint,

the goodness/badness of the acts or the goodness/badness of the consequences?

DISCUSSION

In this chapter we will discuss:
1. The concepts of metaethics and normative ethics.
2. The theories of moral objectivism and moral subjectivism.
3. An argument for, then criticisms of, the theory of moral subjectivism.
4. The concept of the moral point of view.
5. The normative ethical theory of utilitarianism, as well as rival theories by John Rawls and Immanuel Kant.

Metaethics versus Normative Ethics

"The Land of Certus" raises **two sorts of moral, or ethical, questions.** First, it brings up—though without much emphasis—**normative ethical questions: questions about what things are good or bad, right or wrong, about what things should or should not be done.** The Rechtsens, the Linksens, Georges, and the people from the narrator's land each have opinions about what is good and bad. It is obvious that there are differences of opinion among them, even if these differences are not elaborated. The following normative questions are noted: "Is torture ever permissible?" "Ought men and women to be treated equally?" "Is it permissible to be intemperate in the pursuit of pleasure if no one else is harmed?"

Second, "Certus" emphatically raises **metaethical questions: questions concerning whether or not we can know which normative ethical judgments are true and, if so, how we can know.** Initially, it seems as if there are no troublesome metaethical issues in Certus. Good things are those that glow green, bad things are those that glow red. If one says that something is good and that thing glows green, then the statement is true. Knowing good and bad is just a matter of looking at the colors. However, it turns out that there are others in Certus who say that the lights do not correctly mark the good and bad. The Linksens say that knowledge of good and bad is really to be found in their book. Georges disregards both the lights and the religious book and identifies good and bad with pleasure and pain, respectively. Here we confront the issue of how moral questions are to be decided.

We shall begin by considering metaethical questions, questions about the nature of morality and moral judgments. What are we saying when we make a moral judgment? Is there such a thing as the moral truth? Can moral judgments be justified and, if so, in what way? We shall focus on two rival metaethical theories: moral objectivism and moral subjectivism.

It should be noted that the terms "moral" and "ethical" are synonymous and that they are similarly ambiguous. The terms "moral" and "ethical" as they shall be used in connection with metaethics do not mean "good," and their opposites are not "immoral" and "unethical." Rather, their meaning is "pertaining to moral, or ethical, questions"; their opposites are "nonmoral" and "nonethical." In this usage, it is uncontroversial to say that Jesus, Marx, and Hitler all had moral, or ethical, theories—that is, theories about what is good or bad, right or wrong.

Moral Objectivism and Moral Subjectivism

The <u>moral objectivist</u> says that where we have a moral judgment and its negation, one of these judgments must be true and the other false. In this sense, moral judgments are analogous to judgments in the domain of science. We would all agree that where we have two statements like "There is life on Mars" and "There is no life on Mars," one of these statements must be true and the other false. We know this, even if we

> MORAL OBJECTIVIST: MORAL QUESTIONS ANALOGOUS TO SCIENTIFIC QUESTIONS

do not know which of the statements is true and which is false. According to the moral objectivist, the same is the case with moral judgments. Where we have two judgments like "All abortion is wrong" and "Not all abortion is wrong," one of the judgments must be true and the other false.

The moral objectivist says that of the various moral theories, at most one of these theories can be true, and the rest must be false. One and only one moral theory could correctly describe the phenomena relevant to moral questions. In this sense, there is such a thing as the moral truth.

Precisely what the phenomena are that moral theories purport to describe is a matter of debate among objectivists. Some have said that moral theories purport to describe the laws of God. Others have suggested that moral theories purport to describe the natural law, some special moral qualities, or some particular set of those characteristics to which scientific theories also refer. But all objectivists agree that moral theories are rival theories about some sort of moral phenomena.

Many objectivists would claim to know which moral theory is true. Almost all objectivists would claim to know at least that certain moral theories are false—for instance, those that endorse human slavery, torture, or the extermination of some racial group. Other moral objectivists would

---

The CD, Ch. 4, *Metaethics,* reviews the definitions in this and in the following section.

claim that some moral theory must be true, but that they do not know which one is true.

The <u>moral subjectivist</u> claims that where we have a moral judgment **and its negation, neither judgment need be false.** There is no one correct answer to moral questions; there is no such thing as the moral truth. Moral questions are not analogous to scientific questions; rather, they are analogous to questions of taste. We all agree that there are questions of taste, for example: "Is yellow prettier than blue?" "Does apple pie taste better than cherry pie?" Most of us would agree that when one person says, "This apple pie is good" and another says, "This apple pie is not good," neither judgment need be false. In such cases, what is at issue are not conflicting descriptions of the apple pie, but differing reactions toward the pie.

> MORAL SUBJECTIVIST: MORAL QUESTIONS ANALOGOUS TO QUESTIONS OF TASTE

Analogously, according to the moral subjectivist, moral judgments express attitudes toward persons, actions, or events, rather than being descriptions of such things. When one person says, "All abortion is wrong" and another says, "Not all abortion is wrong," each is expressing a different attitude toward abortion and neither judgment need be false. Moral goodness or badness, rightness or wrongness—like prettiness, like deliciousness—are "in the eye of the beholder." Moral issues are fundamentally "subjective."

To elaborate further on moral subjectivism at this point would involve us in subtleties best reserved for later in the discussion. But the above explanation should give you a sense of what moral subjectivism is, and the position should seem to you a familiar one. It is dramatized in much existentialist literature: The universe contains no intrinsic values, so each individual must "invent" his or her own. It is presupposed by much of the current talk about "value-free" scientific theories: True science, it is thought, should deal only with factual matters, because matters of values are too subjective.

An Argument for Moral Subjectivism

Having outlined the theories of moral objectivism and moral subjectivism, let us now consider an argument for moral subjectivism.

When we consider a scientific question, we do not always agree on the answer. But we do agree on what evidence would decide the issue. For example, we may not know whether there are intelligent creatures on a particular planet, but we do agree on what evidence would show that there are such creatures on that planet.

With regard to questions of taste, however, there is no conceivable evidence that would resolve such issues to everyone's satisfaction. There is no conceivable evidence that would demonstrate that yellow is prettier than blue or that apple pie is better than cherry pie.

If moral questions are indeed analogous to scientific questions, then we ought to be able to specify what evidence would decide moral questions to everyone's satisfaction. According to the moral subjectivist, we cannot do this. There is no evidence that would demonstrate that abortion is right or wrong, that an equal distribution of goods is or is not better than competition for goods. Thus, says the subjectivist, moral questions cannot be analogous to scientific questions. Instead, they are analogous to questions of taste.

Put formally, the moral subjectivist argument is this:

1. Moral questions are like either scientific questions (objective) or questions of taste (subjective).
2. Being like scientific questions implies that one can always specify what evidence would decide the questions.
3. With moral questions one can't always specify what evidence would decide the questions.
4. (Therefore) moral questions are not like scientific questions (objective) (from 2 and 3).
5. (Therefore) moral questions are like questions of taste (subjective) (from 1 and 4).

"The Land of Certus" explores the possibility of decisive moral evidence, and the story is slanted in favor of the moral subjectivist. In Certus, apparently, the good is clearly marked with a green light and the bad with a red light. Seemingly, there ought to be no moral disputes in Certus. But there are such disputes. Georges and some of the younger people claim that one ought to ignore the lights whenever they conflict with the principle that one ought to do what gives one pleasure. The Linksens abide by a religious book that sometimes contradicts what is indicated by the lights. The Linksens say that their book, not the lights, shows what is truly good and bad.

> "CERTUS" AND DECISIVE MORAL EVIDENCE

Toward the end of the story, the narrator is shocked when the green light illuminates an act of torture, but decides that if the green light so indicates, then the act of torture must be good. Presumably, many readers formed the opposite conclusion: The act of torture would not be good no matter what the lights indicated.

Here the subjectivist could issue the following challenge: Suppose that an act that you found personally repugnant were labeled as good by some law or by public opinion or by some magical light as in Certus. Would you conclude that the act you find repugnant is good? Or would you conclude that the act cannot be good, since you find it repugnant? Wouldn't you say the latter? And doesn't this indicate that morality is basically a matter of how you feel about things?

Many readers may have an ethic based on what they believe to be divine commands, and they may feel that this argument for moral subjectivism seems forceful only because it neglects religious considerations. Such a reader might argue that throughout history, our ethical beliefs have been reflections of what we believed to be the wishes of the gods, or God; if an omnipotent, omniscient creator was revealed to all and was to make known what we were to do and not do, that would show everyone what things are good or bad, right or wrong.

Some quasi-subjectivists have claimed that moral disputes are unresolvable only because no God exists to "answer" moral questions. However, full-fledged moral subjectivists would deny that even the clear commands of a God would resolve all moral disputes. This is not to say that such a God could not force everyone to follow these commands. But "might" is not necessarily "right." The issue here is whether the clear commands of a God would result in a rational resolution of moral disputes.

Moral subjectivists might begin an attack on the good-is-what-God-commands argument by asking a question that is still a live, if aged, one in theology: **Is something good because God commands it, or does God command something because it is good?**[*]

Those who say that something is good just because God commands it are in an uncomfortable position. They are committed to the view that even if God advocated gratuitous, terrible acts of torture, such acts would necessarily be good. To those theists who are willing to accept these consequences, subjectivists could say the following: Even if you would be willing to accept something as good just because God commanded it, many people, including many theists, would not. These other theists would say that even God must have some satisfactory justification for a command if that command is to be good. This shows that the clear commands of God per se would not be the supposed evidence that would resolve all moral disputes.[†]

---

[*] The God in "A Little Omniscience Goes a Long Way" voices the first of these alternatives: "I don't do things because they're best. Rather, they're best because I do them."

[†] "Surprise! It's Judgment Day," in Chapter, 3, imagines just such a dispute between an individual and God.

Those who say that God commands something because it is good avoid having to say that a terrible act of torture would be good by the simple supposition of God's commanding it. They can say that torture is objectively bad, and God wouldn't command something that was bad. But this position undercuts the argument against moral subjectivism given above. That argument supposes that the clear commands of God would be the evidence that would resolve all moral disputes. But to say that God commands something because it is good supposes that God decides what is good or bad on the basis of some evidence. Now the theists must start all over again and specify what, if any, evidence would resolve all moral disputes—including moral disputes between human beings and God.   ◉

Moral Subjectivism Reconsidered

If this argument for moral subjectivism seems forceful, note that this position still has not been stated very precisely. If we are to evaluate moral subjectivism properly, we need to describe it in greater detail.

There have been some terribly implausible versions of moral subjectivism. We'll start with a crude version of moral subjectivism and then see how, and why, it has been altered to yield a more sophisticated version. It is interesting that this refined theory of moral subjectivism bears a resemblance to a version of moral objectivism that is different from, and perhaps more plausible than, the type of objectivist theory indicated earlier.

One crude form of moral subjectivism claims that moral judgments or theories are simple descriptions of the speaker's attitudes. The statement "X is right" means "I approve of X"; the statement "X is wrong" means "I disapprove of X." According to this theory, all sincere moral judgments are true. When one person says, "All abortion is wrong" and another says, "Not all abortion is wrong," neither statement need be false because the second does not really contradict the first. One person is saying, "I (John Smith) disapprove of all abortion" and the other, "I (Mary Jones) do not disapprove of all abortion."

That this version of moral subjectivism is implausible—or, at least, incomplete—can be seen by noting certain features of our moral discourse that are highlighted in the story, "Those Who Help Themselves." The people on Omega debate moral issues and come to considerable

> WE DISPUTE
> MORAL JUDGMENTS

agreement. We on Earth may not reach so much agreement, but we certainly do debate moral matters. We attempt to persuade others of our moral views and occasionally succeed. We have a saying: "There's no

◉   The CD, Ch. 4, *An Argument for Moral Subjectivism,* has a drag-and-drop quiz re this argument.

disputing matters of taste." Yet we dispute matters of morals. How can this be, if moral judgments are nothing more than statements about one's own tastes or preferences?

"Those Who Help Themselves" assumes there is at least a theoretical distinction between doing what is in one's self-interest and doing what is morally right. In part, at least, this relates to the distinction between what is in one's own interest and what is in the interest of others. On Omega, in practice, there is little real conflict in this matter.

SELF-INTEREST VERSUS THE MORALLY RIGHT

The moral efficacy of the Omegan's belief in perpetual, random reincarnation is that it leads them to believe that in promoting a society that helps others, they are helping themselves. On Earth there is considerable conflict between a person's own interests and that which is morally right or between one's own interests and the interests of others. This conflict is not only external, but internal: We sometimes feel pulled between what we want to do and what we feel we ought to do. Yet there is no hint of the distinction between one's self-interest and that which is morally right in the subjectivist view that moral judgments are only statements of preference.

These are forceful objections to the simple form of moral subjectivism presented earlier. Moral subjectivists have recognized the force of these criticisms and have attempted to revise subjectivism to meet them.

Moral judgments, say these subjectivists, do not merely have the function of stating preferences. They also have the function of attempting to influence the preferences and actions of others. The I-approve-of-it analysis of moral judgments is not adequate. The judgment "It is good, or right" would be better analyzed as meaning "I approve of this; you should approve of this as well; you should do this sort of thing."

Furthermore, present-day subjectivists would say that moral preferences are a particular type of preference. **One's moral preferences express how one would like to see all people treat one another; they express general prescriptions, rules for human behavior.** Moral preferences are not the I-prefer-to-do-this type of preference. Rather, they imply the message: I approve of this kind of human behavior; let us all act in this sort of way. Moral preferences are one's preferences from the standpoint of a hypothetical legislator for all human beings. A person's preferred rules count as moral rules only if they are not prejudiced in favor of one's particular circumstances. To propose moral rules is to imply that such rules should apply even if one were in the other person's position. In the words of the eighteenth-century philosopher Immanuel Kant, moral judgments are "universalizable."

A person who, using imagination, discounts his or her particular circumstances, surveys the human condition, and decides what rules all hu-

man beings should follow, is said to be taking the "moral point of view." To express a moral preference is to express a preference from the moral point of view.

In addition to "moral preferences," people have "personal preferences." Our personal preferences have to do with what we each want for ourselves. Our personal desires often conflict. Our desire to spend two weeks at the beach may conflict with our desire to save money for some new clothing. In an analogous way, says the subjectivist, our moral preferences and our personal preferences may conflict. From the moral point of view, we may wish that people would keep their promises. From the personal point of view, we may wish to break a promise we find very inconvenient to keep. Thus it is that there is often a conflict between self-interest and that which is morally right, says the subjectivist. This is not a matter of a clash between personal preferences and the dictates of some objective moral rules. Rather, it is a matter of a clash between personal preferences and moral preferences.   ●

PERSONAL VERSUS
MORAL PREFERENCES

From the Moral Point of View

Most subjectivists feel that the recognition of the special nature of moral preferences, of the moral point of view, has important implications for ethical debate. Some objectivists have even claimed that this supposed emendation of the subjectivist theory actually yields a form of moral objectivism. Let us examine these claims.

One cannot deduce a particular morality from the definition of the moral point of view. This is as it should be. The definition, after all, is supposed to represent something implied by all moral judgments.

Nonetheless, it is conceivable that many people make judgments that they claim to be moral judgments, but that they would not endorse if they seriously took the moral point of view. They may be proposing rules that they say are moral rules but that they would not be willing to acknowledge if they were in the other person's position. Such people are inconsistent in that they are claiming to take a point of view that they are not really taking.

Some philosophers have claimed that human psychology is such that people who seriously took the moral point of view would all endorse the same set of rules. This claim implies a form of moral objectivism: Only one moral theory is compatible with the moral point of view and the facts of

●   The CD, Ch. 4, *Moral Subjectivism Revised*, reviews the discussion in this section.

human psychology. Moral subjectivists deny that this is so. But most subjectivists do believe that many people would have to modify their moral judgments if they seriously took the moral point of view.

Some people are fortunate enough to make millions of dollars. They may endorse a survival-of-the-fittest morality and say: Let the poor fend for themselves. Suppose these people were to be deprived of their money and their ability to make more. Would they then say: "I'm not fit, let me perish"? Or would they say: "Let's have a good social welfare program"? If the latter, then their original judgments were not moral preferences but personal preferences.

Would anything be gained by persuading people to admit that certain of their views constituted personal preferences and not moral preferences? In some cases, no. Some people are content to be amoral. But many people care very much about morality. After all, to engage in moral dialogue is to engage in a kind of intellectual arbitration. As in any kind of arbitration, one may sometimes lose, but the arbitration procedure does offer one certain protections. To abandon morality would be to agree to let human relations be governed by whim and strength. This prospect bothers many people very much. Also, the psychology of most adults seems to be such that believing they are moral is crucial to their feelings of self-respect. Few adults like to admit that they are amoral or immoral; instead, people tend to adjust their morality to agree with their self-interest. But such adjustments are not really compatible with having a morality.

In any case, the question at issue here is whether or not there can be a rational resolution of moral questions. Whether, and to what degree, people are willing to be moral, willing to act on their moral preferences rather than on their personal ones, is a very serious question, but it is also a quite different question from the one we are considering.

In "Those Who Help Themselves," the metaphysical beliefs of the Omegans motivate them to take the moral point of view constantly. They believe in a perpetual, random reincarnation of souls that will eventually place each of them in different social positions and circumstances. They are motivated continuously to ask: What if I were in the other person's position? Probably this is a question most of us manage to avoid a good deal of the time.

In the story, taking the moral point of view does not resolve all moral questions. There remain disagreements about whether there ought to be competition or an equal distribution of goods, whether one ought to promote happiness over excellence, and so forth. Nonetheless, the story implies that people who really did take the moral point of view would be in close enough agreement that they would be able to get along quite well. 🌑

Utilitarianism versus John Rawls

Let's consider a couple of normative ethical issues with related debates that make explicit reference to something like the moral point of view.

We are all familiar with the issue of how the goods of a society ought to be distributed among its members. Should all the goods be distributed on the basis of competition? Or should all the goods be distributed equally? Or should every individual be guaranteed a certain minimum of goods, and the remaining goods be distributed on the basis of competition? If the last, how much should the guaranteed minimum be?

One normative ethical theory that is favored by many British and American philosophers is utilitarianism. **The premise of <u>utilitarianism</u> is that the only thing valuable in itself is happiness and that a society ought to promote the greatest happiness of the greatest number.** The emphasis here is on "greatest happiness" rather than on "greatest number." If the greatest total happiness in society would be achieved by, say, a competitive system that allocated most of the goods to seventy-five percent of the members, rather than by a less competitive system that distributed goods more equally, then utilitarianism would favor the first system.

This is not to say that utilitarianism per se favors competition and unequal distribution. We would also need factual information about what social system would create the greatest total happiness in a particular society. Nonetheless, it is the case that utilitarianism does not insist upon a guaranteed minimum for all individuals.

A number of philosophers have criticized utilitarianism as "unjust" in this respect: They have said that a more acceptable normative theory would be one that insisted upon substantial guarantees for every individual. One of these critics is **John Rawls,* who puts forward the principle that society should deviate from an equal distribution of goods only if, and only to the extent that, every member is at least a little better off, over time, under a system that distributes unequally.** If, for example, a competitive

---

* See *Justice as Fairness.* Cambridge, Mass.: The Belnap Press of Harvard University, 1971. What follows is a simplification of Rawls's main views. For instance, Rawls seems to claim that liberty is valuable in itself, quite apart from its effects on happiness. That claim will be ignored. What we shall focus on is that part of Rawls's principle that has to do with the effect of the distribution of goods on happiness.

🌑   The CD, Ch. 4, *From the Moral Point of View,* offers an illustrated discussion of the moral point of view, with examples. *Rockin' Review: The Moral Point of View,* offers a song on this topic.

system would produce more goods and more happiness, then the competitive system would be acceptable—but only if, and to the extent that, every individual gained something by such a competitive system relative to less competitive systems.

As with utilitarianism, no specific answer to the question of how goods ought to be distributed in a society can be derived from Rawls's principle. Again, we need information about benefits that might accrue through competition. But it is clear that Rawls's principle insists on a relatively sizable guarantee for each individual, whereas the utilitarian principle does not insist on any.

What is of special interest in the context of this chapter is the way Rawls attempts to defend his principle with an appeal to the moral point of view. He asks us to imagine that we are about to enter life. We do not know what our interests and abilities will be; we do not know what our position in society will be. We must choose some general normative principle that will guide us in determining what sort of social system we will have. According to Rawls, being in such a situation would be the literal equivalent of taking the moral point of view. Obviously, such a situation would be analogous to the situation on Omega, with the—possibly important—difference that each Omegan is already living a life and believes that there are a great number of lives to go. Rawls claims that in such a situation people would choose his principle rather than that of the utilitarian. His principle is the one most compatible with the moral point of view (and with the facts of human psychology).

The utilitarians have responded by claiming that the selection of the utilitarian principle would be the more rational by normal standards of rationality. Suppose you were to "bet your life" on one of two societies. In the first society, ninety-five percent of the people would be very happy, and five percent of the people very miserable. In the second society, fifty percent of the people would be mildly happy, and fifty percent mildly miserable. Which society would you choose? The first, of course, says the utilitarian. Rawls's principle, however, would favor the second society and hence is less rational.

But Rawls argues that people wagering an entire lifetime would adopt the more conservative betting strategy. The idea of living one's life in great misery would be such a fearful prospect that people would be willing to take lesser odds on happiness to ensure that they would not suffer great misery.

"Those Who Help Themselves" imagines that all would insist on at least some guaranteed minimum but would differ as to the distribution of goods beyond that. "Apparently, those supporting the largest opposition party were gamblers: They were willing to risk the possibility of some misfortune in the next life for the possibility of gaining great wealth in this life. Those on the opposite end of the political spectrum were unwilling to gamble at all with their future lives: They wanted to be guaranteed an equal share of the wealth. Those who supported the majority party wanted some guarantees and some chances to gamble. But none was willing to gamble too much with his or her future life, to risk being diseased, mentally defective, or hungry, and being without help."   ✸

Utilitarianism versus Immanuel Kant

We have already mentioned Immanuel Kant (1724–1804) in connection with the idea that moral rules are universalizable.* Kant held a "deontological" type of ethical theory, in contrast to utilitarianism, which is a "consequentialist" type of ethical theory.

<u>Consequentialist</u> ethical theories claim that what makes actions right or wrong are their consequences in terms of increasing or decreasing certain properties that have been identified as intrinsically good or bad. Obviously utilitarianism falls into this category. As we've seen, utilitarianism identifies happiness as good and unhappiness as bad and judges actions in terms of increasing happiness and diminishing unhappiness.

<u>Deontological</u> ethical theories deny that what makes actions right or wrong is simply consequences. Judeo-Christian ethics has a heavy deontological cast: There are prohibitions against such things as stealing, lying, and the shedding of innocent blood, as well as injunctions to share one's bread with the hungry and to act as peacemakers. However, it isn't only religious ethics that are deontological. Anyone who believes rights and duties have a weight that can't be accounted for in terms of consequences alone is a deontologist.

In "The Sheriff's Wife" there are dilemmas as to whether an action should be judged morally right or wrong in terms of certain traditional rules or in terms of the specific consequences of the act.

Alma takes very seriously the Biblical commandment: "Thou shalt not lie." She's not sure the rule admits of exceptions. She's not sure lying could ever be right, even if lying would help save an innocent man. Finally she does lie, though not without qualms. It turns out her lying is a partial cause of that innocent man being killed. How does this result affect the moral evaluation of what she did? Is it confirmation that she was wrong to lie? Or

---

*We also mentioned Kant in Chapter 3 in connection with his critique of the ontological argument.

✸   The CD, Ch. 4, *Utilitarianism vs. John Rawls,* reviews the main ideas in this disucssion.

is it just an unfortunate outcome that doesn't affect the point that she was right to do what she did?

The Sheriff is faced with a choice: Turn an innocent man over to the townspeople to be killed or try to protect that one man at the probable cost of many lives—not only the lives of the Sheriff and his deputies, but also the lives of other Native Americans who are suffering under the town's frustration and rage.

Apparently the Sheriff's motives, unlike those of his wife, are not very admirable, but let's leave that aside and focus on the choice. The Sheriff decides to turn the innocent Moon over to the townspeople to be killed, and the "good consequences" of this unfortunate act go far beyond what the Sheriff could have hoped for. Not only are several lives saved, but the guilty man is found, and the shame felt by the townspeople over their vigilanteism could well lead to moral reform in both individual lives and the life of the town.

One can ask: How relevant—and important—are such consequences in evaluating the morality of actions?

Kant's answer is: Consequences are essentially irrelevant.

Kant distinguishes between two kinds of "ought" (imperative) statements that he calls "hypothetical" and "categorical."

Hypothetical imperatives have the form, If you want X, you ought to do Y. For example, "If you want to impress your socially conscious date (or get a good grade in your class on Hunger in America), you ought to spend an afternoon sorting food items for a hunger-relief organization and then make a point of discussing what you did." This "ought" is not moral, according to Kant. A moral "ought" is categorical: You ought to help feed the hungry.

Kant wants to find an objective basis for morality. He claims to find it in human rationality and in this general Categorical Imperative: "Act only according to that maxim by which you can at the same time will that it should become a universal law." Specific maxims (rules) were to be derived from the Categorical Imperative. Deriving those rules would go something like this:

A man, jealous that someone else has more money, is tempted to steal some of that money. With an eye to the Categorical Imperative, the man must ask himself this: "How would it be if there were a universal rule saying that it's all right to steal from anyone who has more than oneself?" If there were such a rule it would lead to so much stealing that the whole idea of private property would become meaningless and hence the idea of stealing would become meaningless. Therefore, the only sensible rule is, "One ought not to steal."

A woman is tempted to lie every time she thinks lying would do more good than harm. She must ask how it would be if there were a universal maxim to this effect? If it were permissble to lie whenever it seemed that the good consequences of the lie would outweigh the bad, then people would be lying all the time and no one would trust what another had to say; there would be no point to lying. Therefore the universal principle ends up undercutting itself. The rule, then, must be, "One ought not to lie."

Kant was rather extreme in that he felt that the rules generated by the Categorical Imperative—rules such as "You ought not to steal" and "You ought not to lie"—were absolute; they admitted of no exceptions.

Kant would say that Alma should not have lied, even if she thought lying might save an innocent man. Not only are moral rules absolute, says Kant, but you can never be sure what the consequences of your lie might be. In one essay,* Kant considers the case of a murderer knocking on your door and asking if a certain person (one you know he intends to kill) is inside. Kant says, if you tell the truth, maybe the neighbors will intervene and stop the murderer before he finds the intended victim. Or perhaps, unbeknownst to you, the intended victim has just slipped outside, and your lie will be a cause of the murderer finding the intended victim outside. Of course, in "The Sheriff's Wife," that's just what happens to Alma: Her lie becomes a partial cause of Moon's death.

As to the Sheriff's action, Kant would not admit the moral relevance of the possible good consequences of a law enforcement officer letting an innocent man be killed. Kant felt you ought to punish the guilty and not punish the innocent. That rule should hold absolutely.

How might the utilitarian evaluate these actions? The utilitarian would likely approve of Alma's telling a lie to try to save an innocent man's life. It turns out that the lying was bad in terms of consequences (it led to the man's being killed), but the utilitarian would not blame Alma for that. One can only act on the best information, and it appeared to Alma that lying would save Moon's life.

It also looks as if the utilitarian principle would approve of the Sheriff's turning Moon over to be killed. It appeared that there would be better consequences by letting Moon be killed than not, and this turned out to be the case.

How would we evaluate the answers of Kant and the utilitarian here? Probably most of us would feel that Kant was too absolutist in claiming that rules like "You ought not to lie" admit of no exceptions; we'd feel that lying

*"On a supposed right to lie from philanthropy," in *Practical Ethics,* ed. Allan Wood. Cambridge: Cambridge University Press, 1999.

with the intention of saving an innocent life would be a good thing. As for Kant's claim that we can never know the consequences of our acts, that seems extreme. Certainly things can go wrong, as in Alma's case (where the situaton was complicated by her own confusion and Moon's trying to guess what Alma would do). There are certainly times when we can have a pretty good idea what's going to happen: We humans would have a hard time surviving in this world if we didn't.

In the case of the Sheriff's choice, we might be a bit closer to Kant than the utilitarian. We might decide that in a situation that was extreme enough (where we *knew* twenty innocent people would die if we didn't turn over one innocent person to be killed), we might reluctantly turn the person over. However, we would start off assuming that protecting the innocent was a duty with a special weight: It would only be in extreme cases that we could consider violating that duty. It looks as if the utilitarian principle would give the idea of protecting the innocent no special weight. One could approach each case with an open mind about whether protecting the innocent would be good or not—and then decide by calculating the consequences.

Both Kant's deontological ethics and the version of utilitarianism we have discussed are extreme views. Most deontologists would not assume that all moral rules were absolute. They would have a hierarchy of rules, with a given rule (e.g., do not lie) to be followed unless it conflicted with a more fundmental rule (e.g., protect innocent human life). Thus, it would be morally right for Alma to lie because the more fundamental rule takes precedence.

The utilitarian view we've considered is **act-utilitarianism**: **The view that utilitarian calculations should be applied to each individual action.** Actually, it's not quite fair to say that the act-utilitarian would necessarily choose as the Sheriff did: The act-utilitarian would consider the long-range consequences of what the Sheriff did and figure in the insecurity it might instill in people in terms of the law. Still, because the results of act-utilitarianism don't always square with what people do and do not approve of morally, it has generally been replaced by **rule-utilitarianism**: **The view that the rules of society should be determined using utilitarian calculations; however, once the rules are established, they should be followed.** Rule-utilitarianism is consequentialist in terms of choosing the rules, but closer to the deontological in terms of day-to-day moral choices.

The rule-utilitarian could say that our society would be chaos if people thought they could not count on general fairness from the law, if they thought that they could be arrested (or taken into custody for some other reason) and then turned over to vigilantes who wanted to punish them. Since a rule of due process would have better consequences that any other alternate rule, due process should be followed even when following it would lead to bad consequences in a particular case.

This brings us back to where we were when we were discussing the views of John Rawls: When determining the best rules for society from the moral point of view, should we follow utilitarian reasoning or are there other principles that would be preferable? 🕸

Questions and Exercises

1. What is the difference between normative ethical questions and meta-ethical questions?
2. Distinguish moral subjectivism from moral objectivism.
3. Present an argument for moral subjectivism.
4. Consider the following moral judgments:
   a. It's wrong to abort a fetus.
   b. A person who murders another person ought to be executed.
   Can you imagine any kind of evidence that would prove or disprove either of these statements?
5. "Moral judgments are simply statements of preference." In what ways, and for what reasons, has this version of moral subjectivism been modified?
6. What does it mean to take the "moral point of view"?
7. Define utilitarianism.
8. In what way does Rawls consider utilitarianism "unjust"? What principle does Rawls substitute for the utilitarianism principle of distribution?
9. Why does the utilitarian think this theory would be chosen from the moral point of view? Why does Rawls think his theory would be chosen from the moral point of view?
10. Four coworkers entered a contest together and have won the right to race through a grocery store/pharmacy and keep whatever they can manage to get outside the store in half an hour. (They must use grocery carts but each can make more than one trip.) The store is huge, and it would be impossible for any one of the four to get around to the

🕸 The CD, Ch. 4, *Utilitarianism versus Immanuel Kant,* reviews the main ideas in this discussion.

different departments in the time allotted. The four people are going to rely heavily on what they collect for their sustenance in the next couple of weeks, since they've all been laid off and are broke. Some other facts:

- No one is allowed to collect anything until all four have agreed on a procedure for collecting goods and dividing them up. (Each can simply collect and keep his own if they agree to that.)
- Since the person running the contest loves extreme sports, a few spots on the floor of the store have been waxed to a dangerous sheen; in the past, several contestants have suffered bad sprains and were unable to complete their collecting.
- All four contestants are competitive and perform at top efficiency when there's a reward for doing better than others.
  - a. What kind of procedure would you suggest if you were one of the four?
  - b. How would the four reason if they were utilitarians?
  - c. How would they reason if they followed Rawls?

11. Explain the difference between deontological and consequentialist ethics.

12. a. What is Kant's categorical imperative?
    b. How are moral rules to be derived from that imperative?

13. What is the difference between act-utilitarianism and rule-utilitarianism?

5

The Right to Die

Fiction: Death on Demand

Mrs. Burke brought the car to a stop across the street from the clinic. She stared at her knuckles clenched on the steering wheel, then took a couple of deep breaths. This was the moment she had dreaded more than all the other dreadful moments in this thing.

"Billy," she said softly, "it's time to say goodbye to Grandpa."

She turned and saw the two of them as they'd been since leaving the house: the eighty-seven-year-old man and the seven-year-old boy, sitting together, holding hands, saying nothing, just staring ahead. She saw the boy's hand tighten on the man's hand.

"No," whispered the boy.

She felt her own hands shake. She hadn't wanted to bring the boy along, but the sitter had cancelled at the last moment and she didn't dare put this off. If only . . . but, no, it wasn't that really. The clinic had told her they had a woman who'd watch Billy, play with him; he'd probably be better off with her than with that harebrained sitter who did nothing but watch television. It was simply the moment of goodbye she dreaded, whether it happened here or somewhere else.

"Billy . . ."

"No."

🌀   The CD, Ch. 4, *Death on Demand*, contains animation and exercises related to this story.

God, the two of them were crying now. For an instant she thought about turning the car around and going home. But she knew she couldn't do that, couldn't bear to have the whole thing start over again: putting up with the old man's incoherencies, his fumblings, his constant demands for attention, his messes—it was obscene to have to change diapers on an old man. And she and Harry'd be at each other again—all that yelling—with Harry drinking too much and getting violent and threatening to leave. They didn't have the money to put the old man in a nursing home, and there were hardly any free ones anymore, what with the government cutting back the funds year by year. And it wasn't as if they'd pushed the old man into it. It wasn't until that day when he'd said, "I want to die," that they'd really taken the idea seriously. So why did she have to feel like the villain?

"Dad," she began, trying to force some firmness into her voice, "it's time to . . . oh, no!"

She saw them then, the people starting to descend on the car, maybe twenty people, mostly women, with grim, angry faces. They were carrying signs like battle-axes, the message blurring with the joggling except for that one word she saw over and over: Murderer, Murderer . . .

"Damn it, we're getting out of this car," she yelled. "Right now!"

******

Nurse Wyman stifled a yawn and glanced at her watch. It was three in the afternoon and it felt like three in the morning. How would she ever manage to stay awake? She'd had no business staying up for the late, late show, not after working a double shift. But the film had been one of her favorites, *Sweet Desire, Part I,* and she hadn't been able to resist. She was an incurable romantic, there were no two ways about it. That's probably why she'd become a nurse, wanting to become an angel of mercy, just like Florence Nightingale. Only it wasn't like in her childhood books at all: there was so much routine, so much boredom. Well, that's just how real life was. At least she had her books and her movies. And tonight there'd be *Sweet Desire, Part II.*

"Ladies and gentlemen, I'm sorry about the fuss out there . . ."

At the sound of the Director's voice, Nurse Wyman straightened quickly in her chair. Then she realized that his voice came from the next corridor. She remembered that he was conducting another one of his tours for foreign visitors; in that case he wouldn't be coming to her department for another forty minutes or so. She let her body slump.

"They call themselves Pro-Lifers," said the Director, with a theatrical laugh. *"As if we weren't all pro-life. But we must consider the quality of life . . ."*

"Not to mention the sanctity of human choice," muttered Nurse Wyman, absently, the way one talks along with a familiar jingle one has heard often. The Director's voice began to fade as he moved away.

"*. . . start with the counseling offices. As you must have noted in my report, we insist that each applicant have a minimum of five sessions . . .*"

Nurse Wyman stared unhappily at the paperwork stacked in front of her. She had almost gotten up the energy to tackle it when she saw Nurse Anderson approaching with . . . what was the woman's name? . . . Evans?

"You remember Mrs. Evers," said Nurse Anderson, as she placed some papers on the desk.

Nurse Wyman glanced up at the applicant—a young, pretty thing, if one discounted the deep pallor on her face. Evers, yes: she remembered now. Husband killed in a water-skiing accident on the third day of their honeymoon. The woman had been treated for depression for almost a year and a half before she'd applied to the clinic. It was rather romantic, really, someone dying for love this way. Just like in that best seller, *Love Lasts Forever.*

The forms were all in order, so Nurse Wyman got up from her desk and went to a cabinet, which she unlocked with a key from the chain she wore at the belt of her white uniform. On the top shelf of the cabinet were several small white cups, each containing two green-and-black capsules. She removed one of the cups and handed it to Nurse Anderson.

"The Blue Room?" said Nurse Anderson.

"Yes," said Nurse Wyman, taking from a wall rack a key attached to a blue-painted metal plate.

The three of them walked down the corridor to a door that Nurse Wyman unlocked. Inside was a small rectangular room containing a single bed, a nightstand, and an easy chair. The bed was covered with a blue cotton bedspread and the walls were papered with a blue flowered print. Nurse Wyman noticed that the paper was beginning to peel just a bit in one corner. Still, it was better than in some of the others.

Hearing Mrs. Evers give a small groan, she said, "Is something the matter?"

Mrs. Evers shook her head. "No. It doesn't matter how it looks."

"We do the best we can," said Nurse Wyman, keeping her voice even. It wouldn't be professional to show annoyance. Anyway, one had to make allowances.

"How long do I have the room?"

"We can allow you an hour. After that we'll need the room for someone else."

"Busy day, huh?" said Mrs. Evers with halfhearted sarcasm. She pointed at the door at the opposite end of the room. "That's where they'll take me out."

"Yes," said Nurse Wyman, summoning her professional patience. All the applicants had all these details explained to them well in advance, yet so many insisted on going over everything again here, at the door. "After a doctor has checked on you."

"You can still change your mind," said Nurse Anderson, with obvious emotion. "Once you're inside you won't be able to call out to us—the room is soundproofed—but . . ."

"Why? Why is it soundproofed?"

"To give the applicants some privacy. But if you push that red button there by the bed, we'll come immediately. However, you'd have to decide before you take the pills. Once you've taken them . . ." Nurse Anderson looked down at the floor.

"I remember now about the button," said Mrs. Evers. "The counselor told me that if I didn't go through with this I would have to wait at least a year before I got another chance."

"That's the rule," said Nurse Wyman. "At least in cases where there is . . . uh . . . no physical illness."

"No physical illness could hurt more than this does."

"Nonetheless . . ."

"I'm not arguing with you," said Mrs. Evers. "There won't be any pain? From the pills, I mean."

"None. It takes only three minutes or so before one loses consciousness. All one feels during that time is some numbness, then drowsiness."

"And there's no chance they won't work?"

"No. As long as you take them both. There's a carafe of water by the bed."

Mrs. Evers took a deep breath. "I'd better get on with it then."

She took two steps to the doorway, hesitated, then walked quickly into the room. As she got to the bed she suddenly bent over, holding her stomach with both hands, and gave a deep, wrenching cry.

"Mrs. Evers," said Nurse Anderson, her voice pleading, "Please recon—"

"Nurse Anderson," hissed Nurse Wyman, as she shut the door quickly, cutting off the sounds of sobbing from within the room. "I don't believe you!"

"I'm . . . I'm sorry."

"That was totally unprofessional. You know we're not allowed to challenge the applicants. Only the counselors can do that. Those poor people have enough on their minds without you trying to confuse them. I'm afraid I'll have to put you on report."

"No, please. I just forgot myself for a moment. The woman's so young."

"That's no excuse and you know it."

"But it's never happened before. It won't happen again. Please."

"I'm sorry, I . . ." Nurse Wyman stopped, and gave a sigh. "Maybe I am overreacting. You're a good nurse and you're entitled to one mistake. That case we had last month has got me on edge: that nurse who was sneaking the applicants pro-life pamphlets at the door. What a terrible thing to do." She gave Nurse Anderson a sharp look. "You're not one of them, are you?"

"No! You know I'm not."

"Of course you're not. As I say, I'm just overreacting. But you must assure me that something like that won't happen again."

"It won't."

"All right, then."

As the two of them walked back to the desk, Nurse Anderson said: "You know, I think the thing that got me was that I was so sure she wouldn't go through with it. I was so sure the counselors would talk her out of it."

"All they can do is try."

"Which one did she have, do you know?"

"Slattery, I believe."

Nurse Anderson gave a groan. "Not him. The man's incompe—"

"*. . . of course, with the Supreme Court decision of '94, everything became complete chaos. We knew what we couldn't forbid, we just didn't know . . .*"

Nurse Anderson jumped at the sound of the Director's voice; she glanced over her shoulder as if she expected him to be right there, listening to her. Instead he was nowhere in sight.

Nurse Wyman smiled. "His voice does carry, doesn't it. It's all right. He can't hear you."

Nonetheless Nurse Anderson lowered her voice to a whisper. "Slattery is incompetent. You know it. Everybody does."

Nurse Wyman shrugged. "He'll be retiring soon. Anyway, Mrs. Evers was in therapy for well over a year. She must know what she wants by now."

"*. . . the period of experimentation was not all to the bad, I suppose, though we did learn some hard lessons. Nevada's policy of issuing the pills without a prescription was an out-and-out disaster, as anyone with any common sense could have foreseen. California's fourteen-day 'reconsideration period' seemed* *an improvement until the Berofsky murders, and those suicides by that Star Children cult, shocked the nation and forced Congress to formulate a national . . ."*

The Director emerged from a side corridor, nodding briefly to the two nurses while continuing his theatrical gestures, giving the absurd momentary impression that he was lecturing to them. But then his real audience appeared in his train, a group of about fifteen dignitaries, who seemed to exhibit every conceivable combination of skin color and style of dress. The group followed the Director away from the nurses.

". . . follow me to the Review Board hearing room . . . what? . . . oh, yes, every case. If a counselor feels an extra five sessions are called for, the Board will generally go along with the counselor, but beyond that the Board will generally rule in favor of the applicant, assuming, of course, that the applicant meets the appropriate criteria in terms of physical condition or psychiatric history . . . what? . . . that is a good question. I do remember one such case involving an applicant involved in strategic research. He was asked to wait until . . . no, I'm afraid not. He jumped off a bridge . . . oh, hello there. Ladies and gentlemen, could we move to the side a little bit to let these people through . . ."

The dignitaries moved to the side, openly gawking, as Nurse Costello led a middle-aged couple through the crowd toward the desk. The woman—Mrs. Lindberg, wasn't it?—had carcinoma of the liver, and her application had been handled quickly: the Board had even agreed to waive three of the five counseling sessions. The woman was terribly gaunt and was having trouble walking, even aided by her husband. It was rather touching the way her husband—a huge, robust man with large workman's hands—held her with such tenderness.

The crowd was gone, along with Nurse Anderson, by the time the three of them reached the desk.

"You know Mr. and Mrs. Lindahl," said Nurse Costello.

"Of course," said Nurse Wyman. "How do you do?"

At that Mrs. Lindahl burst into tears, and Nurse Wyman felt a pang of guilt at the thoughtless phrasing of her greeting. She'd gotten rattled by that episode with Nurse Anderson. But her guilt subsided as she saw that Mrs. Lindahl was smiling through her tears.

"I'm fine," said Mrs. Lindahl. "At least I will be in a few minutes. Finally. You don't know what I've been through these . . . I mean . . . that's silly . . . you're nurses . . . of course you know . . . I just mean I don't think I could have stood it any . . ."

Her words were lost in a fresh burst of tears, and her husband pulled her tighter to comfort her. Nurse Wyman checked the forms, got the medication, and took them to the doorway of the Pink Room. As the couple glanced inside, the husband said, "Is it all right if I lie there with her and hold her?"

"Of course," said Nurse Wyman, reassuringly, patting him on the shoulder. She glanced down at the pill cup in her hand and said, "Nurse Costello, would you help Mrs. Lindahl into the room while I have a word with her husband?"

When the wife was out of earshot, Nurse Wyman handed Mr. Lindahl the pills, studying his face as she said, "She must take both pills. If a person took one, it wouldn't be enough. Both pills. Do you understand?"

Mr. Lindahl nodded, but it was obvious he didn't understand her underlying meaning. Good. There had been two cases a couple of months back where a distraught spouse had tried to die along with the applicant, holding back a pill to take after the applicant was unconscious. Both partners had awoken eight to twelve hours later, and the situation had been terrible for everyone. One of these days they'd be able to concentrate enough of the chemical in one capsule. Meanwhile the spouse would just have to be warned.

As the door closed on the couple, Mrs. Lindahl was saying, "Bless you. Bless both of you for the work you're doing . . ."

"Well, that was nice," said Nurse Costello.

"I'll say," said Nurse Wyman. "I can't remember the last time I heard an applicant express any gratitude. I suppose it's understandable, but it would be nice if they thought of us occasionally."

"I can do without the gratitude," said Nurse Costello, "just as long as I don't get the complaints. In that nursing home where I worked, all I got were complaints all day. This place is such a relief after . . . what's wrong?"

Nurse Wyman realized she was frowning. But she wasn't frowning at Nurse Costello, or at the elderly man—Mr. Burke, wasn't it?—approaching with his daughter. She was frowning at the sight of the other nurse, Nurse Morley. Talk about complaints. That nurse was always complaining about something. Today it was some slight she thought she had gotten from Dr. Mellon. Nurse Wyman hadn't been in the mood to discuss it that morning, and she was even less in the mood to discuss it now. She'd have to find some way to put Nurse Morley off after the applicant had been seen to.

"It's not you, dear," she said to Nurse Costello. "It's just something I have to attend to. You run along now. I do want to tell you, though, that I'm very pleased with your work."

"Oh, thank you."

As Nurse Wyman approached her desk, Nurse Morley said, "You remember Mrs. Burke. And her father, Mr. Carpenter."

Nurse Wyman nodded, avoiding the other nurse's eyes as she got the pills and the key and led them all down to the Yellow Room. She opened the door, thinking about what excuse she could use to get rid of Nurse Morley, and then noticed that old Mr. Carpenter seemed to be trying to pull his arm loose from his daughter's grip.

"Come on, Dad," said Mrs. Burke.

The old man shook his head.

"Dad, come on now," said Mrs. Burke, with exaggerated pleasantness that didn't hide the undertone of exasperation. "We're going to go inside."

Once again the old man shook his head. Mrs. Burke gave a tug on his arm, and he stumbled forward a step before he regained his ground.

"Dad . . ."

Nurse Wyman gave a sigh. She could sympathize with the daughter. The cases of old people who were only intermittently lucid were the most difficult of all. Testimony from the family and what testimony there was from the applicant were gone over in great detail, trying to sort out the lucid from the confused, the long-term from the momentary. Mr. Carpenter's case had taken a full ten counseling sessions plus two Board reviews. If he balked now, the family would have to go through the whole exhausting process again, assuming the Board would allow them another review. Nonetheless, the rules had to be observed.

"Just a minute, Mrs. Burke," said Nurse Wyman. "You know the rules. No one is to be forced."

"But . . ." Mrs. Burke started to protest, then seemed to see it was useless. "Dad, please."

The old man shook his head once more.

"Can you give me a minute with him," said Mrs. Burke.

"Of course," said Nurse Wyman. "But just a minute."

Nurse Wyman took a few steps back toward the desk, to give the two of them some privacy, and noticed that Nurse Morley was following.

"Dad, why are you doing this to me? We're only here because you said this was what you wanted. You told everybody. Look at all the trouble you've put these people through. Why do you always have to make so much trouble?"

"Nurse Wyman, about Dr. Mellon . . ."

"Not now, Nurse Morley."

"You're just doing this to spite me, aren't you, Dad? You like to make me unhappy, don't you? You always have . . ."

"I won't be put off, Nurse Wyman. Something has to be done about that man. Dr. Mellon is downright insulting—not just to me but to the other nurses as well. I'm a professional and I insist on . . ."

". . . do you want to go home, is that it? Well, good, we'll just go then. And then you can explain to Harry why you're doing this to us. You know what Harry will do, don't you? He'll . . ."

". . . and the other day, in front of one of the patients . . ."

Nurse Wyman tuned them all out. She could see Mrs. Burke gesturing to her father off to the side, could see Nurse Morley's insistent mouth working like a spastic clam just in front of her, but she heard none of it. Instead she was reviewing that scene from *Sweet Desire* where the arrogant pirate ripped off Lucinda's bodice and . . .

"Nurse. Nurse!" The insistence of Mrs. Burke's voice finally broke through her reverie. "He's ready now."

Nurse Wyman turned away from Nurse Morley and walked back to the father and daughter. The old man was staring down at the floor and working his hands together nervously. Mrs. Burke was standing next to him, not touching him now.

"Mr. Carpenter," said Nurse Wyman, "are you ready now?"

The old man gave an almost imperceptible nod.

"Please say so, if you are."

The old man's lips moved. The word was perceptible, though barely so. "Yes."

"All right, then," said Nurse Wyman.

Mrs. Burke let out a sigh of relief. She turned to the nurses.

"I'm sorry for the trouble."

"It's quite all right," said Nurse Wyman. "Old people can be difficult sometimes."

The door to the Yellow Room was barely shut before Nurse Morley started in again: "So I absolutely must insist that you . . ."

". . . of course, many of your countries will not be able to afford the same kind of individualized attention, but then it's doubtful your people would expect it. . . ."

Thank goodness, the Director. The sound of his voice had the power to jolt even Nurse Morley, and, as the other stopped in mid-sentence, Nurse Wyman said, "You'll have to excuse me. The Director will be needing me."

Nurse Wyman rushed over to her desk, anticipating her part in the Director's tour. She eyed the rack of keys: yes, the Green Room would be empty now.

"*. . . follow me to the Resting Rooms, as we call them, I'm sure you'll be im-pressed with the privacy and pleasantness of . . .*"

As Nurse Wyman grabbed the key, she glanced at her watch. Still forty-five minutes to go, but after that there'd be a couple of stiff drinks, then a nice dinner, then *Sweet Desire, Part II,* then a nice long weekend to catch up on her sleep.

"Thank God, it's Friday," she muttered as she waved to the Director.

******

"Billy seems pretty upset," said the woman who'd been taking care of the boy. She held out a slip of paper. "I've written down the name of a counselor you might . . ."

"Yes, yes," said Mrs. Burke, as she crumpled the paper into her purse and reached for her son's hand. "But right now I just want to get out of this place."

She yanked her son with her as she rushed out of the room and down the stairway. At the street door she paused, looking for protestors, then saw, with relief, that they were gone. She rushed across the street, pushed the boy ahead of her into the car, then got in and started the engine.

It was only after she was a mile from the clinic that she felt herself start to breathe normally again. She turned cautiously to look at her son and saw that he was crying. Suddenly she was crying too. And yelling.

"God damn it, stop it, do you hear me? What about me? I had to be there with him. Do you understand? Your father wants this, and you want that, but I was the one who had to be there. How about somebody thinking of me for a change!"

The hysteria in her voice only made the boy cry harder and she knew she had to get control of herself. She took a couple of deep breaths, then gave that up and reached into her purse for some Valium. Fortunately they'd given her more.

When she felt a little calmer, she said, "I'm sorry I yelled at you, Billy. I really am. I know this is hard on you. But you're not being fair. One day you'll understand. Believe me."

Whether because of her words, or because she'd become calmer, or be-cause his tears had run their course, her son gradually quieted. But he kept staring ahead, his forehead wrinkled up, biting at his lip.

"Billy?"

No answer.

"Billy, please speak to me. There was nothing wrong in what we did. I promise you you'll understand that when you're much older."

He turned toward her then, seeming to study her for a moment with an expression she couldn't decipher. When he finally spoke, his voice was flat. He said:

"How old will you be then, Mama?"

Questions

1. In "Death on Demand," three people take their own lives at the Clinic: Mrs. Evers, Mrs. Lindahl, and Mr. Burke. Relative to each of these people, ask yourself whether it was morally right for society to let them / enable them to die as they did. Explain your answers.
2. The applicants in "Death on Demand" must go through certain procedures before they are allowed to die. What are those procedures? Do you find them adequate? Are there other procedures you think would be better?
3. Do you believe that a person has the right to end his or her own life by positive means? If not, why not? If so, why, and under what circumstances?
4. Do you believe that any system enabling people to die (under certain specified conditions) would be subject to certain abuses? If so, what abuses? Could the abuses be minimized, or would they be so great as to make any such system objectionable?

DISCUSSION

In this chapter we will discuss:
1. Euthanasia in its various forms: active versus passive; voluntary versus involuntary.
2. Developing general moral principles re euthanasia.
3. The distinction between consequentialist and deontological ethical theories.
4. Questions as to how legal euthanasia might work out in practice.

The Right to Die

The story "Death on Demand" imagines a clinic, in the near future, where one can get one's own death "on demand," as now, in many places, one can get an abortion "on demand." It is supposed that society gives people who "meet the appropriate criteria in terms of physical condition or psychiatric history" the right to get medical assistance in ending their lives. The conditions/criteria aren't spelled out in the story, but the patients provide examples of what would be allowed. Mrs. Evers has been suffering from severe depression since the death of her husband, a depression, presumably, that did not respond to psychiatric treatment. Mrs. Lindahl is suffering from terminal cancer. Mr. Carpenter is suffering from intermittent senility and lack of bowel control, as well as other disabilities of old age.

The evolution of the situation portrayed in the story seems to have

HISTORY OF RIGHT-TO-DIE CLINICS IN THE STORY

been this: "Right-to-die" laws were passed on a state-by-state basis, with those laws defining how the means of suicide (only pills are mentioned) were to be dispensed. Nevada allowed people to get the pills without a prescription and without any waiting period. California apparently required both a prescription and a fourteen-day waiting period. Other states, presumably, had different policies. When the pills were involved in a series of murders and a mass cult suicide, Congress stepped in and formulated a national right-to-die law, which established the clinics. Though these clinics seem radical to us, the story supposes they were actually part of a conservative backlash against an even more radical situation. The clinics are, among other things, a way of more carefully controlling who would get the pills and how they would be used.

As far as we can ascertain from the story, the right-to-die procedure goes something like this: The law defines certain medical and psychiatric conditions that make people eligible to be assisted in dying. A person who wants to die has his physician certify his condition, and then the person applies to the clinic. There are a mandatory five counseling sessions in which

RIGHT-TO-DIE PROCEDURES

a counselor talks with the applicant about the decision to die. If the applicant remains determined to die and if the counselor is convinced that the applicant satisfies the legal criteria, the applicant's case goes before a board of review. (If the counselor isn't satisfied, she can request that the applicant have further counseling.) If the board approves the application, the applicant is given a date at the clinic, where she is taken to a small room with a bed and given the pills. She may change her mind up until the moment she swallows the pills (apparently there is no antidote); if she does change her mind, she must wait at least a year before being given another chance to die.

The story invites you to consider the issue of who, if anyone, has the right to die, whether or not these persons (if any) have the right to ask so-

ciety to assist them in dying, and how such assistance would/should be implemented. There are other sorts of related cases, not brought up in the story, that we should also consider: the hospital patient with terminal cancer, in excruciating pain, who begs her doctor to give her some injection that will end her life; the same sort of patient who asks his doctor for stronger doses of medication that will kill the pain but will also probably weaken him and shorten his life; and the patient who refuses some treatment that will prolong her misery with no chance of saving her life. All these cases, along with others, come under the heading of euthanasia, or "mercy killing."

Some Definitions and Distinctions

The term <u>euthanasia</u> **means deliberately bringing about, either by action or by inaction, the painless death of people with certain incurable conditions, conditions that usually involve great suffering.** In order to properly evaluate euthanasia, we need to make two important distinctions.

The first distinction is between active and passive euthanasia, often distinguished by the words "killing" and "letting die." **Active euthanasia involves an action intended to cause the person's death.** The administering of suicide pills in "Death on Demand" is active euthanasia. A doctor who administers what she knows to be a lethal injection of morphine would be another instance. <u>Passive euthanasia</u> **involves intentionally inflicting death by inaction.** Not hooking a near-death cancer patient to a respirator or not performing some operation that would give her a few more days of life would be examples of passive euthanasia.

The second distinction is between voluntary and involuntary euthanasia. <u>Voluntary euthanasia</u> **involves the consent of the person who is to die;** <u>involuntary euthanasia</u> **does not.** The phrase "involuntary euthanasia" has an awful sound to it, suggesting someone shoving suicide pills down the throat of some protesting, struggling patient. Actually, the phrase generally refers to cases that are much more benign, such as the person who has spent years in a coma, kept alive only by some elaborate machinery; "pulling the plug" would be involuntary euthanasia. Another example would be the case of a terribly deformed infant who will die immediately unless some operation is performed; not operating would be involuntary euthanasia.

In this chapter we shall be concerned primarily with voluntary euthanasia, whether active or passive. We can't exclude involuntary euthanasia entirely, since cases arise in which it's not clear whether the person is acting voluntarily; we need to know how we would feel about that particular kind of involuntary euthanasia. However, cases like those of the deformed infant, where the consent of the person to die is not an issue, will not be discussed here.

In considering the issue of voluntary euthanasia, you'll need to answer at least **two categories of questions:**

a. **General moral principle:** Do people have the right to take positive means to end their lives? If so, under what circumstances? Do people have the right to ask society to assist them in this? If so, in what ways?

b. **Social policy and practices** (if the answers to the above are, in any sense, positive): What social system might be implemented to support the right to die? Would this system be likely to have any unfortunate consequences? If so, what consequences? Would those negative consequences be so severe as to warrant further limiting the right to die? If so, how should the right be further limited? Would those consequences be so severe as to warrant overriding the right altogether?

Questions related to (a) and (b) often get muddled together in right-to-die discussions. It is important to clarify how you and others feel about (a) before you think about moving on to (b). ✹

General Moral Principle

In the previous chapter the following view of morality was suggested:

> . . . To propose moral rules is to imply that such rules should apply even if one were in the other person's position . . . moral judgments are "universalizable."
>
> A person who, using imagination, discounts his or her particular circumstances, surveys the human condition, and decides what rules all human beings should follow is said to be taking the "moral point of view." To express a moral preference is to express a preference from the moral point of view.

If you accept this view of morality, try to examine the right-to-die issue from the moral point of view. Start with your personal preferences. Would you want to be able/enabled to take your own life under any circumstances? Under what circumstances? Imagine yourself in various circumstances: You have a very painful illness that doctors agree is terminal and untreatable. You have an illness with a slim chance of a cure where the attempted cure would take months of terrible pain. You are going through

FROM THE MORAL POINT OF VIEW

✹   The CD, Ch. 5, *Some Definitions and Distinctions*, reviews the various types of euthanasia.

a cure that will probably work but the pain and debility of the cure have made you suicidal. You have suffered years of debilitating depression for which no psychiatric treatments have been helpful. You have a terrible depression that makes you want to die but that others have good reason to believe will be short-term. If you feel you should have the right to die in any of these circumstances, ask yourself: Do I have the right to die immediately or should I have to go through certain processes first? What processes?

Now imagine that, as you face such situations, you have differing personal circumstances and personality characteristics. You do or don't have a sound mind. You are elderly or young, rich or poor. You have a family or no family. You have a family that desperately wants you to live; you have a family on which you are a burden. You do or don't have a life's work that's important to you, friends to comfort you, the ability to enjoy life under difficult circumstances, a lot of willpower, a great tolerance for pain. Look at all this not only from the standpoint of the person wanting to take his or her life, but also from the standpoint of family, friends, and any other members of society who might be affected.

As you go through these various cases, you may begin to evolve a complex moral principle with various qualifications and conditions.

In discussing an ethical issue like the right to die, it is helpful to remember a distinction we made in the prior chapter between consequentialist and deontological ethical theories. To review:

Consequentialist ethical theories claim that what makes actions right or wrong is their consequences in terms of increasing or decreasing certain properties that have been identified as intrinsically good or bad. Utilitarianism, as we saw, identifies pleasure/happiness as good and pain/unhappiness as bad and judges actions in terms of increasing happiness and diminishing unhappiness.

Deontological ethical theories deny that what makes actions right or wrong is simply consequences. We noted that Judeo-Christian ethics, as normally interpreted, has a heavy deontological cast and we talked about Kant as a deontologist.

During the discussion, we noted that the distinction between the two sides is not normally as sharp as it appeared when we contrasted the deontologist, Kant, who allowed no exceptions to moral rules, and the act is utilitarian, who seemed to judge the rightness and wrongness of each act in terms of the consequences of that act. Most deontologists have a hierarchy of rules: It's permissable to violate a rule against lying if it conflicts with a higher-order rule, such as not assisting a murderer. Most utilitarians are now rule utilitarians, feeling that one should justify one's act with reference to a set of rules and the set of rules in terms of the principle that you should promote the greatest happiness of the greatest number—thus giving utilitarianism a sort of deontological dimension.

However, even though the distinctions between consequentialist and deontological theories are not as sharp as they would first appear, they are real, and they have an important bearing on right-to-die debates.

Most of those who would deny or severely limit a person's right to die are deontologists who are against taking another's life or one's own life. Those who support a broad right to die can be either consequentialists or deontologists. Utilitarian consequentialists would support a broad right to die in terms of avoiding unnecessary pain. Deontologists who support the right to die might appeal to something like a right to self-determination.

Many who take a position against euthanasia base their position on religious reasons. In Chapter 3 it was argued that the mere fact of God's forbidding something would never be sufficient to make it morally wrong. It would seem that a religious deontologist who cares about justifying

EUTHANASIA AND RELIGIOUS BELIEFS

his position should either try to show what's wrong with that argument or come up with another justification for a prohibition against one's *ever* taking one's own life or offering assistance to a loved one who wants to die.

On the other hand, I don't want to make too much of this point. The only requirement that's been insisted on for having a morality is that one's rules be compatible with taking the moral point of view, and there is nothing contradictory about being a deontologist taking a position against suicide and assisted suicide from the moral point of view. The moral point of view is not equivalent to just adding up wants and satisfying the most possible (to a kind of utilitarianism). It simply entails a commitment that one ought to stand by a rule, whatever one's position. One could certainly decide from that standpoint that no one has the right to actively take his own life. The only question would be whether, if the commandment-of-God aspect were stripped away from certain prohibitions, those prohibitions would have quite the same attraction.

An important difference between consequentialist and deontological ethical theories is the role of motives. Consequentialists aren't uninterested in motives for actions. For instance, encouraging and discouraging certain motives is a way of encouraging and discouraging the actions that tend to result from those motives. For consequentialists, motives are important as means, not ends. For many deontologists, however, particularly those with a religious ethic, the motive is often as important as, if not more important than, the act itself in determining the rightness or the wrongness of the act. (We saw this with Kant.)

Suppose a man who is on a date with a social worker gives twenty dollars to some homeless person with the sole motive of impressing his date. The consequentialist, stressing the result, would probably say that giving the money was a good thing, even though the motive wasn't so good (that is, wasn't as likely to lead to giving in the long run as would sympathy). To some deontologists, however, the act would not be good at all—it's totally hypocritical—and some might even argue that it would be better not to give money at all than to give it hypocritically.

Motives play a particularly important role in the ethical theories of those deontologists who place severe limits on the right to die.

We've discussed the difference between active and passive euthanasia, between "killing" and "letting die." **Many deontologists who disapprove of active euthanasia do approve of passive euthanasia ("letting die").** They feel that while a terminally ill patient does not have the right to take his own life, neither does he have the obligation to endure great discomfort while fighting hopelessly against the natural course of an illness. For instance, he is not required to undergo one painful operation after another when the only result could be a few more days of life. (Similarly with the doctor: She is not allowed to take the patient's life but isn't obligated to implement "heroic" measures.)

In the middle ground between active and passive euthanasia lie some tricky cases: A terminally ill patient is in great pain. Painkillers will weaken the patient, causing her to die sooner. The doctor gives, and the patient accepts, these painkillers. Is this active or passive euthanasia? Is this "killing" or "letting die"?

Here's where the deontologists' emphasis on motives plays a crucial role: Many would say that while the consequence of the act was the shortening of life, the act was not the act of killing because the motive for giving the painkillers was not the shortening of life, but the relief of pain. Thus the giving and taking of such painkillers is morally acceptable (as passive euthanasia) to some deontologists.

MOTIVES RE LIFE-SHORTENING PAINKILLERS

Social Policy and Practices

Once you have formulated your moral position on euthanasia, you should ask yourself what social policy and practices should be used to implement such a position. The further you get from the status quo, the more

The CD, Ch. 5, *General Moral Principles,* reviews the main points of this discussion.

thinking you'll need to do. This will be true particularly if you support active euthanasia.

It's possible, however, that the following thought might occur to someone who supports active euthanasia: "Why bother worrying about some elaborate social mechanism to help people kill themselves? People are capable of killing themselves without that. In fact, why even worry about making suicide legal? Someone who's dead hardly needs to worry about getting punished."

There are a number of reasons someone who believes active euthanasia is morally acceptable might want it made legal. For example, some people don't learn they are terminally ill until they are trapped in hospital beds, too weak to do what is necessary to kill themselves. For people who are capable of taking their own lives, there are other considerations in favor of making suicide legal. Keeping it illegal makes the act furtive, and makes those who wish to end their own lives feel like outlaws. Loved ones can't assist or be close to the suicide at the moment of death without putting themselves in legal jeopardy. It bars the person who is to die from doing things that would help others adjust to the death: If the person tries to prepare people, those people would be legally obligated to inform the police, and the police would be obligated to intervene.

There are a number of reasons someone who believes active euthanasia is morally acceptable might want some social mechanism to assist people in dying. It's true that people do successfully kill themselves, but it's also true that people botch suicides. For example: People take the wrong quantity of pills and end up with brain damage; they shoot themselves in the temple and end up blind; they jump off something and end up paralyzed. Even when suicides are successful, they are often violent (obtaining the necessary pills isn't always easy) and for the people who know and love them, discovering successful suicides is traumatic. The answer here wouldn't have to be a clinic, as in the story; it might be a more easily available, relatively gentle means of suicide, along with easily available education on how to utilize those means.

As you try to formulate social policies and practices, you may find that theory may have to be adjusted in practice. For instance, you may find that some policy that was acceptable to you in the abstract is open to too many abuses in practice; you may end up settling for a policy that is more restrictive than you'd like. Is it possible that any social policy/practices would be so open to abuse that you might decide that active euthanasia, though acceptable to you in theory, simply can't be made workable in any form?

Often deontologists who are against active euthanasia argue that any social mechanism aimed at assisting suicides would have horrible conse-

quences. One might wonder why deontologists are speaking in terms of consequences at all, whether they aren't being inconsistent in this. In fact, there's nothing wrong with a deontologist arguing as follows: "I happen to believe that active euthanasia is wrong, apart from any consequences. But I think if you really look at the consequences seriously, you'd see that allowing active euthanasia would be a mistake from that perspective as well."

However, what emerges in many of these debates is the <u>slippery slope fallacy</u>: assuming, without specific evidence, that any move in a certain direction will inevitably lead you to slide past other possibilities to some terrible extreme. The slippery slope fallacy comes up when you are dealing with a continuum of positions, say, A1, A2, A3, A4, A5, where A1 is the status quo and A5 is something obviously bad. The fallacy is to assume, without specific evidence, that there is no way you can move from A1 toward A2 without sliding all the way to A5—so, since A5 is bad, you shouldn't move at all. One example of this fallacy arises in gun control debates: "If you let the government take away the AK-47 assault rifle, pretty soon they'll take away all our rights and we'll be living in a fascist dictatorship." To see how absurd this argument is, turn it around: "We can't let any citizen have any kind of weapon because pretty soon they'll all have tanks and tactical nuclear weapons and be blowing up the whole world."

SLIPPERY SLOPE ARGUMENTS

In real life, we constantly draw boundaries that more or less hold. For example, we eat some sweets without becoming obese; we have a couple of drinks without becoming alcoholics; we have laws against some things without having laws against everything; we pay some taxes without the government taking all our money away. Slippery slope is simply a reflex— a lazy way of arguing that is constantly contradicted by life around us.

On the other hand, there are real slippery slopes in life (stepping off a skyscraper would be an obvious example). If you passed a law allowing a certain ten percent of the population to take anything they felt they really needed from the other ninety percent, you might well be creating a situation that would lead to inevitable disaster.

In order to make a nonfallacious slippery slope argument, you must present evidence that demonstrates the existence of a particular danger in a particular case, showing why it is different from the everyday cases in which we do draw boundaries that hold.

With any social institutions there are going to be abuses, and with life-and-death institutions there are going to be life-and-death abuses. For most people, this is an unfortunate but inevitable consequence of having social institutions at all. Ideally, you will anticipate abuses and do your best to formulate policies and procedures that will minimize them. When you evaluate the result, the important question is not "Will there be abuses?" (there will be, of course), but rather "How many abuses are there likely to be and is that number acceptable?" As you formulate your position here, remember that the minimum required of you, as in any rational endeavor, is consistency. For instance, you can't reject the practice of active euthanasia on the grounds that a few wrongs will be done, and then endorse capital punishment, which obviously inflicts a few wrongs.   ✹

Questions and Exercises

1. Define euthanasia.
2. Distinguish:
   a. Active and passive euthanasia.
   b. Voluntary and involuntary euthanasia.
3. For each of the following cases decide, Is it euthanasia?, and if so, Is it active/voluntary, active/involuntary, passive/voluntary, or passive/involuntary?
   a. A terminally ill infant is not given an operation that would extend her life by a month (no more).
   b. A physician gives a terminally ill infant a lethal injection.
   c. An elderly woman is killed by a son who wants her money.
   d. A comatose woman who left a will saying she never wanted to "be a vegetable" is taken off the life-support systems.
   e. A terminally ill man knowingly takes an overdose of sleeping pills.
4. Take the moral point of view and develop a moral position (or, reconsider your current position) on euthanasia. Explain this position.
5. Explain the difference between a consequentialist and deontological ethic.
6. Is your position in #4 consequentialist or deontological?
7. Whether or not you believe in active euthanasia, outline the social policy/practices that, while allowing active euthanasia, would allow the fewest number of abuses.
8. Do you think that the policy/practices you outlined in #7 would keep abuses down to a relatively small number? Explain.
9. Explain the slippery slope fallacy.

✹   The CD, Ch. 5, *Social Policy and Practices*, reviews the main points of this discussion; *Your Views*, "interviews" you regarding your stance on the right to die; *Rockin' Review*, "Euthanasia Blues*," has a song about the euthanasia dilemma.

6

The Nature of the Mind

Fiction: Life After Life

My funeral was quite moving, I thought. I chose a spot at the front, next to the minister, so that I could observe the faces in the crowd while I listened to the eulogy. There wasn't a dry eye in the house. Reverend Franks reviewed my long career with the Omega Life Insurance Company, my "meteoric rise," as he called it, from messenger boy to president. He said I had always insisted that Omega sold insurance for living, not dying: insurance for the happiness of policyholders should they live full term, insurance for the happiness of the loved ones should they not. He was sure that Charlie—my name's Charles R. Smith, but everyone calls me Charlie, even my secretary—that Charlie would want his funeral conducted in the same optimistic, life-loving spirit with which he had conducted his business. That was a nice touch, I thought, and I hoped that the boys from the office were duly appreciative.

Death, said Reverend Franks, was, above all, the opportunity to reflect on life. Though I had lived but fifty years, everyone, he was sure, would agree that my life had been "full term" in the most meaningful sense. I had been not only a business magnate but also a Boy Scout leader, an Elk, and a church deacon. I had been the beloved husband of Ruth and the beloved father of Tim and Marcie, a good provider in life and beyond. I had been a

The CD, Ch. 6, *Life After Life,* contains animation and exercises related to this story.

man to whom any friend could turn in legitimate need; a man who could laugh with the fellows and cry, so to speak, for an unfortunate boy; a man who had a fifteen handicap as a golfer but no handicap as a human being.

I was feeling a bit smug at that point, I must admit, and I began to feel more so as Reverend Franks started to speak, somewhat uncomfortably, of his hope for "life after life." Our church has always been vague on that particular issue, tending to stress the vast potential for human moral development in "this life." But I knew now, of course, and he didn't. I knew there was life after this life. Or I guess I should say: life after that one.

In all honesty, though, this development was as much of a surprise to me as the next guy. When I got that fish bone caught in my throat and couldn't breathe, and everything started getting dark, I said to myself: This is it, fella. Nothing else, just: This is it, fella. And you know, in the back of my mind, I was a bit pleased with how it was ending. You spend a lot of your life worrying about death and imagining how awful it is going to be. But when the time comes, it's just something you go ahead and do, or rather something that gets done to you, like getting punched in the nose in your first fight. When it happens, it happens quickly, and you're kind of numb, and there isn't that much pain, or fuss, or fear at all.

Then I opened my eyes and I thought: I guess that wasn't it, fella. Ruth was kneeling next to me, wringing her hands and crying, and Tim, who'd been having dinner with us, was yelling into the phone. I said, "I'm all right, Ruth." But she kept on crying, and I realized she was sobbing too loud to hear me. So I got to my feet to show her I was okay. Even that didn't get her attention, so I put my hand on her shoulder. Only then I noticed there wasn't any hand. That was a shocker, I can tell you. I looked down at myself and there was nothing there—no hands, no arms, no feet, no legs, no nothing. I looked in the mirror over the dining room table, and there was nothing there either, just the image of the living room behind me. I looked at Ruth again and there, at her feet, was a body that looked just like mine, only the face was kind of waxy and blue. And I thought: This is too much. You're having some kind of weird dream. You're on the floor, unconscious, dreaming that you're moving around the room without a body. In a little while you're going to wake up in a hospital bed with your body connected to you the way it's supposed to be, and everything will be all right.

But if this was a dream, it was awfully vivid. Tim hung up the phone and helped Ruth over to the couch. He held her as she cried, and occasionally he glanced over her shoulder at the body on the floor, showing little emotion, just as I'd always taught him a boy should do.

And I thought again: Yes, this has to be a dream. You can't be dead. If you were dead, you'd be standing before Saint Peter at the Pearly Gates, getting fitted for your wings, or something like that. But then I thought: Maybe it doesn't happen that fast. Your soul has just left your body. Maybe it takes the Lord a little while: After all, there are people dying in houses all over the world tonight. You could hardly expect the Lord to make the rounds of all those houses so quickly. You'll just have to wait your turn. And maybe you'd better get yourself ready. So I started in with "Our Father Who Art in Heaven" and when I finished that I started singing, "Nearer My God to Thee." Only no one appeared except for the policemen and the ambulance attendants. All that commotion distracted me, I guess: the sirens, the chatter, the neighbors gathered outside, the ride to the hospital.

At the hospital they pronounced me dead and gave Ruth a sedative. I wasn't all that concerned about Ruth. I don't mean to say I was unsympathetic. I knew how frightened and unhappy she was, and I knew it would be hard for her to get along without me. But I also knew now that death wasn't the end of everything. Ruth would have a few years of loneliness and fear, but then she would find out that life goes on and on, and she would be with me again. From where I stood, so to speak, that looked like a pretty good deal. Anyway, I had my own problems.

In the days following my death, when I wasn't diverted by my funeral arrangements, I was absorbed with the perplexities of my new situation. It was hard to get used to. Some friend would enter the house and I'd say "hi," and he'd walk right through me. I mean right *through* me. And then I'd look down at where my body had been, and I'd be brought back to reality—whatever that was.

My perception of things was much as it had always been, at least visually. I saw the same shapes, sizes, and colors, in the same three dimensions. And my perception of sounds was about the same. But I had no sense of touch, taste, or smell. I really regretted my lack of taste when I looked at a steak and a beer, not to mention my lack of wherewithal when I glanced at a naked woman. Still, I didn't have hunger anymore, and I wasn't in pain. I just missed those pleasures.

I wasn't able to move objects in any way, which is kind of puzzling when you think about it. Of course, my soul didn't have a body anymore. But if a soul can't move objects, how does it ever move a body? Some special kind of connection, I suppose. In any case, my connection had snapped.

However, if I couldn't move objects, I could move through them without difficulty. I would walk into a wall, get a quick impression of darkness, and then emerge from the other side. I found I was able to rise to a height of about forty feet from the ground, and to move laterally at a top speed of ninety-five miles an hour. I checked that speed when I went into Los Angeles for a Dodger game, two days after the funeral. I had a great time. I was able to move around the infield, getting close-ups of the action, without fear of getting hit by the ball. I had the best "seat" in the house, and it didn't cost me one thin dime.

It goes without saying that I could go anywhere I wanted, unobserved, and observe anything I wanted. I didn't abuse that privilege. The naked woman I mentioned earlier was my wife. Any others I saw were by accident, and I departed almost at once. It was fun, at first, dropping by the office, or a neighbor's house, or Larry's Bar, listening to plans for an ad campaign, or to local gossip, trying to guess along with the fellows on the baseball pools. But as time went on, I found myself less and less interested in those conversations, I suppose because I was not involved in the things they were talking about. Occasionally I heard cutting remarks about me, and those hurt. But perhaps I felt even worse when they stopped talking about me altogether.

The real hurt was from my family. Tim took his share of the inheritance, bought himself a flashy SUV, packed it with surfboards, and left college for the beach. When a friend asked him how he got his money, he said, "My old man kicked the bucket." That's all. No fond recollections, no good words, just "my old man kicked the bucket." I never heard my daughter Marcie talk about me at all. l visited her college dorm once and only once. I mean, you teach a girl what's right and wrong, and how no one will buy a cow if the milk is free, and how pot leads to stronger stuff, and she says, "Yes, Daddy, of course," and then you see what she does when she's away. Just once. I wouldn't want to see anymore of it.

But my wife, Ruth, gave me the greatest pain—Ruth, with whom I spent all those years, Ruth, whom I trusted. My old friend Arnold kept dropping by to "pay his respects," which I thought was nice of him until I saw what his respects amounted to. I remember vividly that evening two months ago when Ruth was wearing her black dress, and Arnold was pouring her brandy to boost her spirits, and she started crying, and he hugged her, then kissed her, and she started muttering "No," and he said Charlie would want it this way, which, of course, I didn't, and later they started moving toward the bedroom. I was screaming at her at the top of my lungs, even though I knew she couldn't hear me. Then I turned and stomped out of the house. I haven't been back there since. I'm never going back there.

Later, when I calmed down a bit, I began to think things over. By this time it was obvious that the Lord wasn't coming. Maybe I'd always felt that there wasn't anyone in charge of things—life, I mean—and I was pretty sure of that now. And if my fundamentalist friends had been wrong about heaven and such, I could count myself lucky that those Eastern religions I'd read about had been wrong too. I mean, at least I wasn't reincarnated and wandering around as a skunk or a radish. What was happening to me was quite natural, apparently, and uncontrolled. What I had to do was take things in hand and make my own way, just as I had in my former life. I've never been one to sit on my thumbs, I can tell you.

Now that all the people in my former life had become uninteresting or disappointing to me, it seemed that I ought to try to make some new friends among my own kind. There had to be a lot of other souls around, and surely I would get along with them just fine. I've always been great at making friends.

But the question was: How do you make friends with people who are invisible, untouchable, and make no sounds? All I could see when I looked around me were bodies, no souls. How to make contact? Obviously, I needed some good advice.

In hopes of finding an answer, I started taking some philosophy courses (unofficially, of course) at UCLA. They were no help. I did get a few proofs for the indestructibility of the soul, but that was the last thing I needed. What I needed was a suggestion about how to chat with silent souls and wouldn't you know those guys would have nothing to say about really relevant topics. I would have asked for my money back if I'd paid any.

After I'd thought about the problem on my own, it occurred to me that extrasensory perception might be the answer. But that didn't help much, considering I didn't know anything about extrasensory perception. The only thing I could think of was to act as if I were yelling to someone. So in my mind I said as forcefully as I could, "Hey there!" "Hello there, guys!" "Speak to me!" "Come in, souls, come in!" For the longest time nothing happened, and I tried everything. I "spoke" loudly and softly, at different times of day, facing in different directions. I would think of departed friends or relatives and speak their names. Or I would simply address myself to strangers. I tried visiting areas where it seemed logical that souls might congregate, such as churches, graveyards, and busy city streets.

Finally, I had some luck of sorts. I was sitting on the shore at Long Beach, watching the water and feeling kind of depressed, when I heard a buzzing, chattering sound, like you might hear over the phone. In desperation I cried, "Speak to me, speak to me!" and then, to my amazement, I heard a voice.

"Who's that?"

"I'm Charlie," I said, "Charlie Smith. Who are you?"

"I'm Mildred."

"Where are you, Mildred, in Long Beach?"

"Long Beach? Heavens no. I'm in Tallahassee."

"Tallahassee?"

It happens like that. You'd think that if you got through to another soul, it would be a soul in your own neighborhood. But that other soul can be anywhere. I remember a teacher at UCLA saying that a soul, being non-physical, would have no spatial location. I wanted to interrupt her and tell her how wrong she was. I mean, I was a soul, and I was right there in her classroom. But I must admit now that that kind of location doesn't seem to count for much when souls communicate with one another.

I had a pleasant chat with Mildred that day and the next. She invited me to visit her in Tallahassee, and I accepted. It was a pretty easy trip. I could move, as I've said, at ninety-five miles an hour and didn't need to stop and rest. I didn't have to worry about traffic jams or stop-lights, or winding roads. With a few side trips for sightseeing, and getting lost once, I made it in about a day and a half.

I guess I had the absurd feeling that I would see Mildred in Tallahassee. Of course, I couldn't. She was a soul and invisible, no matter how close you got. Our communications in Florida were still like phone conversations, only this time they were local calls. Still, we were able to share experiences and see the sights together.

The first few days were fun. Then Mildred reverted to her "normal" routine. It turned out that the only sights she really wanted to see and share were at the television department at Sears. Mildred loved soap operas. She was a real fanatic. When she wasn't watching the soaps, she would listen to women talking about them or peer over someone's shoulder at the pages of *Soap Opera Digest*. It was all too much for me. I wasn't about to spend eternity watching "The Guiding Light" and "One Life to Live." I thought I'd better find a woman with other interests. I'd made contact once, and I was sure I would again.

And I did—this time with Alice in Cheyenne, Wyoming. That visit went badly from the start. All Alice wanted to do was hang around her husband and spy on the women he'd taken up with after she'd died. I would have left right away, but I happened to see Alice's picture on the mantelpiece in her house. She was gorgeous, I mean really gorgeous. I'd never been with a woman who looked like that. So I tried to get her interested in me. I told her about my bad experiences with my wife and how I'd decided I should forget about my former life and associate with my own kind. I told her she should forget about her husband and try to have some fun.

I took Alice out on a couple of dates. Her mood seemed to be picking up, and she seemed to be getting to like me. One night I took her to a drive-in movie. We sat near the front, about twenty feet in the air, over the cars. It was a very romantic, sensual movie. I got really involved in the film. I began to feel a deep regret at not having a body. I was longing for some kind of human warmth.

"Oh Alice," I said, "I wish so much that I could hold your hand."

"It wouldn't be proper," she said. "I've only been widowed for five months."

That was the last straw. An hour later I was heading back to California.

That's the way it's been going. Every soul I meet seems to be interested only in the past. But the past is past, and you can't live on memories. On the other hand, what else can you live on? There doesn't seem to be anything interesting that you can do for, or to, or with, another soul. Or vice versa. It's not much fun floating around like a bubble, not able to do anything in the world.

What on earth am I going to do with myself? I don't know. I've got to figure out something. I've just got to. I'm bored as hell.

Fiction: Strange Behavior

What first startled us about the civilization on the planet Gamma was not its strangeness but its familiarity. It was as if a piece of southern Europe from the year 2050 had been transported fifty years ahead in time, and millions of miles out into space, to that small planet. Of course, the similarity is not exact. The Italians of fifty years ago did not have quite the same enthusiasm for spherical constructions, nor for the colors pink and orange. Also, the brown-skinned Gammas are nine feet tall and hairless, and they hear through slits located just below their cheekbones. But with all the strange life forms recently discovered in the universe, these minor dissimilarities between the Gammas and the mid-century Italians go almost unnoticed. When we landed on Gamma, we felt as if we had stepped into a living museum.

The technological sophistication of Gamma is virtually the same as that of Earth fifty years ago. But there is one notable difference. The Gammas'

 The CD, Ch. 6, *Strange Behavior*, contains animation and exercises related to this story.

skill in robotry is more advanced than is ours even today. In fact, we spent our first six hours on Gamma in the company of robots we thought to be living beings. In our defense, I should note that the Gammese robots have a tremendous flexibility of response and fluidity of motion and that their metallic parts are covered with a brown, skinlike exterior. It is only when a Gammese robot is standing next to a Gamma that one notices, in the robot, a hint of the mechanical. But I don't think one is thoroughly convinced of the difference between the Gammas and the robots until one has toured the hospitals where the living are treated and the factories where the robots are repaired.

It was from the robots that we got the rudiments of the Gammese language. After letting them know that we were friendly, we coaxed them over to the Q-35 Computer Language Translator. We showed them the green patch on the screen of the Translator's Sensitivity Panel and indicated that they should say aloud the Gammese word for what they saw. The robots said something like "rooga"; the Translator said aloud "green." We said "green" and the Translator said "rooga." We continued this process until we were able to produce, via the Translator, several basic sentences in Gammese. Then the robots realized that the Q-35 was recording all the word translations and would soon enable us to converse by voice alone, without constant reference to the pictures on the Sensitivity Panel. Thereafter, the robots concentrated on teaching the Q-35 their language, responding in quick succession to the series of sights, sounds, textures, tastes, and scents produced by the Sensitivity Panel.

The real Gammas appeared eventually, and we laughed at ourselves for having mistaken the robots for living beings. The Gammas were very friendly and intensely curious about the civilization on Earth. Of course we had more to tell them than they us, for they were like the past to us, and we were like the future to them. The first days on Gamma were a constant series of conferences, largely of a Show-and-Tell variety, as we struggled to make ourselves understood through the less than fluent Q-35 Translator. Fortunately, we had with us an instruction kit filled with models, maps, and photographs designed to aid us in explanations of life on Earth.

With so much on Gamma already familiar to us, we tended to focus our attention on the robots. We became more and more puzzled by what we observed. It was not only that the robots were so lifelike but also that the Gammas seemed to treat the robots as their equals. True, there was a preponderance of robots in jobs that demanded only strength or great memory, but there were Gammas in such jobs as well. And some Gammese robots held high-level positions in which they supervised the activities of the living Gammas. Furthermore, the Gammas seemed to treat the robots with the same sort of courtesy, affection, or, occasionally, anger that they showed toward other Gammas.

Our most frequent guide was a Gamma whose name is unpronounceable. We simply addressed him as "Mr. A," and the Q-35 made the sound that he recognized as his name. We were eager to question him about the Gammas' attitude toward the robots, but we approached the subject cautiously, not wishing to seem critical. His initial responses to our inquiries were bewildering. It seemed as though he were teasing us.

"Would you say that flesh is so much better than metal?" he asked. "I should think it would be just the opposite."

Or again: "Would you treat someone differently just because he is produced in a factory? Personally, I think our mode of reproduction—which is similar to yours—is rather inefficient and even comical."

Mr. A was asked why only robots had been sent on the potentially dangerous mission of meeting us when we landed on Gamma.

"Because, of course, they're more easily repaired than we are. It is a quality we envy them. Just as they sometimes envy us our greater flexibility."

Phrases like "they envy us" and "they also want" were constantly employed by our guide. Finally Ms. Washington, a member of our group, blurted out the question that all of us wanted to ask.

"Mr. A, do the Gammas really believe that their robots have minds?"

"Of course," said Mr. A, looking puzzled.

"Then that explains the confusion," said Washington. "We did not mean to say that one should treat a creature differently simply because it is made of a different substance or is produced differently. Rather, we believe that creatures made of metal cannot possibly have minds. On the other hand, you believe they can and do. Now we understand each other better."

We were all quite pleased with the quick and tactful way in which we had solved the mystery. At the same time we all felt more than a little superior to a people who believed that machines could think. However, Mr. A did not seem pleased. He seemed absolutely bewildered.

"I don't understand," he said. "Please explain yourselves."

"You believe that these robots have minds," said Washington. "So you treat them as your peers. We don't believe that robots have minds. Therefore we treat them as we might treat, say, expensive watches. Of course, there is room for disagreement on this point. I mean, one doesn't actually see minds."

"Of course you see minds!" said Mr. A.

He was quite emphatic and seemed quite serious. We were all startled.

"Well, one's own mind, yes," said Washington. "But one doesn't see other minds."

"You do see other minds!"

"No, no. At least not according to our beliefs. We believe that one sees the behavior of other people, but not their minds."

Mr. A glanced toward the Q-35 Translator and then back at Washington.

"Your words don't seem to translate. What I hear from the Translator makes no sense."

Washington looked thoughtful for a moment and then continued.

"Does the word 'behavior' make sense to you? The actions of the body?"

"Yes."

And the word 'pain'?"

"Yes."

"Do you understand me when I say that a person in pain behaves in a special sort of way?"

"Yes. Of course."

"Well, what we call 'pain' is not the behavior but the thing inside."

"What thing inside?" said Mr. A. "There are many things inside."

"I mean the thing that is inside whenever you show the pain behavior."

"Oh, you mean the state of the brain, or the state of the robot's computer?"

"No, no, no. You could observe the brain state or the computer state under certain conditions. I mean the thing that you could never observe no matter how extensively you examined the body. I mean the feel of the pain, the sensation of pain."

"Those last words don't translate."

Washington was obviously feeling frustrated, but he pressed on.

"Perhaps the example of imagination would be easier. Suppose you close your eyes and imagine something round and orange. Form an image of it. What we call the 'mental' is not the closing of the eyes or the verbal description 'orange and round' that you might give us. What we call the 'mental' is the round and orange picture inside of you."

"What picture?" said Mr. A.

The conversation went on in this absurd fashion as Washington tried to phrase the obvious in a way that would be obvious in Mr. A's language. But gradually the truth of the matter began to dawn on us. The reason the Gammas saw no essential difference between themselves and their robots was that the Gammas, like the robots, were creatures without minds, without consciousness.

Our words like "think" and "want," and the generic term "mind," had seemed, at first, to translate into Gammese because we constantly correlated our mental events with behavioral patterns. The Gammas had thought all along that we were talking about behavior. In fact, our mental terms didn't translate into Gammese at all, for the Gammas have no minds. They only behave as if they did.

As we were staring at Mr. A in astonishment, it occurred to us that we might be frightening or offending him. We were very vulnerable on this faraway planet. So we turned the conversation from the topic of minds to the topic of interplanetary travel. Our talk of the overtly strange life forms we had encountered on our travels seemed to reestablish our kinship with the Gammese people.

When the subject of minds arose again, as it inevitably did, we tried to deemphasize the dissimilarity between ourselves and the Gammas. We implied that our word "mind" referred to behavior plus that "something else." This allowed us to say that the Gammas and the robots had minds without pretending, as would have been hopeless now, that there was no difference between them and us. Eventually, the whole matter turned into a kind of joke. Mr. A asked us what the "something else" inside the people from Earth did for them. Of course, we had to admit that it produced no overt effects that could not occur without it. After that he began to joke about us as "the people with the something else that does nothing at all." In fact, this phrase threatens to become the general designation for us on Gamma.

****

It is truly amazing to observe just how little external difference the lack of mind has made to the Gammese civilization. With only a body and a brain, they have almost managed to keep pace with the civilization on Earth. Without thoughts, they have been able to develop a sophisticated technology that has brought them to the verge of interplanetary travel. Without feelings, they can discriminate between beauty and ugliness, goodness and evil, and they have produced sophisticated treatises on ethics and aesthetics. They act as if they have the normal variety of human emotions, even to the point of enjoying very sentimental love stories.

The only noticeable differences appear in their metaphysical writings, and even these are minor. One philosopher on Gamma began a philosophical treatise with the argument, "I think, therefore I am." Of course, this is not really the same as Descartes's argument. The correct translation would be something like, "I behave (in a thinking way), therefore I exist (as a physical being)."

On Gamma there is a fairly widespread belief in God, though they have their religious skeptics just as we do. They identify God with the universe and claim that He is (or rather behaves as if He is) omnipotent, omniscient, and perfectly good. They certainly do not imagine God to be nonphysical. The word "nonphysical" translates into their language as "not-being" or "nothing," which is to say that it does not translate at all. Some Gammas believe in life after death, which they imagine to be a physical resurrection of the body that occurs at some far distant time. They include the robots in this resurrection. "The robots worship Him as we do," they say, "and our Heavenly Father would not neglect them." Of course, they do not believe that the mind exists during the period between death and the resurrection. Said one philosopher: "To take the mind from the body is as impossible as taking the shape from a flower while leaving its color and weight behind."

I often wonder about our future relations with the Gammas. I doubt that we would provoke hostilities with these creatures. There are enough hostile beings in the universe already, and we need whatever allies we can find. The Gammas may be able to provide us with valuable information about their solar system. And no doubt our scientists and philosophers will want to study the Gammas at great length. But the issues here will be strictly practical. There can be no question of extending moral rights to mindless, unfeeling creatures, whether they are made of metal or protoplasm.

Mr. A was there to bid us goodbye as we prepared to leave the planet Gamma. He told us how much he had enjoyed our visit and how sad he was to see us depart. He said the Gammas would always look forward to visits from the people of Earth. Then he laughed softly:

"We shall always welcome the people with the something else that does nothing at all."

I laughed with him, but in my heart I felt only pity. He did not, could not, possibly understand that the "something else that does nothing at all" is the very essence of life, the point of it, and that it makes all the difference in the world.

Questions

1. In "Life After Life," Charlie is a disembodied soul. Is there any difference between a soul and a mind? Explain.
2. Charlie says that he can't understand how souls or minds manage to move human bodies. What is his reasoning here?

3. Do you believe that the perceptions and capacities of a disembodied soul would be any different from those described in the story? If so, in what ways do you think they would be different?
4. Which of the following statements are true of the Gammas?
   a. They act and speak intelligently.
   b. They treat the people from Earth in a friendly way.
   c. They exhibit a good sense of humor.
   d. They have a fairly sophisticated technology.
   e. They write and read love stories.
   f. They philosophize.
   g. They have a religion.
5. Explain the differences between body, brain, and mind. Which of these are the Gammas supposed to have?
6. The narrator of "Strange Behavior" says that the Gammas have no minds. What does she believe the mind to be?
7. What are the Gammas supposed to be missing in not having minds?
8. What outward differences, if any, would there be in the Gammese culture if the Gammas had minds?

DISCUSSION

In this chapter we will discuss:
1. The dualist theories of interactionism and parallelism.
2. The materialist theories of behaviorism, the identity theory, and functionalism.
3. Minds and machines.
4. Different concepts of life after death.

Two Dualist Theories of Mind

The narrator of "Strange Behavior" holds a view of mind and body that is shared by many people in our culture. It is sometimes dubbed **"the official view."** According to this view, the mind is radically different from any physical object. For one thing, physical objects (including human bodies) are publicly observable, while minds are necessarily private. That is, one can observe another person's body just as one can observe the chairs and tables in a room; but one cannot observe another person's thoughts. Furthermore, physical objects occupy space, while minds do not. A mind is not located in some part of the physical body, nor anywhere else in the physical world. Because the mind is radically different from any physical object, it is claimed, the mind is nonphysical. Persons holding this "official view" of mind and body are called "dualists."

Dualism is the view that the world is composed of two radically different kinds of things—physical bodies and nonphysical minds.

We will discuss **two forms of dualism**, each holding a different view about the relation between mind and body. The two theories are interactionism and parallelism.

Interactionism says that there are nonphysical minds and physical bodies and that the two are causally related (have effects on one another). Stubbing the toe causes pain. The desire to wave causes the arm to move.

Parallelism says that there are nonphysical minds and physical bodies, but that the two are never causally related (never have effects on one another). Stubbing the toe may occur just prior to pain, but it does not cause the pain. The desire to wave occurs just prior to the moving of the arm, but it does not cause the arm to move.

Interactionism seems, at first glance, to be a sensible view of mind and body. (In fact, it is probably this specific version of dualism that warrants the label "the official view.") Parallelism, on the other hand, seems ludicrous. Why believe it?

PARALLELIST ARGUMENT

Parallelists invoke the principle that a thing cannot produce characteristics that it does not have. Employing this principle, they say that the nonphysical, containing nothing physical itself, could not produce physical effects. And the physical could not produce nonphysical effects.

The principle that a thing cannot produce characteristics that it does not have seems to be acknowledged in everyday life. A brush that is dipped in clear water could not paint a wall red, because there is no red in the paint brush; a feather could not topple a sturdy wall, because the feather is not sufficiently powerful. Suppose that, while watching a knife-throwing act, you learn that the knives in the performer's hand are made of flimsy rubber. You would conclude that the act is a fake. True, each time the man appears to fling a knife, a knife appears in the wooden backdrop, perilously close to the body of his assistant. It seems as though he is throwing the knives, but he is not. The rubber knives do not contain sufficient

GHOST STORIES RE MIND/BODY

strength to penetrate the wood. The movements of the man's hand are not causing the knives to appear in the wood; the hand movements are merely correlated with the appearance of the knives. Actually, the knives are hidden in the wooden backdrop and are popping out, handle first, at the appropriate moment. The illusion of the supposed "knife-throwing" act is analogous to what the parallelist sees as the illusion of the relation be-tweeen mind and body.

The specific impulse to deny causal relations between the physical and nonphysical appears, to some extent, in ghost stories. If a ghost passes through a room, it is not tripped by chairs, nor does it knock them over. It is not stopped by a wall, nor does it dent the wall as it enters.

In "Life After Life," it is quite natural to imagine that Charlie, as a soul, would not interact with physical objects. To Charlie, as to many philoso-phers, this suggests a philosophical problem about the mind and body: "I wasn't able to move objects in any way, which is kind of puzzling when you think of it. Of course, my soul didn't have a body anymore. But if a soul can't move objects, how does it ever move a body?"

In fact, ghost stories clearly illustrate our confusion about this issue. Though ghosts do not normally interact with the physical world, they do so when the plot demands that they rattle chains or start fires. Ghost stories would be pretty dull if ghosts didn't do such things. But, philosophically, it seems as though we ought to make up our minds on this matter. Could the physical and nonphysical be causally related? Parallelists say no.

Parallelists, of course, are confronted with the following challenge: "If mind and body are not causally related, what accounts for the constant correlations between them? Surely this is not just coincidence!" In the case of the knife-throwing act, we would conclude that the act is a fake: The movements of the man's hand are not causing the knives to appear in the wood. But, having drawn that conclusion, we would suppose some other explanation for the constant correlation between the hand movements and the appearance of the knives. Perhaps there is some mechanism in the backdrop that springs out the knife handles at intervals known to the man; he is timing his arm movements accord-ingly. Or perhaps there is a third person backstage who presses a button, re-leasing a knife handle each time the performer's hand moves. We certainly would insist that there is some explanation. We would reject the supposi-tion that the correlations are coincidental.

PARALLELISTS RE MIND/BODY CORRELATIONS

Parallelists have been unable to provide any satisfactory explanation as to how mind and body happen to be correlated if they are not causally related. Some have said that God causes the correlations, either moment by moment or through some predestined synchronization of mental and physical events. But this supposition won't do. If God is a spirit, then, according to the logic of parallelism, He cannot affect the physical; if He is physical, then He cannot affect the mental. If He is both mental and physical, how do these aspects of God happen to be correlated? Parallelists are uncomfortable with the idea of extensive, happenstantial correlations between minds and bodies. But they say: "However astounding this may seen, it is more plausible than the theory that nonphysical minds and physical objects are causally related."

Today there are few, if any, parallelists. However, the parallelist argument against interactionism has made a lot of thinkers uncomfortable with any form of dualism.   ⊛

Three Materialist Theories of Mind

Some of the critics who reject dualism are called "materialists." <u>Materialism is the view that everything that exists is physical, including the mind.</u>

ARGUMENTS FOR
MATERIALISM

Many materialists believe this view of mind is most compatible with a "scientific view" of the world. They believe that the higher life forms evolved from physical matter. In their view, the emergence of physical mind from physical matter is theoretically plausible; however, the emergence of nonphysical mind from physical matter is preposterous. Moreover, some materialists believe that their view is supported by considerations of theoretical simplicity. The dualist narrator of "Strange Behavior" has to admit that the "something else" she calls "mind" produces "no overt effects that could not occur without it." In theory, a sophisticated brain-nervous system would be quite sufficient to produce the full range of human behavior. To suppose a spirit (nonphysical mind) is behind the workings of the human body would be as unscientific, materialists say, as to suppose a spirit is behind the workings of a car engine. (Twentieth-century British philosopher Gilbert Ryle has called dualism "the myth of the ghost in the machine.")

Three forms of materialism that have received considerable attention in the twentieth century are **behaviorism, the identity theory, and functionalism.** (It should be noted that the philosophical theory called "behaviorism" differs from the psychological theory of the same name; sometimes the philosophical theory is called "logical behaviorism" because it is a theory about the logic and meaning of mental terms.)

The narrator of "Strange Behavior" says that the Gammas are "mindless": ". . . the Gammas have no minds. They only behave as if they did." A

⊛   The CD, Ch. 6, *Dualism: Two Theories,* reviews definitions and arguments regarding the two theories; *Interactionism and Parallelism,* has an animation that illustrates the difference between these two theories.

behaviorist would disagree with the narrator. The Gammas behave intelligently and kindly, the behaviorist would point out. To behave intelligently and kindly is to be intelligent and kind. The term "mind" designates

ARGUMENTS FOR
BEHAVIORISM

such characteristics as intelligence and kindness. Therefore the Gammas do have minds.

According to the dualist, one never sees another mind; at most, one sees the physical behavior of another person. But, says the behaviorist, if we were really talking about unobservable entities when we talk about other minds, then each of us would naturally be skeptical about other minds: We would be reluctant to make judgments about the mental states of others; we would even be dubious about the very existence of other minds. Yet the opposite is the case: We feel certain that other minds exist; we are all quite confident about pronouncing others to be more or less intelligent, kind, or happy. Such confidence indicates that the mental states of others are not hidden at all, that other minds are things we can observe. What we observe when we judge other minds is physical behavior.

According to <u>behaviorism</u>, when we say that someone has a mind, we're saying that person is exhibiting certain complex, overt, physical behavior or would exhibit such behavior under certain circumstances. When you have seen someone's behavior, you have seen their mind. Behavior isn't *evidence* for the existence of mind: This would imply that the mind and behavior are two different things. The mind *is* behavior.

The word "overt" in the definition indicates external rather than internal bodily behavior. According to the behaviorist, when we talk about minds we are talking about speech, facial expressions, and the movements of the arms and legs, as opposed to the workings of the liver, heart, or brain. The behaviorist would not deny that a functioning brain is essential to our exhibiting complex, overt, physical behavior. But, in the behaviorist view, the mind is not the brain; the mind is behavior.

Behaviorism has been important in showing us that many of our mental terms do imply behavioral components. Consider generosity, for instance. In the absence of all behavior, a person could conceivably be sympathetic, but he or she could not be generous. The term "generosity" implies some physical act of giving. Knowing how to ride a bike implies a physical ability component; simply having some theoretical knowledge of bike-riding wouldn't count as knowing how to ride a bike.

However, behaviorism is difficult to defend as an analysis of all our mental terms. Most, if not all, of them indicate something over and above behavior and dispositions to behave. They indicate events that we are inclined to call "internal" and "private." As Lewis says in "Strange Be-

havior": "Suppose you close your eyes and imagine something round and orange. Form an image of it. What we call the 'mental' is not the closing of the eyes or the verbal description 'round and orange'
that you might give us. What we call the 'mental' is the round and orange picture inside of you."

The difficulties with behaviorism are most apparent when that theory is applied to oneself. Sit still, fold your hands, close your eyes, and think, "Two plus two equals four." Now report what you have just thought: "I just thought 'two plus two equals four.'" Is it at all plausible to believe that this statement is merely the report of some behavior or some disposition to behave? The crucial thing that you are reporting is an internal, private event, the thought, "Two plus two equals four."

Put formally, this particular argument against behaviorism is as follows:

1. Behaviorism implies that all talk about minds is talk about behavior.
2. When I report the thought "2 + 2 = 4," I am not talking about behavior.
3. (Therefore) it's not the case that all talk about minds is talk about behavior (from 2).
4. (Therefore) behaviorism is not true (from 1 and 3).

The mind doesn't seem to be simply overt physical behavior. But perhaps it is physical nonetheless. There is an internal bodily organ, the brain, that is intimately associated with mental processes. Perhaps the mind and the brain are not two different entities, closely related; perhaps the physical brain is the mind. Philosophers who claim that the brain and mind are identical are identity theorists. As has been noted, the identity theory is a form of materialism.

According to the identity theory, the mind (that which produces thoughts, images, sensations) is identical with the brain (the mass of nerve tissue inside the skull). Mental events are nothing but electrochemical brain processes. Mental events are "internal" only in the sense that they occur inside the skull. They are "private" only in the sense that brain processes are very infrequently observed.

By saying that the mind and the brain are identical, the identity theorist is saying that they are literally one and the same thing. It is easy to mis-

interpret this claim, because in everyday speech the word "identical" often has the meaning of "very similar." For example, we call some twins "identical," even though they are not one person. They are two different people who are similar in most, but not all, respects; for instance, they occupy different positions in space. However, the identity theorist is not saying that the mind and brain are two different things that are quite similar, but rather that the mind and the brain are one and the same thing.

The identity theory is widely discussed today, and there are some philosophers who consider it plausible. But there are objections to this theory that seem to have weight.

Critics of the identity theory appeal to what might be called a **principle of nonidentity: Two things cannot be identical if they have different characteristics.*** This principle is one that we seem to accept readily in everyday life. That pen you have can't be my pen if my pen is blue and the one you are holding is green. My brother can't be the axe murderer if my brother is short and the murderer is tall.

> ARGUMENT AGAINST THE IDENTITY THEORY

Having claimed that two things having different characteristics cannot be identical, critics of the identity theory go on to claim that mental events and brain events do have different characteristics. Consider, for example, mental images. When one imagines something round and orange, presumably the image is round and orange. But is there a round, orange brain process occurring at the same moment? Our best evidence indicates that there is no orange brain event: The brain does not have the range of colors that our images display. If the image is orange and no brain events are orange, then the image cannot be a brain event. Mental events and brain events, however closely they might be related, are different things.

Put formally, this argument against the identity theory is as follows:

1. The identity theory implies that the mind and brain have all the same characteristics.
2. Mental images have colors the brain doesn't have.
3. (Therefore) it's not the case that the mind and brain have all the same characteristics (from 2).
4. (Therefore) the identity theory is not true (from 1 and 3).

---

*This informal wording of the nonidentity principle has the virtue of simplicity, but the phrase "two things" may be confusing. How could two things be one thing (identical), whatever their characteristics? Actually, what is at issue in identity questions is whether two descriptions refer to the same thing or to different things. Do the phrases "My neighbor" and "the axe murderer" refer to the same man? Do the phrases "the mind" and "the brain" refer to the same thing? A more exact statement of the principle of nonidentity would be that if the thing referred to by one phrase has characteristics differing from those of the thing referred to by another phrase, then the two phrases do not refer to the same thing. Once this is understood; the simpler wording of the nonidentity principle allows for less cumbersome exposition.

The difficulties with behaviorism and the identity theory have led to a third materialist theory called functionalism, which today is the most popular theory of mind among cognitive psychologists and researchers in artificial intelligence.

According to <u>functionalism</u>, **all mental states are physical states; what makes a physical state a mental state is the kind of causal relationships it has with the environment, with other mental states, and with behavior.**

In opposition to the behaviorist, the functionalist says that mental states are internal states that are causally related to behavior. This was another problem with the behaviorist analysis: We talk about mental states as causes

> ARGUMENT FOR
> FUNCTIONALISM

of behavior: "He's dieting because he wants to fit into his suit for the wedding"; "She said those things because she was hurt." But how can mental states be causes of behavior if they *are* behavior?

The functionalists agree with the identity theorists that mental states are internal physical states, but they don't agree with the identification of mental states with brain states. **The implication of the identity theory seems to be that no conceivable creature without a human-like brain could have a mind.** The functionalists argue that it's implausible to rule out in advance the possibility that an alien being made of different stuff—or even a very sophisticated robot or computer—could have a mind.

Functionalists argue that it's irrelevant, in theory, what materials the mind or mental state is composed of; what matters is how it functions

> "IT'S IRRELEVANT
> WHAT MINDS ARE
> MADE OF"

causally. We define a lot of things in terms of function rather than materials. Consider clocks: To measure time, you can use falling grains of sand, the turning of gears, or the vibrations of

atoms; what makes something a clock is not the materials that constitute it but how it functions to measure time. Similarly, argue the functionalists, what makes something a belief—for example, that it's raining—is its causal relation to the environment (it was caused, say, by the sight or sound of rain, or someone's words, "It's raining"), and how it functions along with the desire to stay dry (another functional state) to alter behavior (I reach for my umbrella).

As you might imagine, critics of functionalism question its adequacy as an analysis of those mental events we think of as quintessentially conscious—sensations of pain or pleasure, emotions like joy and sadness, and images such as our orange circle. Before discussing that point, however, **let's consider for a moment how much of mind does *not* have a vividly conscious quality.**

You're rushing across campus, worried about being late for a test, trying to remember what you just read about an objection to the identity theory, looking forward to class being over so you can go play softball with your friends. Think of all that your mind is doing that you're barely conscious of in terms of manipulating your muscles to keep you balanced and moving as you rush along. It seems simple to you now, but it's an enormously complicated ability you had to learn painstakingly as a young child.

Think about all the processing your mind is doing in terms of the visual, auditory, and tactile sensations that are impinging on your senses. Think about all the information you have in your head that you don't seem to be conscious of but could easily recall if the need arose—memories of where you were and what you were doing at various times in your life, all the facts you know about family and friends, all the facts you know about, as well as the sensory recall you have of, the movies you've seen and the songs you've listened to. Think of all your beliefs about where things are located and how things work. Think of the system that catalogs and coordinates all these memories, beliefs, preferences, and bits of information.

All of this is mind, but almost none of it is obviously conscious in the way that the thought, "I'm late," is. To many of those who study the human mind with its trillions of neuron connections and its complicated processing, what's obviously conscious at any given moment seems the tiniest fraction of what the mind is doing—of what's "in" the mind. It doesn't seem implausible to imagine most of the processing that the mind does being done by sophisticated physical processing units. Even where there are conscious events like pain, there are complex processes underlying those events that a machine could, in theory, duplicate; even now, computers can be programmed with a degree of self-monitoring, self-diagnostic, and self-repair capabilities. (You could certainly program a computer to moan and complain while doing these tasks.) Given that so much of the mind could, in theory, be done by physical processing, the idea that nonetheless the essential ingredient of mind is nonphysical spirit seems suspiciously like a bit of superstition held over from an earlier time. The natural world, our bodies, and our brains are susceptible to a physical explanation; why shouldn't those oddities like pains and dream images be explainable physically as well? Maybe the idea of the nonphysical simply arises from our ignorance about mind, and will eventually disappear—like many outdated concepts—when we learn more.

In spite of the energetic defense functionalists give for their position, many philosophers and scientists remain unconvinced. Dualists argue that the claim that the mind is nonphysical doesn't rest on the strength of some speculative theory of mind formulated centuries ago in less sophisticated

ARGUMENT AGAINST
FUNCTIONALISM

times. Conscious mental events are what we experience firsthand. And it is what we experience about them—their privacy aspect, their subjective qualities—that makes it seem unlikely that they could be physical.

Dualism Revisited

What was presented in our initial discussion of dualism was more or less the classical version of this theory. We now need to bring dualism up to date.

Several hundred years ago when the French philosopher René Descartes (1596–1650) and others were formulating their dualist theories in the light of the beginnings of modern science, it was taken as a given that human beings had a mind/soul that would survive the death of the body; it was thought that the mind/soul, having free will, was not subject to the laws of what was beginning to seem a thoroughly mechanistic physical world. The mind was considered a substance radically different from any physical substance and existing in its own nonphysical realm. This form of dualism, which views the mind as a nonphysical substance, is now known as <u>substance dualism</u>.

There are still many substance dualists—especially among those who hold traditional religious views. However, there are other dualists who view mental events as nonphysical *properties* of a physical mind—different in kind from the physical properties of mind, but still incapable of existing without the physical mind. **The view that mental events are nonphysical properties of the physical mind is called <u>property dualism</u>.**

What might lead one to property dualism? **One might agree with the functionalists that the vast majority of mental activity going on at any given time isn't obviously conscious and that it would make sense to account**

REASONS FOR
BELIEVING IN
PROPERTY DUALISM

for such activity with a physical model. One might be impressed with the progress the physical sciences have made in analyzing our mental activity in terms of the workings of the brain. (Think, for example, of how our view of depression has changed now that we know something about the chemical causes of depression and can alleviate depression by changing those chemical processes.) One might also feel that insofar as we ever understand workings of the mind, it will

---

The CD, Ch. 6, *Materialism: Three Theories,* reviews definitions and arguments regarding the three theories.

come mostly through the study of the physical aspects. (Psychodynamic models of mind—the Freudian, Jungian, and countless more modern versions—though useful therapeutically, have never come close to yielding a scientific model of mind.)

One might agree with all this, but disagree (perhaps even reluctantly) that the mental events that seem to us most obviously conscious—the "look" of the image, the "feel" of the pain—could ever be completely accounted for in physical terms. One might feel, however, that these nonphysical mental events don't constitute a separate thing: Mental events are too closely correlated with—and seem dependent on—the physical. Rather, mental events seem like nonphysical aspects or properties of the physical mind. This is the kind of reasoning that might convince one to be a property dualist.

Some property dualists liken these nonphysical properties to the kind of "emergent properties" we're already familiar with in the physical realm. "Emergent properties" are properties that emerge at a higher level of organization and seem different in kind from properties at a more basic level. One uncontroversial example of an emergent property would be solidity. At the atomic level, a table, for instance, consists of a small percentage of atoms and a huge percentage of empty space. Yet at the macroscopic level, there's no sense at all of the empty space: What emerges is "solidity." In the same way, some property dualists argue, what emerges from certain brain processes is the property of pain-feeling.

> EMERGENT PROPERTIES

Viewing conscious events as nonphysical properties of the physical brain, rather than as aspects of a nonphysical mental substance, doesn't itself take care of the mind-body interaction problem we discussed earlier; we still have the physical producing the nonphysical. However, a dualist today might argue that the whole mind/body interaction problem depends on an outmoded view of causation. In the seventeenth century it might have seemed reasonable to talk about objects having essences and to worry about whether or not something with essence A could be causally related to something with essence B. Today we don't believe in such essences anymore; we decide questions of causation in terms of the relationships among objects and events. We don't get physicists wondering if electrical current really has the right sort of essence to create a magnetic field; we judge the causality in terms of certain sorts of associations between the two things.

> A "MODERN" VIEW OF CAUSATION

Critics might agree that we don't share the same view of causation held by the interactionists and parallelists of several centuries ago. Nonetheless, they'd say, it is the dualists who create problems of causation between mind and body by insisting that the mind is so much unlike the body; it's the very extreme characterization of mind as nonphysical that still raises legitimate questions as to how mind and body could be causally related.   ⚙

Minds and Machines

In the story, "Strange Behavior," the narrator expresses a dualist position: However sophisticated the behavior/functioning of the Gammas and their robots may be, the Gammas and their robots do not have minds: They lack conscious mental events, such as feelings of the pain or experiences of the image.

What would our three materialists say about whether or not the Gammas and the robots have minds?

	Gammas: Mind?	Robots: Mind?
Behaviorist:	Yes	Yes
Functionalist	Yes	Yes
Identity Theorist	No	No

The responses of the behaviorists and functionalists should be pretty obvious from our discussion: They would say that both the Gammas and their robots have minds, since having a mind is just a matter of behaving/functioning in a certain way. These materialists would likely share Mr. A's bemusement at the dualist insistence that the "something else," which produces "no overt effects that could not occur without it," makes "all the difference in the world."

The identity theorists would say no in both cases: Neither the robots nor the Gammas have the physical structures that constitute mind. This may seem more obvious in the case of the robots than the Gammas. After all, the story does indicate that the Gammas have brains. However, if we accept the statements of the Gammas that they do not have such internal events as images and feelings, then, even though the Gammas have brains, they do not have those sorts of brain states that would qualify them as having minds according to the identity theory.

There are a couple of points in the story that deserve clarification. One has to do with the attitude of the dualist narrator toward the "mindless" Gammas:

⚙   The CD, Ch. 6, *Dualism Revisited*, reviews the main points in this section.

I often wonder about our future relations with the Gammas . . . the issues here will be strictly practical. There can be no question of extending moral rights to mindless, unfeeling creatures, whether they are made of metal or protoplasm.

A dualist narrator wouldn't have to take this extreme a position. The dualist could have at least as much respect for the Gammas as she might have for something wondrous in nature or for some beautifully complicated and successful type of machine. Perhaps a dualist who spent time among the Gammas would fall into thinking of them as creatures with minds and would have to keep reminding herself that they were mindless. But there's no doubt that a being's capacity to feel is an important element in assigning it moral rights: This is why it's plausible to talk about the rights of animals, but not the rights of plants and rocks. If it was believed that the Gammas did not have feelings, it is doubtful the Gammas would be accorded full moral rights—assuming they were accorded any moral rights at all.

MINDS AND MORAL RIGHTS

Since the behaviorists and functionalists would see the Gammas and the robots as having feelings (since feelings are either just behavior and dispositions to behave or any sort of internal features that cause pain behavior), presumably they'd be more inclined to ascribe moral rights to the Gammas and their robots.

A number of futurists and sci-fi writers seem to see themselves as advanced crusaders for the rights of the enormously sophisticated robots they foresee sharing the future with us. But how we treat these robots in the future will depend on what theory of mind we accept and what related facts we believe to be true of the robots.

If our descendants favor a functionalist-type view of mind, then the only facts relevant to according robots moral rights will be how they compare to us in functioning. If our descendants favor a dualist view of mind, then the relevant facts will be whether or not the robots have feelings and the other "stuff" of consciousness.

ROBOTS AND MORAL RIGHTS

Of course, it's entirely possible that these issues won't be resolved among our descendants, and society will be divided among at least these three possible positions regarding the (let's assume) very human-like robots:

a. Functionalists who believe that of course these sophisticatedly functioning robots have minds and should have full moral rights.
b. Dualists who believe that these sophisticated robots have developed nonphysical consciousness in addition to all their physical properties and so should have full moral rights.

c. Dualists who believe that the robots have not developed nonphysical consciousness in addition to their physical properties and so should not have full moral rights.

One can imagine a partial social compromise in which there are laws governing the treatment of robots, laws that can be agreed to either on the basis of the robots' moral rights or on the basis that they are an important societal resource that must be protected and optimized. But this compromise would only be partial given the division of positions noted above. There could be fierce right-to-life, abuse, and discrimination issues raging— in other words, the more things change, the more they stay the same.

Of course, living among, and interacting with, robots—especially if they became very human-like and developed a great deal of autonomy—might change our moral views. Even if we didn't believe they had feelings in our sense, proximity and interdependence might lead us to accord them the equivalent of moral rights. They might even demand this as a condition of continuing to help us.

The idea that **we might not know if future robots had consciousness** may seem odd in light of "Strange Behavior." In that story, it is through questioning the Gammas that the Earth people learn that the Gammas don't have minds. Couldn't we learn if future robots have minds by questioning them in the same way?

There are problems here that the story glosses over in order to dramatize other points. It's not just that a robot might say it wasn't conscious when it was or vice versa. The deeper issue is connected with how the robot would learn language. Even today, when robotics is at an elementary level, scientists—especially the Japanese—are working at having robots mimic human facial expressions and feeling-like language. The idea is that if robots are to be used extensively in society (the Japanese are thinking they might eventually help with elder care, for example), people are going to have to feel comfortable with them. If robots are developed to use feeling language before they have feelings (this on a dualist view), how would the arrival of real feelings be noticed?

ROBOTS AND LANGUAGE LEARNING

Even that doesn't get at the real problem. Robots sufficiently complex and autonomous to be candidates for moral rights might well learn language from others the way children do now. They would learn to talk about their internal states in the same language we use, whether or not those states are the same as ours. The robot would learn to use the expression "feeling of pain" to refer to the signal that went off within it when it suffered damage, a signal that would cause behavior aimed at getting away from the source of the damage and getting repair help. Imagining "something round and orange" would be to call up those same processes that normally went on when it detected something round and orange. It's not clear we could ever tell the difference between a robot like this and a robot with "real" pains and images.   ❀

Life After Death

In "Life After Life" Charlie survives the death of his body as a disembodied soul. The word, "soul," like the related term "spirit," has a familiar metaphorical usage having to do with deep feeling or vivacity, as in "he has a lot of soul" and "I like her spirit." We're not concerned with this usage, but rather the meaning of soul as it relates to life after death.

In this respect, the word "soul" means "a nonphysical mind that survives the death of the body." To claim that a person has a soul is simply to make such claims about the mind; it is not to claim that the person has a mind plus some other thing.

Of the positions we've considered, only substance dualism is compatible with belief in the existence of a soul. All materialists and property dualists would deny the existence of the soul. For the materialist, there is no nonphysical mind. For the property dualist, there are nonphysical mental properties, but these depend on, and could not survive without, the physical brain.

The belief that the mind survives the death of the body is often, though not always, linked to religious beliefs. Some who believe in an afterlife claim that people have had experiences that are most reasonably interpreted as contacts with disembodied spirits. Some claim that people occasionally have what are most reasonably interpreted as memories of a past life; thus, the mind existed before the

FOR AND AGAINST MIND SURVIVING DEATH

birth of the present body and will probably live after the death of the present body. Some claim the "white light" experiences reported by people who have been near death are most reasonably interpreted as contacts with an afterlife. Of course, there are many who doubt that there is an afterlife and are critical of the arguments in favor of it: They claim that there is no persuasive evidence of the existence of a God who will preserve the mind after death. They claim that supposed contacts with spirits and supposed memories of a previous life and supposed glimpses of an afterlife are most

❀   The CD, Ch. 6, *Minds and Machines,* discusses the above issues in the context of a march for robots' rights.

reasonably explained naturalistically. They claim that there is evidence that the mind, if not identical with the brain, is dependent on the brain and will cease to function when the brain ceases to function. These are ongoing debates of considerable complexity, and we shall not attempt to deal with them here.

Only a substance dualist can consistently believe in the existence of a soul. Does that mean that only a substance dualist can consistently believe in life after death? The answer is no.

Throughout history, many religious polemicists have equated the terms "materialist" and "atheist"; however, while these beliefs have usually gone together, they are not strictly speaking equivalent. As is illustrated by the Gammas in "Strange Behavior," a materialist could believe in a physical God. Materialism can also be reconciled with a belief in life after death,

MATERIALISM AND LIFE AFTER DEATH in the sense that the physical body, with its mental characteristics, could be resurrected at some future date. Here the person wouldn't be surviving the death of the body. Rather the body/physical mind would die (be broken down into chemical substances) and then the body/ physical mind would be reassembled—and thus start existing again—at some future date. A property dualist could presumably hold a similar belief, imagining that the nonphysical properties of mind would reappear when the brain was resurrected.

The hope for life after death does persist among some non-religious materialists. "Cryogenics" is one example: The idea here is that you freeze and store dead bodies in the hope/belief that some time in the future hu-

CRYOGENICS AND CLONING mans will be technologically capable of thawing, reviving, treating and improving the bodies in ways that will allow the once-dead people to live many more years. Cloning seems to offer a similar sort of promise, where storing one's DNA would allow one to be recreated in the future. Those who live in the future when cloning has been perfected might be able to keep recreating themselves as the current self is damaged or begins to wear out. (The Schwarzenegger movie, *The Sixth Day,* deals with this sort of cloning.) There are even fantasies of one day transfering individual human minds into computers or robots, extending the life of those minds indefinitely.

Whether you believe such visions are likely to be realized one day or are pure fantasy, there's one philosophical issue worth considering as you survey these various visions: the issue of personal identity.

The important distinction is one we have already made in connection with the identity theory: that between identity and exact similiarity. The

hope of life after death is presumably the hope that *I* will survive, not that something a lot like me will survive. The idea of the soul surviving death is that the same mind that I have identified with all these years will keep on going after my body has ceased to exist. The idea of materialist resurrection—whether by God or your cryogenics team—is that the same body/brain I have identified with all these years will begin functioning again.

If, like Charlie, you found yourself floating around, viewing your body on the floor (and this went on long enough to convince you it wasn't a dream or hallucination), you would feel *you* had survived death (even if, in Charlie's case, in a diminished form.) If you had a heart attack and then found out a few days later (through witnesses you trusted) that you had been brain dead for twelve hours, but thanks to an experimental technique developed at the hospital where you were taken, the doctors were able to get your brain and body refunctioning with only minor brain impairment, you would feel that you had survived.

But consider the following scenario: After you are revived through the experimental procedure above, you are congratulated on your recovery by a cloned copy of yourself in the next bed. It turns out that the hospital was also doing advanced work in cloning, and your spouse and your boss, fearful the revival procedure wouldn't be successful, ordered the hospital to clone a copy of you. You express gratitude that the revival procedure did work and they wouldn't be needing the clone. But it turns out that your wife and boss have conferred and since the clone is as much you as you are—except that it is not at all impaired—they have decided to take the clone instead of you.

Would you say, fine, you understood? Or would you protest that the clone is not you, just a copy of you, and that they should care about you, not the clone; that it was with you, not him or her, that the marriage and employment contracts were made?

Presumably you would make the latter response. And that response would be based on the claim that the clone isn't really you, but a copy of you—isn't (identical with) you, but a person exactly similar to you.

Such reflections remove a lot of the comfort that fantasies of life after death through cloning might bring. Initially living again through cloning seems a lot like living again through resurrection: First you're alive, then you're dead, then you're alive again. But the similarity blinds us to the fact that there is a fundamental difference between the two "you's" in these cases. Suppose you were cloned while alive and then were about to be killed, knowing the clone would go on. I don't think you would find the traditional comfort in this that the idea of life after death is supposed to bring.

Having your mental processes copied and put in a computer which then "runs" your program isn't resurrection either. It would be different, of course, if your actual soul began to inhabit the robot or if your own physical brain were somehow attached to the computer; however, this is not what's envisioned in such fantasies. (One reason it's easy to gloss over the identity/exact similarity issue in such fantasies is that the details are left vague.)

I don't want to overstate the point. There are bound to be borderline cases where it is difficult to decide if it is the "same" person existing before and after certain transformations. Also it wouldn't necessarily be irrational to prefer having a copy of you survive your death than having nothing survive. (And it certainly wouldn't be irrational for others to prefer to have a copy of you rather than nothing at all.) The question is whether or not the comfort to be derived from traditional concepts of life after death really makes sense in some of these more modern life-after-death scenarios. You might find it interesting to consider that question as you encounter such scenarios in movies, TV, and books. 🌐

Souls

For substance dualists who believe the soul survives the death of the body, questions arise about the nature and capacities of a soul that's separated from the body. **What would survival as a disembodied soul be like?** What kind of perceptions would such a soul have, what kind of relations with physical objects? How could such a soul communicate with other souls or, for that matter, with God? Could survival as a disembodied soul be any fun? Charlie, in "Life After Life," finds his disembodied existence to be "hell." Is this because he does not have his mind on higher things? Or is that the way such an existence would inevitably be?

We could not even begin a general discussion of such questions without also introducing the various religious beliefs to which one's answers are so often linked. This we shall not do. Instead, we shall simply consider the kind of rational scrutiny one might bring to bear on the subject of what survival as a disembodied soul might be like. Of course, if any topic tempts people toward mystical pronouncements, the concept of an afterlife is it. Ask someone how disembodied souls might communicate and the reply is likely to be "in some mysterious way that we can't even begin to fathom." Although such a response cannot be dismissed as nonsense, one could be forgiven for thinking of it as a glib device to avoid serious thinking. Even if

🌐 The CD, Ch. 6, *Life After Death*, reviews some conceptions of life after death.

we don't pretend to be able to comprehend all the possibilities of an after-life, it would not seem overly presumptuous to suppose that we can determine some impossibilities.

Let us examine, as examples, two general statements implied by "Life After Life":

1. A Disembodied Soul Would Have Impressions of Sight and Sound But Would Not Have Impressions of Touch and Taste.

Many people would be inclined to believe this statement. In part, this inclination may result from a more explicit awareness of the role played by the sense organs in our perceptions of taste and touch than in perceptions of sight and sound. However, it seems that our perceptions of sight and sound are the effects of light rays and sound waves impinging on the eyes and ears. If, indeed, all our perceptions are the effects of the world on our sense organs, is it reasonable to assume that a disembodied soul would have only limited sensory impressions, as opposed to either the full range of them or none at all?

Still, one might claim that the (image of the) body has an important orientation function with respect to taste and touch that it does not have with respect to sight and sound. I need the impression of a hand to show me what I am feeling; I do not need the impression of eyes to show me what I am seeing. At the very least, sensations of touch and taste would be confusing to a disembodied soul in a way that sensations of sight and sound would not be. If one assumes a benign deity or some principle having to do with the survival of the fittest souls, one might go on to argue that disembodied souls would not have the confusing impressions of touch and taste. But is it really impossible to conceive of some way in which a disembodied soul might receive impressions of taste and touch without confusion? Consider the following supposition: Whenever the disembodied soul had the kind of visual impressions it once had when it put its nose up against some object (object in the center of the visual field, close up), it would experience tactile sensations of that object. Could not the soul thus receive impressions of touch without confusion? Is there something nonsensical about this supposition? Perhaps taste might work in the same way, though the combination of touch and taste might be awkward—if, for example, the soul had to taste whatever it felt.

2. A Disembodied Soul Could, at Best, Communicate With Other Souls by a Kind of Quasi-Verbal "Mental Telepathy."

"Life After Life" makes the following suppositions: that dualism is true; that no mind could directly perceive another mind; that life after death is a natural, rather than a supernatural, phenomenon; that a disembodied soul would have normal visual and auditory perception of our world; that a disembodied soul would not interact with any physical objects. Of course, it is not claimed that such suppositions are true, nor that this combination of suppositions is even coherent. But, given these suppositions, communication between disembodied souls by a kind of quasi-verbal mental telepathy is the only kind of communication that I can imagine without contradicting one of the suppositions. Even such "mental telepathy" may be inconsistent with the other suppositions. But assuming all these circumstances, an afterlife would seem to be a rather dismal state, even if one were not as shallow an individual as Charlie. Perhaps you can do better than this. Perhaps my judgments are only indicative of some triviality and lack of imagination on my part.

Many theists, of course, believe that after the death of the body, the soul joins God and other souls in a community of spirits that either goes on forever or lasts until a time when all bodies will be resurrected. Can one make sense out of this supposition of a community of souls?

GOD AND A COMMUNITY OF SOULS

One suggestion (borrowed, in part, from a philosophy called "idealism"*) would be that after death, God links these bodiless human souls and Himself together through something analogous to coordinated dreams. God would present these souls with the kind of images they would have if they lived together in some magnificent physical world. Each soul would receive sensory images that represent other souls: It would seem as if every other soul had some sort of body and could gesture, talk, and so forth. This suggestion may seem a bit too "earthly" for some theological tastes, and it might be offensive in its implication of an image body for God. Still, one might be able to work out something like this along more "spiritual" lines. In any case, this conception of the afterlife would be "other-worldly" in the sense that it is hard to imagine experiencing simultaneously this community of souls and our world.

---

* You may have noticed earlier that in opposing the positions, "everything is physical, including the mind" (materialism) and "there are physical bodies and nonphysical minds" (dualism) we left out another possible position: "everything is nonphysical, including objects." This latter position is called "idealism" and holds that nothing exists but minds and perceptions. If you and I are sitting together eating, we're both getting similar visual impressions of the room, the table, and the food, as well as similar taste sensations. Only there's no room, no table, and no food out there—just our coordinated impressions of them. How does the coordination take place? The usual explanation is that the coordination is done by God or results from the fact that we are all aspects of the same world mind. The view that everything is nonphysical was popular in the nineteenth century, but has few adherents today.

Questions and Exercises

1. a. What is dualism?
   b. What is the difference between interactionism and parallelism?
   c. Give the reasoning behind being an interactionist.
   d. What reasons would a parallelist give for believing interactionism is false?
2. a. What is materialism?
   b. What is behaviorism? What are some problems with this theory?
   c. What is the identity theory? What are some problems with this theory?
   d. What is functionalism? What are some problems with this theory?
3. Name some modifications many current dualists have made to that theory.
4. What factors would one have to consider in deciding whether or not supersophisticated robots were entitled to moral rights?
5. What would be some problems with the idea of quizzing robots to determine whether or not they had minds?
6. Explain how a materialist could believe in life after death; give some examples of what would count as life after death for a materialist.
7. If some person in the future were to seek life after death through cloning, what personal identity issues would this raise?
8. Why does it seem plausible to assume that a disembodied soul would have sensations of sight and sound, but not taste and touch? What could be said against this assumption? ✺

✺   The CD, Ch. 6, *Rockin' Review: I Can't Decide What Makes Up My Mind,* offers a musical review of the various theories of mind.

7

Appearance and Reality

Fiction: The Fantasy Machine

Orange yellow bright red flashing yellow pulsing . . .

Have a seat there, if you will, Mr. Fuentes. From here you get a clear view of the operating room and of all our special equipment. The woman on the table is . . . uh . . . let's just call her Ms. C. Like you, she has a terminal illness that has not impaired the brain. Like you, she has no living family to complicate our security precautions or the legal intricacies of our arrangements. She's a nice person—comes from southern California, just as you do. The two of you are somewhat different in temperament, but I'm sure you would have liked one another.

Right now, Ms. C is being programmed with the fantasy of her choice. We're sure that some patients would volunteer for our project out of a desire to help others through helping science. But it is so much nicer that we're able to offer them something in return, don't you agree? In any case, Ms. C is now experiencing her selected fantasy, and I can assure you that she is happier than either of us could imagine. You'll notice that we are keeping a careful eye on things. The physicians and technicians are monitoring the Fantasy Machine to make certain that nothing goes wrong.

Before the fantasy comes the research part of the operation—which, of course, is the real purpose of our project. With the patient anesthetized,

---

The CD, Ch. 7, *The Fantasy Machine*, contains animation exercises related to this story.

but conscious, the upper part of the skull is removed—you're not getting nauseated, are you? I thought not. You knew roughly what to expect, and you've had surgery before. Anyway, with the skull removed, we begin an experiment on the brain that lasts an absolute maximum of four hours per patient. Years ago such experiments were concerned with, oh, monitoring the subject's moods or attempting to evoke a single, complex mental image. We are much more advanced than that now. But still, there is so much more to learn about the mind.

In Ms. C's case, the project was conducted as follows: Prior to the operation, Ms. C made a list of thirty vivid memory impressions. Actually, she listed them twice. One was a chronological list: She gave that one to us so we and the computer would know what the memory impressions would be. On a second piece of paper, she listed these same impressions in a different sequence that she had spent some time memorizing: This was the sequence in which she would recollect the memories on the operating table. That second list was sealed in an envelope and put in the vault.

Once on the operating table, Ms. C recollected the first five memories and described them aloud into a microphone. Her descriptions were fed into the computer and correlated with the brain patterns recorded by the brain-probing mechanisms. Then, without making any verbal reports, Ms. C recollected the other twenty-five memory impressions, concentrating on each for a minute to distinguish them quite definitely from any random thoughts. It was up to the computer to deliver a properly ordered list of her memory impressions. And you know what? The list was ninety-two percent accurate. Quite amazing, don't you agree?

In your case I shall attempt to conduct a complete, coherent conversation with you, lasting a full hour, without either of us overtly "speaking" to the other. First, we shall conduct a brief conversation in the normal way, while the computer gets an accurate reading of the relevant patterns in your brain. Then you will think a sentence that the computer will attempt to interpret from your brain activity; its interpretation will come to me on a printout sheet in that booth over there. I will formulate a reply that will be fed into the computer and translated into brain stimulation. If this works as it should, you will get the impression of hearing me speak, just as you might hear some figure speaking in your dreams. You will then think a response to my statement, and so on. After the experiment is over, we shall compare notes. And after that will come your fantasy. But before we get to the selection of your fantasy, are there any questions?

No, there's no chance of that. The anesthetization process we use takes care of all pain and all anxiety. By the way, if you are at all worried about trickery on our part, don't be. There are strict governmental regulations and supervisory procedures in effect here. We are not mad scientists or brainwashers or any such thing. We are engaged in important scientific research that is humane in its intent and positively beneficent in its treatment of the patients. True, we are engaged in a politically sensitive area of research, which is the reason for the secrecy. But every person here has been screened by the government for mental stability, high moral standards, scientific expertise, and whatnot.

Furthermore, at each operation there must be two scientifically competent outside observers, who are rotated constantly to keep them free of influence by any overzealous researchers here. As you will recall, the government agent who gave you your final screening had credentials from another agency, one you have known of all your life. There is no question of malice or trickery here, and absolutely no question of unfortunate mistakes.

Now—shall we get to the good part? The fantasies. I enjoy so much discussing the fantasies with the patients, anticipating their decisions, enjoying secondhand their fun. It is a bit like watching a friend select a gift from a pile of Christmas packages, knowing one's turn will come next. Only I cannot be sure that my turn will come. I can only hope. If I should be run over by a truck or develop a brain disease or die suddenly in my bed, then I would miss out. You're very lucky, Mr. Fuentes.

> Terrible stench terrible thirst so hot burning my skin got to stop it want to get away can't move can't stop it so hot suffocating can't breathe hot things tearing at my skin burning oh it's horrible loud screaming hurts can't stand it stop oh please stop . . .

Some day, I'm sure, we'll have a large selection of fantasies, and the patients will pore over a catalogue before making their decisions. At the moment, we have only a few fantasies—most with male and female versions. At the our current stage of technology, they are tremendously difficult and costly to produce. However, I shouldn't put too much emphasis on "only." You would be thrilled with any one of them, I can assure you. To be truthful, I don't know that any particular fantasy would make you happier than the others, since we program you to love whichever fantasy is used. But having a selection of fantasies does seem to be important to the patients and does help us recruit participants.

Summaries of the fantasies make them sound simple, but the experiences are rich and profound beyond the wildest expectations of those tinkering with virtual reality machines. We are talking about a coordinated experience, programmed directly to the brain, stimulating the areas associated with the five senses, with pleasure, and with one's sense of time. Your fantasy will seem as real to you as anything you've experienced in real life.

How long do the fantasies take? Only an hour—but don't worry about that. We alter your sense of time so that the fantasy seems to last for something like four weeks. And we program you to be completely satisfied with your experience.

Inducing the fantasy is a straightforward matter, now that we've developed the Fantasy Machine. After the brain research experiment I've described is completed, we simply bid you *bon voyage*, connect your brain to the Fantasy Machine, push the button for the fantasy you've selected, and give you the time of your life. When the fantasy is over, that's it for you, of course, but there is no intimation of what is to come—no pain, no fear—simply the conclusion of a delightful story. Could one conceive of a better way to complete one's life? I doubt it very much.

Now. Shall I describe the fantasies to you? Each of them has a long serial number and some horribly long name invented by some bureaucrat with no imagination. The staff here is a bit more lively and, if you will allow me, I shall simply use the names they have given the fantasies. All right?

First, there's the Nirvana fantasy. That was the earliest one we developed, and it's the simplest in conception, though quite intricate in detail. It is what you might call a "light show," to use a somewhat out-of-date phrase. It's also a sound, taste, touch, and scent show. Lovely music, beautiful, gently swirling colors, soft touches, delicious tastes and fragrances. It is amazing how many people still select it. I suspect that as life draws to a close, many people have had too much of "plot" and simply want beauty.

Then there are the Romance fantasies. In your case, you would be living in a grand house on the French Rivera where you enjoy racing your stable of fast sports cars—that is, when you're not on your yacht or schooner. You would have relations with several gorgeous women, but you would be a cynic about love—at least, until you meet the mysterious beauty who claims she's in danger and needs your help.

The female version takes place in Paris in the spring. There are museums and shopping and fabulous restaurants. There's the invitation to the party at the beautiful country estate owned by the gorgeous, elegant young prince who falls in love with you at first sight. Um. I'm certainly going to be tempted by that one when my time comes. The life of a scientist can be so restricting and the idea of just letting oneself . . . but, sorry. I'm rambling. Where was I?

Yes. Besides the Nirvana and Romance fantasies, there's the Olympic one. How would you like to be a champion ski jumper—can't you just imagine the thrill of soaring through the crisp air against the backdrop of the Swiss Alps? In this fantasy you dream of being in the Olympics, train your young body hard (though not so hard it actually hurts), and finally win the gold! We've had a lot of takers, both male and female, on that one. Though, to be honest, I'm not sure whether the main attraction is the sports glory or all the wild partying that comes after the competition.

You're a teacher, I know, and perhaps you'd like an intricate mystery. We have two of those, roughly patterned after Agatha Christie stories. How would you, as Hercule Poirot, like to use your "little gray cells" to discover who killed the long-lost heir who appeared suddenly and, just as suddenly, was killed in a locked room in a house containing twenty larcenous relatives? What? Well, yes, I suppose it is a bit dated. The people in our production department want to do something more in line with contemporary tastes—wise-crackin' buddy-detectives, lots of shooting and car chases, lots of bars and beers—and, I suppose, flatulence jokes. Oh, dear. I'm afraid I'm too old-fashioned to appreciate such things.

For scholarly types, we have the Descartes Fantasy, which puts you back in the seventeenth century as the father of modern philosophy. You sit in your study, then go to bed and dream you're in your study, then wake and return to your study once again. As you sit at your desk, wearing your heavy dressing gown, warmed by the fire, jotting down your philosophical meditations, you begin to wonder if everything you believe exists might be mere illusion. As you doubt your beliefs, you decide that the very act of doubting proves your existence. You consider the idea of a perfect God and conclude that such a being must exist: a perfect God, lacking nothing, could not lack existence. You decide that a perfect God would not allow you to be deceived in what you perceive, so the room in which you are sitting must truly exist as you perceive it. All this takes place while you are really lying on the operating table! Whoever decided on that fantasy must have had an odd sense of humor, don't you agree? Still you, as Descartes, would be sure you were right. The Church would applaud you, and Gassendi would write you congratulations instead of all those endless objections. It must be nice to feel secure in one's beliefs. One does get so tired of the constant skepticism one confronts.

A little too esoteric for you? Well, think about the others; you have several days to decide. Then you will be where Ms. C is now, and you, rather than she, will be the happiest person on earth. Just look at her. Of course, you can't see what she's experiencing. But take my word for it. It is fantastic.

What? Are you joking? Is this the teacher coming out, or did the mention of Descartes get you going? All right, I'll play along. But, in fact, the answer to your question is quite simple.

No, of course we don't literally see the contents of Ms. C's mind. But then the doctor doesn't see the virus causing a disease either. She knows it's there because of the symptoms. Do you play the skeptic with your doctor? Of course not. No sensible person would. And do you doubt the existence of atoms because you don't see them? No.

But to get quite specific. When we program a fantasy, we are causing certain observable processes in the brain. We know what mental experiences are produced by these brain processes, because we have correlated them with the patient's reports of his or her mental experiences. We have checked these correlations over and over during our experiments with hundreds of patients. And we double-check the relevant correlations with each patient before we induce the fantasy. Of course, the computer is not one hundred percent accurate, as in the listing of Ms. C's memory experiences. But that was new ground. The fantasies are contrived so that they need involve only very limited and familiar areas in the brain. Certainly, you could imagine that Ms. C is having an experience quite unlike the one in the fantasy. In the same way, you could imagine that the normal patient under anesthesia is in great pain. But would you take such a hypothesis seriously? Of course not . . . Ah, I see you were just teasing me . . . No, it's quite all right. I enjoy such discussions very much.

Look, what do you say we continue this chat in my office? They're almost finished here, and they won't be needing me anymore. There are only twelve minutes left on the fantasy, though to Ms. C that will seem nearly a week. Which one did she pick? The Nirvana Fantasy. Another week of her ecstatic light show to go. Then it will end, of course. But with all that Ms. C has experienced, I can assure you that she will have no regrets.

Help me help me please can't stand it orange yellow too bright flashing burning my eyes hurting me burning can't move make it stop oh please make it stop.

Fiction: Why Don't You Just Wake Up?

I'm in the living room at home, and Dad's there, all serious, saying, "John, where's your mind these days—you've got to wake up," and it seems like I wake up, and I'm at my desk at home. I straighten up and yawn and pick up my history book, and just then Mom comes in, saying, "Johnny, you're just not concentrating—you've got to wake up," and again it seems like I wake up, and I'm sitting in class. I look around, and Teresa's sitting next to me looking all upset, saying, "John, what's with you these days—why don't you just wake up," and I think I wake up, and I'm lying in bed in my dorm room.

It was all dreams within dreams within dreams, and what I thought was waking was just more dreaming. I lie in my dorm bed and wonder who is going to come in next and wake me from this, only no one comes in, and the digital clock blinks slowly toward seven-thirty, and I guess this must be real.

It doesn't seem real, though. Nothing does these days. Everything that happens seems sort of vague somehow and out of focus and not all that important. I have trouble concentrating—taking things seriously—and everybody's on my case. That's the reason, I think, for all those dreams about dreaming and waking.

One reason, anyway. The other is that philosophy class and all that talk about Descartes and whether all reality could be a dream. That's not helping much either.

I'm late picking up Teresa again, and she's had to wait, and there won't be time for us to have coffee together. She gives me that exasperated look I see a lot these days, and we walk across campus without talking. Finally, she says:

"I don't know why I took that stupid philosophy class. I can't wait 'til it's over."

I know it's not really the class she's annoyed at. It's me and the way I've been lately. I know I should say something nice. But I'm feeling pushed and kind of cranky.

"I like the class," I say, to be contrary.

"You do not."

"I do. It's kind of interesting."

"Interesting. Right. Like I really want to sit around all day wondering whether I'm dreaming everything in the world."

"Maybe you are."

 The CD, Ch. 7, *Why Don't You Just Wake Up?*, contains animation and exercises related to this story.

"Sure." She shakes her head. "That's so stupid."

"Just because you say 'stupid' doesn't make it wrong. How do you know you aren't just dreaming this all up?"

She glares at me, but her eyes begin to dart the way they always do when she's thinking hard. She's not in the mood for this, but I've gotten her mad.

"Because . . . I know what dreams look like. They're all hazy. Not like the world looks now."

"You mean what you can see of it through the smog."

"Funny."

I know what she means, though. A few weeks back I would have said that being awake looked a lot different from dreaming. But the guy in class is right. That's just a matter of how things look. It doesn't prove how things are.

"Look," I say, "nobody's denying that what we call 'dreaming' looks different from what we call 'being awake.' But is it really different? Maybe 'being awake' is just a different kind of dream."

"Yeah, well, if I'm making all this up, how come we're talking about something I don't want to talk about?"

"Because you're not in control of this dream any more than you are your dreams at night. It's your unconscious doing it."

"This is so much bullsh—"

"Why?"

"It's crazy. You're standing here trying to convince me that everything is my dream while you know you're real. That doesn't make any sense."

"Yeah, it does. I'm saying you can't know that I really exist, and I can't know that you . . ."

I stop suddenly, because something scary is happening. It's like a ripple moving through the whole world, coming from the horizon to my left, but moving fast as if the world is really much smaller than it appears. And where the ripple is, everything becomes elongated and out of focus. The ripple passes over Teresa, distorting her for a moment, like a fun house mirror. Then it's gone, and everything's back to normal.

"John, are you okay?" says Teresa, giving me a worried look. "You look white as a sheet."

"I don't know. I just got the weirdest feeling. I guess I'm okay."

"John, are you on something?"

"No. I told you. Really."

She looks at me for a moment and decides I'm telling the truth.

"Come on," she says, taking my hand. "The last thing you need right now is philosophy class. Let's go get something to eat and then sit in the sun for a while. I bet you'll feel better."

"Hey, Ter, I'm sorry I'm being such a jerk. I . . ."

"Don't worry about it, John. It's okay. Come on."

Later I do feel better. I feel like things are almost back to normal. But my night is full of dreams within dreams, and the next day the world seems full of unreality once again. And then, at midday, the world ripples again.

I go to the university health service, and of course the doctor thinks it's drugs, and we go round and round on that until I insist he test me and then he begins to believe I'm not lying. He becomes nicer then, and more concerned, and schedules some tests and an appointment with a specialist he'd like me to see, though he's "sure it's nothing, just stress."

Walking across campus, I see the world ripple again and suddenly I realize what it all looks like. It's like when you are watching a movie in class, and the screen on which the movie is showing twists, distorting the image, and you're aware that it wasn't a world in front of you at all, but just an illusion on a not-very-large piece of material. I put my arm out to feel the ripple, only my arm ripples too because it's part of the movie.

I don't know what's happening, and I'm afraid. At night I keep myself from sleeping because the idea of dreaming is something I suddenly find disturbing. In the morning I'm exhausted, but I stumble off to class because I want something to divert my attention; however, once there I have trouble paying attention. I guess the professor must have asked me something I didn't hear because I feel Teresa nudging me in the ribs, and hear her say, "Come on, John, wake up."

I look up then at the professor standing behind his lectern, and just above and in back of him a dark line seems to appear in the wall. It looks like the slow fissure of an earthquake, except that the edges fold back against the surface of the wall like the edges of torn paper, and I see that behind the tearing there is nothing at all, just darkness. Then I see that the tear isn't in the wall at all but in my field of vision because as it reaches the professor he begins to split apart and then the lectern and then the head of the student in the front row. On both sides of the tear, the world distorts and folds and collapses. The fissure moves downward through the students and then, I see as I glance down, through my own body. No one is moving or screaming—they take no more notice than movie characters on a torn movie screen would. In a panic I reach out and touch Teresa, then watch as she and my hand distort, as everything, absolutely everything, falls away.

******

It is night. It's always night. A night without stars, without anything—just an infinite emptiness falling away on every side. And so I float, an invisible being in a nonexistent world.

How long have I been like this? I don't know. It feels like years, but that's just a feeling because there is nothing here by which to mark the time.

I try to remember how it was, but my memories are such pale things, and they grow more pale as time drags on.

I would pray, but there is nothing to pray to. And so I hope, for hope is all I have: that one day, as inexplicably as once I did, I will begin to dream the world again.

Questions

1. In "The Fantasy Machine," the narrator admits that she does not have firsthand knowledge of the experiences of her experimental patients. However, she claims to have strong indirect evidence of the experiences they are having. What is this evidence? What is the reasoning of the narrator here? You might want to answer this question in two steps:
    a. On what evidence does the narrator rely in determining the experiences had by patients who are awake?
    b. On what evidence does the narrator rely in determining the experiences had by patients who are not awake?
2. Presumably, you believe that you often know what others are thinking and feeling. How do you know this? What is your reasoning on this matter? How does it compare to the reasoning of the narrator in "The Fantasy Machine"?
3. When patients in "The Fantasy Machine" are being programmed with a fantasy, they believe they are experiencing the real world. Is there some way that the patients could find out that what they are experiencing is illusion? Can you know that what you are now experiencing is not a programmed illusion? If so, how? If not, why not?
4. According to the story "Why Don't You Just Wake Up?" which of the following are real and which illusion?
    a. John's father talking to John.
    b. The college campus.
    c. John's feelings of fear.
    d. The exasperated expression on Teresa's face.
    e. Teresa's feelings of annoyance.
    f. Endless darkness.
    g. Teresa's mind.
    h. John's body.
    i. John's mind.

5. Critique the following arguments: This world can't be just my dream because:
   a. What I'm seeing right now looks much more vivid than it does when I am asleep and dreaming.
   b. I can't control what the world is like.
   c. I just asked my friend if I were dreaming this all up and she said, "No."

DISCUSSION

In this chapter we will discuss:
1. Our commonsense beliefs about the world.
2. Grounds for doubting the existence of the external world.
3. Descartes's "cogito" as proof of one's own mind.
4. Whether or not we can prove an external world.

Commonsense Beliefs

"The Fantasy Machine" imagines the following: A secret brain research study seeks volunteers from among terminally ill patients with unimpaired brains. The volunteers have the tops of their skulls removed (painlessly) and have various instruments connected directly to their brains. In the experimental part of the procedure, the instruments interpret brain activity in terms of thoughts, images, and sensations. The experiment begins with something that allows the establishment of certain correlations—between, say, specific memories and brain activity—by coordinating instrument data with the patient's reports. Then the machine tries to interpret from brain activity alone without the patient speaking aloud or describing the memories.

Once the experiment is over, the patient (as a reward) is hooked up to the Fantasy Machine, which programs the brain with a fantasy of the patient's choice, a fantasy that seems as real as anything the patient has experienced in real life.

The story imagines that in a particular case, the scientists have made a horrible mistake. Ms. C is supposed to be experiencing a light show that's also "a sound, taste, touch, and scent show. Lovely music, beautiful, gently swirling colors, soft touches, delicious tastes and fragrances." Instead Ms. C is having a grotesque experience—"terrible stench . . . terrible thirst . . . suffocating . . ."

The narrator in "The Fantasy Machine" admits she has no firsthand knowledge of the mental states of others. Rather, she relies on indirect evidence. She, like most of us, takes it for granted that behavior, particularly the speech behavior of people, when they are awake, is a generally accurate indicator of their mental states. She finds that the patients' verbal reports can be correlated with particular kinds of brain processes. The narrator concludes that these brain processes are accurate indicators of mental states. Consequently, when patients are asleep, the narrator judges their mental states in terms of their brain processes.

Is the narrator reasoning well by our normal standards of reasoning? It seems so. Perhaps she is a bit overconfident. Perhaps she has not carried out enough experiments in the precise correlations between verbal reports and brain states to justify great confidence in her inferences of particular mental states from particular brain states. Perhaps she could be blamed for not taking the degree of care required by the risk involved. But her general reasoning is in line with how we normally reason about the mental states of others.

However, there are skeptics who question the whole inference from the behavior/speech of other people to the mental states of those people. The skeptics point out that we are reasoning from something we experience all the time—physical behavior/speech—to something we have never experienced—the mental states of others. The skeptic says, How do you know other people have any mental states at all? How do you know that other people aren't like the Gammas in "Strange Behavior" who act and talk like humans, but lack actual mental states? Such beings are at least theoretically possible.

The considered response to this skeptical challenge has often been this: "I have a mind, and I exhibit certain kinds of complex physical behavior (including speech). Other creatures who look very much like me exhibit very similar physical behavior. Therefore, (it is very probable that) those other creatures also have minds."

At first glance, this argument may seem quite satisfactory. But skeptics have argued that it is quite weak. The argument claims that, because behavior and mind are associated in one case (my own), it is very probable that behavior and mind are associated in millions of other cases. But this would be analogous to a Gallup poll election prediction based on a "survey" of one voter. It would also be analogous to a lifelong prison inmate's argument that because he lives in a small cell with gray walls, everyone lives in a small cell with gray walls. (Like the prisoner, apparently, one can experience only one's own situation or mind.)

The skeptic could pick another point out of "The Fantasy Machine." The story suggests that the people programmed with the fantasies think they are experiencing real life. The skeptic could ask how we can ever know if what we're experiencing is real life versus the type of illusion mentioned in the story. This point is emphasized in the story with reference to those who select the Descartes tape and confidently "prove" that the world they perceive must be real.

"The Fantasy Machine" uses a familiar sci-fi theme that tends to be referred to as the "brain in the box" or the "brain in the vat." An archetypal version might go like this: Some time in the future, a new genetic disease develops in which five percent of all infants are born with healthy brains but bodies so grotesquely deformed as to make any kind of pleasurable life impossible. Society, being wealthy and technologically advanced, decides to remove the brains of these infants at birth, put the brains into specially designed vats, and program the infants with a satisfying virtual life made up entirely of inner experiences. The question is, How could such children ever know that the worlds they inhabited weren't real?

This same theme is used in the enormously popular movie, *The Matrix,* in which all humans (with bodies and brains intact) are programmed with a totally artificial world (though one resembling life as it had been) by beings who have taken over the planet. In the movie the conditioning wasn't perfect and occasionally someone (like our hero) would wake to find himself lying among a gigantic network of human bodies in the process of being programmed. But it's just as easy to imagine a similar situation in which no one "wakes up."

As we begin to glimpse a future in which science might be able to develop increasingly real virtual reality worlds, themes of appearance and reality have taken on a new importance and appeal. 🌀

The World as a Dream

"Why Don't You Just Wake Up?" suggests a possibility more radical than the idea that the real world might be totally different than the world of my experience. It suggests the possibility that there may be no world "out there" at all, that the world is nothing but my dream. It suggests the possibility that our everyday commonsense beliefs are false.

Presumably you, like virtually everybody else, believe in the existence of the following:

1. Other minds
2. Physical objects
3. Your own mind

🌀 The CD, Ch. 7, *Common Sense Beliefs,* reviews the concepts in this section.

To believe in <u>the existence of a mind</u> is, at a minimum, to believe that there exists a collection of thoughts, images, emotions, and sensations. To believe in <u>the existence of a physical object</u> is to believe in the existence of some such thing as a tree, a hand, a river, a flash of lightning, or a molecule and to believe that such a thing would or could continue to exist if all minds ceased to exist. (In other words, dreams or desires could not exist in the absence of the mind: such things, then, are mental.)

The possibility that the world is a dream challenges some of these commonsense beliefs, but which ones? Imagine that you dream you are a glamorous movie star getting out of your limousine at the Academy Awards, with people cheering you and snapping pictures; then you wake up in your same old bedroom, wearing pajamas or nightgown or underwear, nobody cheering, nobody (we hope) snapping pictures. What has remained constant from dreaming to waking? Very little. The location has changed, the objects have changed, even your body has changed. The one constant has been that the same mind (in some sense) was dreaming and waking. Everything in addition to your mind is often dubbed "the external world."

The skeptic is asking how we know there is an external world. How do we know that we're not just dreaming it up? ❈

Doubting the External World

The possibility that the world is a dream is likely to evoke from us the same response it evoked from Teresa in "Wake Up." "That's so stupid . . . I know what dreams look like. They're all hazy. Not like the world looks now."

All of us constantly distinguish dreams from reality, and we don't find any particular difficulty with this. True, while we are dreaming we can be confused about whether we are dreaming or awake, but when we are really awake, it's obvious that we are.

How do we distinguish dreams from reality? In both dreams and waking life, we seem to see, hear, touch, taste, and smell things. But in dreams, perhaps, those sensory impressions are not as vivid and persistent as in waking life. More strikingly, the experiences of waking life are more consistent from episode to episode. In a series of dream episodes, one may be able to fly, then only able to walk, then not able to move. In a series of waking experiences, one's abilities to act are more fixed. In waking life, impressions of a burning building are followed by a familiar set of long-term impressions that continue through subsequent episodes: fire engines,

---

❈   The CD, Ch. 7, *Dreams and Reality*, contains animation and discussion re the distinctions between dream and reality.

smoking ashes, cold ashes, clearing away debris, rebuilding. Such need not be the case when one merely dreams that a building is burning.

In most cases, then, it seems that we can easily distinguish dreams from reality. Dreams can be distinguished from waking life by their relative haziness and relative inconsistency from episode to episode. However, **consider two meanings of the word "dream":**

1. Dreams are experiences that are hazy and relatively inconsistent.
2. Dreams are experiences that are purely mental and do not represent things existing outside the mind.

THE POSSIBILITY THAT THE WORLD IS A DREAM Perhaps the preceding commonsense view of waking and dreaming indicates that there is no serious problem about determining when we are dreaming in the first sense. But is this sufficient to show that we are not always dreaming in the second sense? "Wake Up" implies no. The story grants our normal distinction between experiences that are hazy and inconsistent and those that are not, but denies this distinction as good evidence for what is only in our minds and what is not. The story issues the following challenge: How do you know that what we experience when we are "awake" isn't as much a product of our minds as what we experience when we are dreaming (in sense 1)? How do we know that reality isn't a dream (in sense 2)?

Consider some other objections to the possibility that the world is just a dream:

QUESTION: How could I perceive images if there were no objects?

REPLY: Your mind could invent them, as in dreams.

QUESTION: How can this chair hold me if it is only an imaginary chair?

REPLY: What is sitting on the chair might be an imaginary body, and, as we know from dreams, imaginary chairs are quite adequate to support imaginary bodies.

QUESTION: If everything I perceive is imaginary, why can't I create a more pleasant world through acts of will?

REPLY: To say that the world consists of mental images is not to say that these images are within your conscious control. You can't control your dreams, but you don't therefore deny that dreams are mental.

QUESTION: How can I be dreaming? Just now, I asked my friend if I was dreaming and she said "No."

REPLY: Maybe you're just dreaming that your friend is here telling you no.

You begin to see what is so insidious about the possibility that one is dreaming everything up. It seems to undercut the evidence against itself by raising the possibility that the evidence is merely illusion.   ✦

Proving My Own Mind

We have seen how the possibility that I might be dreaming challenges my belief in the external world. Is there a comparable problem with the internal world? That is, is there a problem justifying my belief in the existence of my own mind? It seems not, and here we can borrow an argument from Descartes, whose philosophical approach was touched on in the description of the Descartes's fantasy.

Descartes* was a seventeenth-century French philosopher who subjected his basic beliefs to the kind of critical scrutiny in which we have been engaged here. Initially, he decided that there were serious grounds for doubting his belief in physical objects and other minds. But Descartes thought there were no serious grounds for doubting his own existence; he could be absolutely certain that he existed. He said: "I think, therefore I am" or, in Latin, "Cogito ergo sum"; the claim is often referred to as the "cogito." (A similar claim can be found in the fifth-century writings of Saint Augustine.)

DESCARTES'S "COGITO"

This traditional, shorthand formulation of the "cogito" seems to indicate that Descartes was presenting an argument with "I think" as premise and "I exist" as conclusion. In fact, what Descartes argued was that one cannot be in error about one's existence as a thinking being, one's existence as a mind. Descartes noticed that one's belief in one's own mind seemed to be immune to the sorts of challenges or doubts that infect one's other beliefs. "Perhaps I am mistaken in thinking that others think." "Perhaps I am mistaken in thinking that physical objects really exist." "Perhaps I am mistaken in thinking that I think." In the third statement, and the third statement only, the conclusion is reaffirmed in the doubting. The very act of doubting my existence proves it.

The "cogito" can be applied to more specific first-person statements, and a consideration of such statements helps clarify the nature of the "cogito." "I seem to see a chair" appears to be an indubitable statement. One cannot be wrong about seeming-to-see, as opposed to seeing, and seeming-to-see is an experience, a mental state. "I am distressed" appears to be an indubitable statement. My seeming-to-be distressed is necessarily a

---

* Descartes was mentioned in Chapter 3 in connection with the ontological argument and in Chapter 6 in connection with dualism.

✦ The CD, Ch. 7, *Doubting the External World,* distinguishes between solipsism, idealism, and realism.

kind of distress, and distress is a mental state. All statements about my present mental states would seem to be indubitable.

Descartes's "cogito" seems to me to be correct if it is properly restricted in scope, but one should be clear about these restrictions.

Descartes's "cogito" is not a proof to each of us that Descartes existed. To each of us, Descartes is another mind. Your "cogito" could not be a proof to me that you exist, and vice versa. I have no direct experience of your thoughts, and you have no direct experience of mine.

My "cogito" does not prove that I have a particular body or, indeed, any body at all. The body is a physical object, and the existence of physical objects is in question at this point. The "cogito" does not prove that I have a particular past or, in fact, any past at all; that I think does not guarantee the reliability of my memory impressions. Insofar as my proper name, Tom Davis, is linked with a particular physical or mental past, my "cogito" does not prove that Tom Davis exists. Perhaps I am Descartes or Napoleon, and I am merely hallucinating that I am Tom Davis. What the "cogito" does guarantee is that there now exist certain thoughts, images, and sensations that I may define as "my mind."

WHAT THE "COGITO" DOES AND DOESN'T PROVE

Can We Prove an External World?

Having proved the existence of my own mind, can I prove the existence of the external world? There are philosophers who say no. They hold a position called **solipsism, which says that the only thing one can prove exists is one's own self.** The solipsist accepts Descartes's "cogito" but claims that one cannot prove the existence of the external world.

The solipsist argues as follows: It is theoretically possible that everything one has ever experienced has been a total invention of one's mind (as in dreams). Since one can judge things only according to one's experience, and since one cannot get "outside" of one's experience to determine its source, one cannot know whether the experience reflects an external world or whether it is merely an invention of one's mind. One cannot show that an external world is more likely to exist than not to exist.

ARGUMENT OF THE SOLIPSIST

The problem of the external world is a difficult one, and the argument of the solipsist is forceful. Can we satisfactorily answer the solipsist? Can we

---

The CD, Ch. 7, *Proving My Own Mind,* reviews issues related to the cogito; *Rockin' Review: The Solipsist,* expresses that condition musically.

formulate an argument that shows that the existence of an external world of physical objects and other minds is more likely than its absence?*

Before we attempt any kind of proof, let's talk a little about what a proof might involve.

Note that we can't prove everything. If no statements are accepted without proof, it will be impossible to prove anything. For example, consider any statement and call it A. If that statement is not acceptable without proof, then we shall have to form an argument in which A is the conclusion and another statement (or statements) B is the premise. This will show that A is true if B is true, but what is the proof for B? Now we will need another argument in which C is the premise and B is the conclusion. This will show that A is true if B is true, and B is true if C is true. But what is the proof for C? Now we shall have to give an argument for C and so on, ad infinitum. Since this process of proof can never be completed, and A remains doubtful until the process is completed, we shall never prove A. If we are required to prove everything, then we can prove nothing.

WHAT A "PROOF" MIGHT INVOLVE

Any theory must begin with axioms—statements accepted without "proof." In fact, this whole discussion has presupposed an unmentioned axiom: that our fundamental principles of reasoning are reliable—that any contradictory statement is false, that no statement can be both true and false, that certain forms of argument are such that the conclusion follows from the premises, and so forth. This general axiom has been presupposed by the "cogito," by the skeptical argument of the solipsist, and by the very attempt to engage in rational discussion.

Some skeptics, more extreme than the solipsist, have challenged the reliability of our principles of reasoning. They have demanded a proof of the reliability of these principles. Of course, this demand could not be met. Any supposed proof would simply assume its conclusion since, as proof, it would assume the principles of reasoning that have been questioned. What we have here is a choice: Either we assume the reliability of our principles of reasoning and go on reasoning about various matters, or we do not assume this and we treat all statements as mere babble. **Of course, we are assuming the reliability of these principles of reasoning.**

RELIABILITY OF OUR PRINCIPLES OF REASONING

---

*Descartes is of no further help to us. He did offer a proof of an external world, but it is not satisfactory. First Descartes presented the "ontological argument" for the existence of a perfect God. Then he went on to argue that a perfect God would not deceive him by presenting him with appearances that were all illusory. Thus, Descartes's experiences must represent an external world. As is explained in Chapter 2, the ontological argument is fallacious. With it the rest of Descartes's argument collapses.

But is this axiom concerning the reliability of our principles of reasoning "mere assumption"? I am inclined to say emphatically no. These principles of reasoning seem to be "self-evident": One simply "sees" that they are correct.

A second general axiom has been presupposed in this discussion: that appearances do exist now (of a chair, of distress, and so on). One could not argue for this claim without simply assuming the conclusion: Any purported proof would have to assume the existence of appearances. But are there rational grounds for doubting this statement? I would say no. The axiom "that appearances do exist" now seems to me "self-evident."

Employing these two axioms, we have considered and then accepted the "cogito." It seemed that one could not be in error in believing that one's own mind exists. Would it be correct to say that we advanced one step and then were halted by the problem of the external world? To say we "advanced one step" might be misleading. The "cogito" is not a proof of some additional entity not stated in the axioms. The "cogito" simply enabled us to use principles of reasoning to clarify the statement that there are now appearances. For example, we noted that the word "distress" indicates nothing more than a certain kind of appearance. **The statement "I exist as a thinking being" is really equivalent to the statement "There are thoughts," which is equivalent to the statement "There are appearances."**

In a sense, then, at the point at which we confront the problem of the external world, what we have claimed are two general axioms. The solipsist also accepts these axioms. He asks us for a proof of the existence of physical objects and other minds. But, instead of attempting a proof, **why not make the statement "There are physical objects and other minds" an axiom and claim that it is self-evident?**

This possibility, though tempting, is troublesome. At what point should one stop claiming that statements are self-evident axioms and start offering proofs for them? Surely, there is some such point. Many of us would be inclined to scoff if someone claimed that the existence of a benign, omnipotent, omniscient God was self-evident (instead of one requiring faith or proof). And we would howl in disbelief if someone claimed as self-evident the statement that there is life on exactly sixteen other planets. What guidelines should we use in determining which statements are self-evident and which are not?

WHAT MAKES A STATEMENT SELF-EVIDENT?

What we might do is determine what essentially distinguishes our two general axioms from other beliefs that almost no one would be inclined to call self-evident. These characteristics could be used as tests to determine which other statements, if any, qualify as self-evident. It seems that our two general axioms share at least the following essential characteristics:

1. They are believed with the deepest conviction.
2. No conceivable experimental evidence would count against them.
3. It seems unimaginable that they are false.*

Clearly, the statement that there is an omnipotent, omniscient, benign God would be disqualified by the third and second characteristics, if not by the first. Even if one has a deep religious faith, one can imagine there not being such a God, even if one is sure there is such a God, just as one can imagine the floor collapsing, even if one is sure that it will not. One can imagine future experiential evidence that would count against the existence of such a God, for example, an afterlife encounter with a being who is powerful but unable to accomplish a difficult task or with an omnipotent being who acts immorally. Obviously, the statement that there is life on exactly sixteen other planets fails to pass any of these tests.

How does the concept of "external world" stand up to these three conditions of self-evidence? At the very least, the third condition presents a serious problem. The implication of the stories, especially, "Why Don't You Just Wake Up?" is that we can at least imagine there being no external world. If we can imagine there being no external world, then a claim for the self-evidence of the statement "There are physical objects and other minds" would seem weak.

What else could we try?

One approach that won't work is to employ the kind of evidence we use in everyday life to prove that something "really" exists—looking, touching, asking other people, etc. As we have seen, the possibility that we are dreaming undercuts such reality checks by raising the question of whether they too are only a dream.

Similarly there is no way we can somehow peek outside our experience to see if there is something causing it. Whatever we perceive is, or at least could be, only our experience.

What about treating the external world as the most reasonable hypothesis explaining why we have the experiences we do? Let's ask along with that: Why am I so inclined to believe in an external world?

---

* It is tempting to word "believed with the deepest conviction" in terms of "universal conviction." But such wording would assume the existence of other minds at a point where their existence is in question. Note that the conversational "we" employed in this discussion of skepticism does not assume what is at issue since it can be taken as merely hypothetical. It would assume what is at issue only if it led to statements that could not be rephrased as first-person statements.

Perhaps one general consideration that sways us toward a belief in the external world is the stark contrast between the relative poverty of those thoughts obviously created by one's mind and the richness of those experiences that seem to be imposed upon one. When I intentionally produce

WHY WE BELIEVE IN AN EXTERNAL WORLD

a mental image, it tends to be hazy and simple, and its content tends to be exhausted at a glance. But much of the experience that seems to come from outside is complex, endlessly explorable, and full of surprises. A similar contrast exists between the ideas that are obviously mine and those that seem to come from others. Through apparent conversations with others, I gain knowledge that I was not conscious of possessing before. Many of those ideas that seem to come from elsewhere are barely comprehensible to me (for example, Einstein's theory of relativity, Russell's *Principia Mathematica*, Joyce's *Ulysses*). It seems absurd to suppose that all these ideas are really just products of my own mind.

Of course, **the solipsist isn't suggesting that this complexity is coming from my conscious mind. He suggests that it could be produced by the unconscious mind. But is that an equally reasonable hypothesis?**

Note, first, that the concept of the unconscious mind is a murky one. We need something like that concept to account for phenomena like the

THE UNCONSCIOUS MIND

following: My mind seems to be processing information even when I'm not aware it's doing so (the solution to the problem I was thinking about yesterday suddenly pops into my head); or, some people act as if they intend to do things they are not aware of intending (a friend engages in self-destructive behavior without seeming to realize it). There is a temptation to view the unconscious as a full-blown second mind deep down below (sort of like the troll under the bridge in fairy tales). But there are alternatives to thinking of the unconscious as a second mind. The brain, for instance, might perform the information processing functions (as a computer would) and deliver the results to consciousness. (Note that the brain is not something the solipsist is allowed, since it is a physical object, part of the external world.) A lot of unconscious intentional activity could be analyzed as habit: If I act self-destructively without realizing it, that doesn't have to mean that deep down inside of me is the intention to self-destruct. It could mean that I once felt self-destructive and set up behavioral habits. Or, more likely, that I was simply trained to act in self-destructive ways by antagonistic parents.

If we do try to think of the unconscious as analogous to the conscious mind, the resulting concept seems to verge on the self-contradictory: awareness without awareness, thought without consciousness.

The solipsist is suggesting that it is equally reasonable to suppose that the world of experience comes from the unconscious as from the external world. But the concept of the unconscious seems to be either close to contradictory or a placeholder for causes that either the solipsist can't employ (the brain) or that won't do the work he wants the unconscious to do (habits). It's questionable whether the all-experience-comes-from-the-unconscious hypothesis even makes sense. It's more questionable whether it is as reasonable as the hypothesis that much experience comes from the external world.

Approaching this from a slightly different direction, **let's ask ourselves what a one-mind universe would look like.** I don't know about you, but I see an image of a bubble floating around in the darkness with video pictures projected inside it. Obviously this won't do because we need some source for the pictures. So mentally we might add a kind of ghostly video camera, and perhaps a computer, to the bubble. Among other things, either this computer contains every bit of information in every library in every language, or somehow (as in "Please Don't Tell Me How the Story Ends") it contains only the information I will happen to look up. Why? How? Saying "it just does" isn't satisfactory. Again, we're not simply asking whether this is possible, we're asking whether it is the most reasonable view.

When I try to complete a picture of a one-mind universe, just at the point where it seems to make some sense, I find it's no longer a one-mind universe at all: It isn't one mind with a huge unconscious, but a mind plus another huge mind (a kind of God) that has actively thought everything up and is feeding me some of the information. But if we reach that point we already have an external world of sorts: God, in addition to my mind. Now we can ask if that is the most reasonable view. What is the evidence for there being such a God? Does it make sense to suppose that there would be a God plus one human mind? If there are other minds, does it make sense to think that there are also physical objects?

People have taken all sorts of different positions concerning the nature of the external world. Philosophers called "idealists" have argued that what exists in the world are God and minds and no physical objects. Other people believe the world consists of God, minds, and physical objects, while still others believe in minds, physical objects, but no God. At this point, though, we are debating what the external world is really like, not whether there is one. ✹

✹ The CD, Ch. 7, *Can We Prove an External World?*, contains a summary of this section of the text.

Questions and Exercises

1. Explain the concept of the "external world." What would, and wouldn't, be part of that world?
2. On what basis do we normally distinguish dreams from reality? What does it mean to say that reality might also be a dream?
3. Explain Descartes's "cogito" argument.
4. Say to yourself, "I think, therefore . . . exists," filling in your name. Is this a good argument?
5. "If we had to prove everything, we couldn't prove anything." Explain this statement.
6. What's the problem with saying that the existence of the external world is "self-evident" and requires no argument?
7. Critique the following claim: "To believe there is no external world is as reasonable as to believe there is."

Glossary

The definitions below are convenient simplifications for quick reference; they are not meant to replace the fuller definitions presented in the discussions.

Agnosticism: Neither believing nor disbelieving in God.

Atheism: The belief that there is no God.

Begging the question: Assuming what one is trying to prove; presenting a version of the conclusion as if it were an additional statement in support of the conclusion.

Behaviorism: A version of materialism, claiming that the mind is nothing but complex, overt, physical behavior.

Big Bang: The theory of the origin of the universe that says that the universe began in a superhot, supercondensed state and that some sort of explosion threw matter outward, creating the expanding universe we know today.

Block Time: The view that the past, present, and future all exist at once, in a "block" or like something "frozen," and that all change is illusion.

Causal laws: Inevitable patterns in nature, such that when certain events occur ("the cause") certain other events must occur ("the effect").

Cogito: "I think, therefore I am."

Consequentialist ethical theories: Those ethical theories that claim that what makes actions right or wrong are their consequences.

Cosmological argument (The):   Attempts to show that given the existence of a world (in motion), God must exist as First Cause (First Mover).

Deontological ethical theories: Those ethical theories that deny that what makes actions right or wrong are simply their consequences.

Determinism: The theory that all events, including mental events, are governed by causal laws.

Dualism: The view that the world is composed of two radically different kinds of things: physical objects and nonphysical minds.

Property dualism: The dualist view that the nonphysical mind is simply a property of the physical brain and can't exist without it.

Substance dualism: The dualist view that the nonphysical mind is a separate substance that can exist without the physical.

Emergent property: A property (like solidity) that emerges at a higher level of organization and seems different in kind from properties at a more basic level. Some property dualists consider mind an emergent property.

Euthanasia: Deliberately bringing about, either by action (active) or by inaction (passive), the painless death of people with certain incurable conditions.

External world (The):   Everything outside of one's own mind.

Fatalism: The view that some specified events must occur in a person's life, no matter what that person may choose to do.

Free will: The concept that (at least some) human choices are not governed by causal laws.

Free-will defense (The):   Claims that it would be contradictory for God to give people free will and guarantee that they not cause suffering; further, that free will and suffering are better than no free will and no suffering.

Freedom of action: The ability or opportunity to perform whatever physical actions one might choose to perform.

Frozen Universe: (see "Block Time").

Functionalism: A version of materialism that says that the defining feature of any mental state is the kind of causal relations it has with the environment, with other mental states, and with behavior.

Identity theory: A version of materialism, claiming that the mind is nothing but the (physical) brain.

Indeterminism: The theory that not all events are governed by causal laws.

Interactionism: A version of dualism, claiming that the (physical) body and (nonphysical) mind are causally related.

Materialism: The view that everything that exists is physical, including minds.

Metaethical: Relating to the nature of moral judgments, especially their meaning and justification.

Moral objectivism: The view that where there is a moral judgment and its negation, one of those judgments must be false; that there is such a thing as the moral truth.

Moral subjectivism: The view that where there is a moral judgment and its negation, neither judgment need be false; that there is no such thing as the moral truth.

Normative ethics: Relating to questions about what is morally good or bad, right or wrong, required or not required.

Ontological argument (The):   Attempts to prove the existence of God from the concept of God.

Parallelism: A version of dualism, claiming that the (physical) body and (non-physical) mind are not causally related.

Principle of nonidentity: If the thing referred to by one phrase has characteristics differing from those of the thing referred to by another phrase, the two phrases do not refer to the same thing.

Problem of suffering (The):   The question of whether the existence of a God who is omnipotent, omniscient, and perfectly good is compatible with the existence of suffering in the world.

Spacetime: Treating time mathematically as if it were a fourth, space-like dimension.

Slippery slope fallacy: Assuming, without specific evidence, that any move in a certain direction will inevitably lead to some terrible extreme.

Solipsism: The view that, with the exception of the belief in one's own mind, one cannot justify any beliefs about the world.

Teleological argument (The):   Attempt to prove that given the complex orderliness of the world, God must exist as designer of that world.

Theism: The belief that there is a God.

Utilitarianism: The moral view that only happiness is good in itself and that one ought to promote the greatest happiness of the greatest number.

Veridical: True; genuine; nonillusory.

Virtue defense (The):   Claims that it would be contradictory to have virtues and no suffering; further, that virtues and suffering are better than no virtues and no suffering.

Further Materials

The following anthologies are referenced below as "Feinberg" or "Lawhead."

"Feinberg": Feinberg, Joel and Shafer-Landau, Russ (ed.). *Reason and Responsibility: Readings in Some Basic Problems of Philosophy,* 11th ed. Belmont, CA: Wadsworth 2002.

"Lawhead": Lawhead, William (ed.) *Philosophical Questions: Classical and Contemporary Readings.* Boston, MA: McGraw-Hill, 2003.

FREEDOM AND RESPONSIBILITY

Philosophy

Feinberg, Part IV. Readings by Honderich, Ayer, and Kane.

Lawhead, Ch. 5. Readings by Holbach, Campbell, and Stace.

Searle, John R. *Minds, Brains, and Science.* New York: Harvard University Press, 1984, chapter 6.

Other

A Clockwork Orange (video). Warner Home Video, 1971. The main character goes through a conditioning process that forces him to be "good."

Dostoevsky, Fyodor. *Notes from the Underground.* New York: E. P. Dutton, 1960. An expression of a man's hysterical insistence on free will.

TIME AND TIME TRAVEL

Philosophy/Physics

Al-Khalili, Jim. *Black Holes, Wormholes and Time Machines.* Bristol (UK): Institute of Physics Publishing, 1999.

Davies, Paul. *About Time: Einstein's Unfinished Revolution*. New York: Simon & Shuster, 1995.

Gott, J. Richard. *Time Travel in Einstein's Universe*. New York: Houghton Mifflin Co., 2001.

Other

Back to the Future (video). A time travel movie that plays with the idea of changing the past.

Borges, Jorge Luis. "The Secret Miracle" in *Ficciones*. New York: Grove Weidenfeld, 1987. A man facing execution gets his wish that time stop for a while.

Frequency (video). A son receives communications from the past from his dead father and tries to change the circumstances of his father's death.

The Sixth Day (video). Schwarzenegger in a cloning adventure.

Heinlein, Robert A. "—All You Zombies—" in *The Unpleasant Profession of Jonathan Hoag*. New York: Ace Books, 1989. The story presents the ultimate in time-travel complexities: A man manages to become the mother and father of himself.

The Terminator (video). MGM Video, 1984. A time travel story in which the past is acted on in a way that fulfills it.

GOD AND SUFFERING

Philosophy

Feinberg, Part I. Readings by Anselm, Aquinas, Paley, Mackie, and Imwagen.

Hick, John. *Philosophy of Religion*. 4th Ed. Englewood Cliffs, N.J.: Prentice-Hall, 1990, chapters 3–5.

Lawhead, Ch. 3. Readings by Aquinas, Paley, St. Anselm, Johnson, and Hick.

Other

Bedazzled (video). CBS/Fox, 1967. There are some delightful discussions between Dudley Moore and Peter Cook (as the devil) on why God allows evil.

The Book of Job. A Biblical exploration of the problem of suffering.

Dostoyevsky, Fyodor. *Brothers Karamazov*. New York: Norton, 1976. The chapter entitled "Rebellion" contains an outcry against a God who would allow suffering.

Huxley, Aldous. *Brave New World*. New York: Perennial Classics, 1989. The discussion between Mustapha Mond and the Savage at the end of the book parallels the discussion between God and Martin in "Surprise! It's Judgment Day."

Stoppard, Tom. *Jumpers*. New York: Grove Weidenfeld, 1989. The main character, a philosopher, presents an amusing discussion of the first-cause argument.

Voltaire. *Candide*. New York: Bantam, 1959. A satire of the claim that this is the best of all possible worlds.

MORAL PRINCIPLES

Philosophy

Beauchamp, Thomas (ed.). *Philosophical Ethics: An Introduction to Moral Philosophy.* Boston, Mass.: McGraw-Hill, 2000, part 1.

Feinberg, Part V. Readings by Rawls, Kant, and Mill.

Lawhead, Ch. 6. Readings by Kant and Mill; ch. 7, readings by Mill and Rawls.

Rachaels, James. *The Elements of Moral Philosophy*, 4th Ed. Boston, Mass: McGraw-Hill, 2001.

Other

Huxley, Aldous. *Brave New World.* New York: Perennial Classics, 1989. Mustapha Mond defends a quasi-utilitarian morality, distinguishing between his personal preferences and a moral perspective.

Sartre, Jean-Paul. "The Flies" in *No Exit and Three Other Plays.* New York: Vintage, 1989. The "freedom" exalted in the play is not so much free will as the freedom to choose a morality without any possibility of being in error. In other words, the play primarily is concerned with moral subjectivism.

Stoppard, Tom. *Jumpers.* New York: Grove Weidenfeld, 1989. The characters discuss moral subjectivism with some sophistication.

THE RIGHT TO DIE

Philosophy

Feinberg, Part V. Articles by Rachaels and Beauchamp.

Levine, Carol (ed.). *Taking Sides: Clashing Views on Controversial Bioethical Issues.* Guilford, Conn.: Dushkin / McGraw-Hill, 1990. Issues 4 and 6.

Pence, Gregory (ed.). *Classic Works in Medical Ethics.* Boston, Mass: McGraw-Hill, 1998, parts 1 and 2.

Other

Whose Life Is It Anyway? (video). MGM / UA, 1981. Richard Dreyfuss as a paralyzed sculptor fighting for the right to die.

THE NATURE OF THE MIND

Philosophy

Churchland, Paul M. *Matter and Consciousness.* Cambridge, Mass.: MIT Press, 1999.

Feinberg, Part III: Readings by Churchland, Searle, Lycan, and Penelhum.

Lawhead, Ch. 4: Readings by Descartes, Ryle, Churchland, Chalmers, Olen, Badham, Evans and Searle.

Searle, John R. *Minds, Brains, and Science.* New York: Harvard University Press, 1984, chapters 1 and 2.

Other

Asimov, Issac. *Robot Visions.* New York: ROC, 1990. A compilation by the master of robot stories.

Ghosts (video). Paramount, 1990. Ghosts can interact with the world in certain ways. It's fun to try to figure out what the rules are and whether they're consistent.

2001: A Space Odyssey (video). MGM/UA, 1987. Of particular interest here is the revolt and death of HAL, the computer.

Vonnegut, Kurt, Jr. "Epicac" and "Unready to Wear" in *Welcome to the Monkey House.* New York: Dell Publishing Co., 1970. The first concerns a computer that falls in love, and the second is about a group of people who have learned to step in and out of their bodies.

APPEARANCE AND REALITY

Philosophy

Descartes. *Meditations.*
Feinberg, Part II: Readings by Descartes and Moore.
Lawhead, Ch. 3: Readings by Descartes, Locke, Berkeley, and Hume.

Other

Borges, Jorge Luis. "The Circular Ruins" in *Ficciones.* New York: Grove Weidenfeld, 1987. In this story, a man discovers that he is only an illusion.

The Matrix (video). Warner Home Video, 1999. The world as a programmed dream of all human beings.

Total Recall (video). Live, 1990. Schwarzenegger on an adventure in which dream and reality become confused.

Index